DOING A
SYSTEMATIC
REVIEW

Sara Miller McCune founded SAGE Publishing in 1965 to support
the dissemination of usable knowledge and educate a global
community. SAGE publishes more than 1000 journals and over
800 new books each year, spanning a wide range of subject areas.
Our growing selection of library products includes archives, data,
case studies and video. SAGE remains majority owned by our
founder and after her lifetime will become owned by a charitable
trust that secures the company's continued independence.

Los Angeles | London | New Delhi | Singapore | Washington DC | Melbourne

DOING A SYSTEMATIC REVIEW

A Student's Guide

2nd Edition

Edited by

Angela Boland
M. Gemma Cherry
Rumona Dickson

Los Angeles | London | New Delhi
Singapore | Washington DC | Melbourne

Los Angeles | London | New Delhi
Singapore | Washington DC | Melbourne

SAGE Publications Ltd
1 Oliver's Yard
55 City Road
London EC1Y 1SP

SAGE Publications Inc.
2455 Teller Road
Thousand Oaks, California 91320

SAGE Publications India Pvt Ltd
B 1/I 1 Mohan Cooperative Industrial Area
Mathura Road
New Delhi 110 044

SAGE Publications Asia-Pacific Pte Ltd
3 Church Street
#10-04 Samsung Hub
Singapore 049483

Editor: Mila Steele
Editorial assistant: John Nightingale
Production editor: Victoria Nicholas
Copyeditor: Jen Hinchliffe
Proofreader: Camille Bramall
Marketing manager: Ben Sherwood
Cover design: Shaun Mercier
Typeset by C&M Digitals (P) Ltd, Chennai, India

Library of Congress Control Number: 2017936782

British Library Cataloguing in Publication data

A catalogue record for this book is available from the British Library

ISBN 978-1-4739-6700-7
ISBN 978-1-4739-6701-4 (pbk)

At SAGE we take sustainability seriously. Most of our products are printed in the UK using FSC papers and boards. When we print overseas we ensure sustainable papers are used as measured by the PREPS grading system. We undertake an annual audit to monitor our sustainability.

Contents

List of Tables, Figures and Boxes

Tables

Figures

Boxes

Online Resources

Doing a Systematic Review is supported by a wealth of online resources for both students and lecturers to aid study and support teaching, which are available at: https://study.sagepub.com/doingasystematicreview2e

- **WATCH** ... A FAQ video series, in which the editors address the most common systematic review challenges. Your very own team of supervisors is on hand to provide advice on everything from writing a protocol and conducting scoping searches to data extraction and meta-analysis.
- **EXPLORE** ... the Links Library, which gives you a host of online resources to help you tackle the systematic review process. Including links to organizations that specialise in conducting systematic reviews, software that can help you organize your own project and additional video. The editors have scoured the internet and carefully curated this tool kit of useful resources just for you.
- **READ** ... example reviews, journal articles and further guidance on the review process. These resources will allow you to see what a systematic review looks like in practice and provide you with a more in-depth understanding of the method generally.

About the Editors

This book is largely the result of the collaboration of researchers who are, or have been, linked to the Liverpool Reviews and Implementation Group (LRiG). This research group was established in 2001 and the major focus of their work is related to conducting systematic reviews of clinical and cost-effectiveness evidence. Members of the group also have experience in supervising and supporting students who are conducting systematic reviews as a part of their academic endeavours.

Dr Angela Boland has worked at LRiG since it was established in 2001. During this time she has carried out many systematic reviews of both clinical effectiveness and cost-effectiveness of healthcare interventions. As Associate Director of LRiG, she has also managed and proofread many others. She has an undergraduate degree in Economics and Spanish, a Master's degree and PhD in Health Economics, and a Postgraduate Certificate in Learning and Teaching in Higher Education.

Dr M. Gemma Cherry is a lecturer in Clinical Health Psychology at the University of Liverpool and an honorary clinical psychologist at the Royal Liverpool University Hospital. Prior to qualifying as a clinical psychologist, she worked at LRiG for several years, conducting systematic reviews, particularly in the field of psychology. She was awarded her undergraduate degree in Psychology from Newcastle University in 2005, her PhD in Medical Education from the University of Liverpool in 2013 and her doctorate in Clinical Psychology from the University of Liverpool in 2016. Gemma is a strong believer in evidence-based practice and that primary research should be underpinned by systematic reviews.

Professor Rumona Dickson has been involved in the conduct of systematic reviews in healthcare for over 20 years and has been the Director of LR*i*G since 2001. During that time she has also been involved in a number of Master's programmes that have promoted the use of systematic reviews as a learning tool to help students better understand the role of research in the evolution of health policy and practice. It is these experiences that prompted her to convince her colleagues to contribute to the first edition of this book.

About the Contributors

Ms Sophie Beale joined LR*i*G in 2011 after having spent 11 years at the University of York carrying out economic evaluations and service reviews in a range of treatment areas for pharmaceutical, National Health Service (NHS) and government clients. Her main role within LR*i*G is to contribute to analyses of the cost-effectiveness of new pharmaceutical products and she also enjoys contributing to other types of studies when time allows. Sophie is midway through her PhD at the University of Liverpool.

Mrs Michaela Brown has worked as a statistician at the University of Liverpool since 2009. During that time she has developed her skills in meta-analysis methods and has worked on a number of systematic reviews of healthcare interventions. Her main areas of expertise are the design, conduct and analysis of randomized controlled trials. She has an undergraduate degree in Psychology and Statistics from Newcastle University and a Master's degree in Statistics from Lancaster University.

Dr Tamara Brown has worked as a systematic reviewer since 2001. Tamara worked at LR*i*G from 2009 to 2012 and is now at both the University of Durham and Teeside University. She has conducted a number of systematic reviews on behalf of the UK Health Technology Assessment Programme and for the Cochrane Collaboration. She has also contributed to National Institute for Health and Care Excellence (NICE) guidance. Her main areas of research are in public health, specifically the prevention and treatment of obesity in children and adults.

Dr Yenal Dundar has worked as a researcher conducting systematic reviews on a wide range of topics in healthcare since 2001. During that time he has developed particular skill in the area of systematic identification of evidence, which is an essential step in the systematic review process. Yenal is a former general practitioner, and is working in Mersey Care NHS Foundation Trust as a consultant psychiatrist. He was awarded an MPhil from the Faculty of Medicine, University of Liverpool in 2006, Membership of the Royal College of Psychiatrists in 2010 and the Certificate of Completion of Training in General Psychiatry in 2013.

Mr Nigel Fleeman has been a researcher at the University of Liverpool since November 1994. Originally working in public health, he conducted a number of relatively short primary and secondary research projects for local NHS bodies before he joined LR*i*G in October 2006. Much of his work since has been to conduct systematic reviews, on behalf of the UK Health Technology Assessment Programme and the Cochrane Collaboration, on a wide variety of topics. Examples include reviews to investigate the effectiveness of cancer treatments, pharmacogenetic testing, interventions aimed at reducing iron overload in patients suffering with chronic anaemia and self-management strategies for people with epilepsy. Nigel has a Master's degree in Public Health from the University of Liverpool.

Dr Janette Greenhalgh has worked as a systematic reviewer at LR*i*G since October 2006. During that time she has conducted a number of systematic reviews on behalf of the UK Health Technology Assessment Programme and also for the Cochrane Collaboration on a wide variety of topics including cardiovascular disease, lung cancer, sickle cell disease and epilepsy. Janette has a PhD in Psychology from Bangor University and a PGCE in Adult Education from Llandrillo College.

Ms Juliet Hounsome began working at LR*i*G in 2005 as a clinical reviewer working on both single technology assessments for NICE and health technology assessments for the Health Technology Assessment Programme. In addition, Juliet carried out large-scale updates of systematic reviews of prevention and intervention strategies, and of risk assessment tools for populations at high risk of engaging in violent behaviour. As a consequence of these updates, Juliet has registered for a PhD and is developing and validating an additional manual for the Structured Assessment of Protective Factors for Violence (SAPROF) to be used with people with intellectual disabilities.

Professor Elizabeth Perkins is Director of the Health and Community Care Research Unit (HaCCRU) and William Rathbone VI Chair of Community Nursing Research at the University of Liverpool. She has spent 20 years undertaking research studies in the field of health and social care policy. Before working at the University of Liverpool, Elizabeth worked at the Policy Studies Institute, undertaking large-scale surveys and small-scale in-depth qualitative studies for a range of funders including the Department of Health. She took up the post of the Director of HaCCRU in 1997 and has since specialized in undertaking qualitative studies, often using grounded theory, in the fields of mental health, ageing and addiction.

Mrs Gerlinde Pilkington worked as a researcher with LR*i*G from 2009 to 2016 and is now at Liverpool John Moores University. She has a background in history and Classics, and an MA in Research Methodology, focusing on social policy. She has worked on systematic reviews covering a wide range of topics including mental health, cancer treatments (focusing on treatment for older people), community well-being and dentistry, and really enjoys the challenges and diversity each project brings. Gerlinde has also contributed to the organization and delivery of systematic review teaching workshops, and is building university-wide networks to support colleagues undertaking evidence synthesis.

Ms Marty Richardson was awarded a BSc in Mathematics in 2011 and an MSc in Statistical Epidemiology in 2012 from the University of Leeds. Since joining LR*i*G in 2013, she has provided statistical support on systematic reviews and meta-analyses. Marty also works with the Cochrane Infectious Diseases Group, and is undertaking a part-time PhD on the meta-analysis of pharmacogenetic studies.

Dr Helen Smith is a senior research associate in the Centre for Maternal and Newborn Health at Liverpool School of Tropical Medicine. She is a social scientist with a disciplinary background in demography and human geography. She has 18 years' experience in leading and contributing to research projects, and teaching on postgraduate programmes in international health. Early in her career, she authored systematic reviews with the Cochrane Infectious Diseases and Pregnancy and Childbirth groups. While recognizing the value of producing systematic reviews on priority health topics, Helen became more interested in how review evidence was being used in policy and practice; this led to her PhD, which in turn led to the implementation of evidence-based obstetric care in South Africa. She has authored several systematic reviews of qualitative research relating to health problems in low- and middle-income countries including tuberculosis, malaria, childhood illness and maternal health. Helen has also led qualitative evidence syntheses commissioned by the World Health Organization for use in guideline development. She believes that policymakers need many different types of evidence for decision-making, and that systematic reviews of views and experiences of interventions and barriers to implementation are just as important as reviews of intervention effects.

Foreword

Conducting a systematic review is a 'journey [where] you want a companion who knows what they are talking about'. In my Foreword to the first edition of this ground-breaking text, I borrowed the authors' extended journey analogy to explain what my students, and myself as their supervisor, need from such a practical guide. I am delighted to report that this expanded pool of authors for the second edition has, if anything, surpassed itself in delivering this revised, updated and extended version.

For my students, I want a text that is both readable and practical; a source of know-how to which they can turn when seeking to add some colour and detail to my monotones on 'what to do'. This text is populated with tables, figures and frequently asked questions that will help my students to consolidate and extend my advice from supervision meetings, delivered in a vibrant, energetic and, above all, convivial style.

But why would I, as a supervisor, the driver of a juggernaut referenced in the 'Further Reading and Resources' sections of this book, want to 'swap vehicles' for the company of this University of Liverpool-based team? Quite simply – to enjoy the view! Placing myself in the capable hands of this trusted guide allows me to draw on their practical tips and concise explanations without the nagging fear that I've missed something. While a guide of this sort can't necessarily have all the answers, the authors have collectively done a marvellous job in identifying all the junctions, landmarks and potential pitfalls. In their preface, the editorial team states that they have enhanced their metaphorical truck with the addition of a trailer: namely the multiple tools that populate the different chapters of the book. From the sample filing system of Chapter 2 to the 'What an examiner is looking for in your thesis' features that conclude most chapters, I found myself continually making mental notes for future reference. If you want to be able to travel light, unencumbered by unnecessary baggage, making steady progress to successfully complete your own personal unique review journey, then climb on board!

Andrew Booth
Reader in Evidence-Based Information Practice
School of Health and Related Research (ScHARR)
University of Sheffield

Foreword

Conducting a systematic review is a 'journey [where] you want a companion who knows what they are talking about'. In my Foreword to the first edition of this ground-breaking text, I borrowed the authors' extended journey analogy to explain what my students, and myself as their supervisor, need from such a practical guide. I am delighted to report that this expanded pool of authors for the second edition has, if anything, surpassed itself in delivering this revised, updated and extended version.

For my students, I want a text that is both readable and practical; a source of know-how to which they can turn when seeking to add some colour and detail to my monotones on 'what to do'. This text is populated with tables, figures and frequently asked questions that will help my students to consolidate and extend my advice from supervision meetings, delivered in a vibrant, energetic and, above all, convivial style.

But why would I, as a supervisor, the driver of a juggernaut referenced in the 'Further Reading and Resources' sections of this book, want to 'swap vehicles' for the company of this University of Liverpool-based team? Quite simply – to enjoy the view! Placing myself in the capable hands of this trusted guide allows me to draw on their practical tips and concise explanations without the nagging fear that I've missed something. While a guide of this sort can't necessarily have all the answers, the authors have collectively done a marvellous job in identifying all the junctions, landmarks and potential pitfalls. In their preface, the editorial team states that they have enhanced their metaphorical truck with the addition of a trailer: namely the multiple tools that populate the different chapters of the book. From the sample filing system of Chapter 2 to the 'What an examiner is looking for in your thesis' features that conclude most chapters, I found myself continually making mental notes for future reference. If you want to be able to travel light, unencumbered by unnecessary baggage, making steady progress to successfully complete your own personal unique review journey, then climb on board!

Andrew Booth
Reader in Evidence-Based Information Practice
School of Health and Related Research (ScHARR)
University of Sheffield

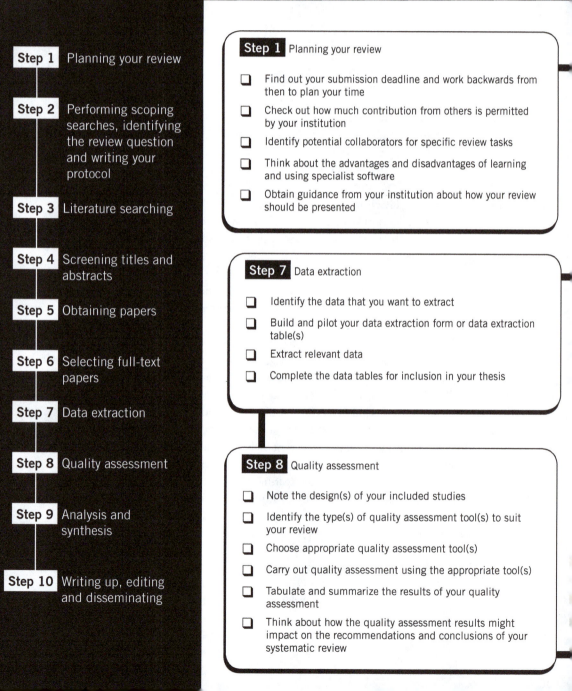

10 STEP
roadmap to your systematic review

Step 1	Planning your review
Step 2	Performing scoping searches, identifying the review question and writing your protocol
Step 3	Literature searching
Step 4	Screening titles and abstracts
Step 5	Obtaining papers
Step 6	Selecting full-text papers
Step 7	Data extraction
Step 8	Quality assessment
Step 9	Analysis and synthesis
Step 10	Writing up, editing and disseminating

Step 1 Planning your review

- ❑ Find out your submission deadline and work backwards from then to plan your time
- ❑ Check out how much contribution from others is permitted by your institution
- ❑ Identify potential collaborators for specific review tasks
- ❑ Think about the advantages and disadvantages of learning and using specialist software
- ❑ Obtain guidance from your institution about how your review should be presented

Step 7 Data extraction

- ❑ Identify the data that you want to extract
- ❑ Build and pilot your data extraction form or data extraction table(s)
- ❑ Extract relevant data
- ❑ Complete the data tables for inclusion in your thesis

Step 8 Quality assessment

- ❑ Note the design(s) of your included studies
- ❑ Identify the type(s) of quality assessment tool(s) to suit your review
- ❑ Choose appropriate quality assessment tool(s)
- ❑ Carry out quality assessment using the appropriate tool(s)
- ❑ Tabulate and summarize the results of your quality assessment
- ❑ Think about how the quality assessment results might impact on the recommendations and conclusions of your systematic review

Step 2 Performing scoping searches, identifying the review question and writing your protocol

- ❏ Identify a topic area of interest to you
- ❏ Carry out early scoping searches
- ❏ Focus your ideas to define the scope of the review
- ❏ Finalize your review question and develop your inclusion and exclusion criteria
- ❏ Consider contacting experts in the topic area
- ❏ Write a review protocol

Step 5 Obtaining papers

- ❏ Obtain the full text papers of all potentially eligible references

Step 6 Selecting full-text papers

- ❏ Use your screening and selection tool to help you identify full-text papers for inclusion in review

Step 9 Analysis and synthesis

- ❏ Report your extracted data in your thesis
- ❏ Choose an appropriate method of analysis/synthesis
- ❏ Combine data narratively or statistically in line with your chosen method of analysis/synthesis
- ❏ Present the results of your chosen method of analysis/synthesis

Step 3 Literature searching

- ❏ Think about how comprehensive your search needs to be
- ❏ Consider the different types of evidence available to you
- ❏ Identify the specific bibliographic databases that you will search for evidence
- ❏ Identify and refine your key search terms
- ❏ Search bibliographic databases using your final search strategies and collate citations
- ❏ Consider complementary searching activities

Step 4 Screening titles and abstracts

- ❏ De-duplicate references
- ❏ Develop and pilot your screening and selection tool
- ❏ Screen all of your titles and abstracts identified via searches against your inclusion and exclusion criteria

Step 10 Writing up, editing and disseminating

- ❏ Ensure that you adhere to institutional guidelines regarding presentation and content
- ❏ Be consistent in use of language and abbreviations, and in reporting and referencing styles
- ❏ Ensure sufficient time for write-up and dissemination

Preface

Welcome to the second edition of *Doing A Systematic Review: A Student's Guide*! It strikes us as odd that the preface to the second edition of a book usually assumes that the reader is familiar with the first edition. We don't want to start our preface by launching into what is different in this edition compared with the first edition. Instead, we want to be different! So, with that in mind, we want to first welcome you to this book, and give you a bit of history about *Doing a Systematic Review: A Student's Guide*.

Why did we write this book?

There are a variety of excellent books written by systematic review experts that provide the 'How to...' of carrying out a systematic review. Why, then, in 2013, did we think it was necessary to write a new one for students? Well, we wrote the first edition of this book for two reasons.

First, we have long held a strong conviction that carrying out a systematic review as a postgraduate research project can yield excellent learning opportunities for students. Increasingly, academic and scientific communities are also acknowledging the value of this research activity. Conducting such a review requires insight into the fundamentals of research. Students learn to develop research questions, critique research findings and, most importantly, synthesize findings and make recommendations regarding how to use results in professional practice. These are valuable skills for students to learn, no matter what their academic or professional discipline.

Second, we wanted to reflect on the systematic review process from the viewpoint of a student working independently (most likely at Master's level, but perhaps at undergraduate or doctoral level) to undertake a systematic review as part of their academic programme. Even though the 'How to...' books are useful to students, they frequently don't focus on the 'But what do I do when...?' type questions that so often arise during the review process. These are the questions that students need to know the answers to more or less immediately so that they can move forward with their theses. While we wanted the first edition of our book to provide a comprehensive guide to carrying out a systematic review, we decided to focus more on the *practicalities* of systematic reviewing rather than on the theory underpinning it. We pitched the first edition of this book at students carrying out a systematic review, not simply learning about them.

Understandably, we were a bit nervous about how the first edition of this book would be received. Luckily, there was no need for nerves. Response proved what we believed: that there was a need for an easy-to-read handbook to guide students through their systematic review journey. Fortunately, our publishers agreed, and, in 2016, we began work on the second edition of our book.

What does the second edition of this book contain?

The second edition of this book contains 12 chapters. The first chapter explains why we think systematic reviews are important, how they came about and why they provide an excellent learning opportunity for students. The remaining chapters focus on the actual systematic review process and offer methodological and practical advice on conducting and reporting this type of research within the format of a postgraduate thesis. As in the first edition, each chapter ends with a 'Frequently Asked Questions' section. These questions have been taken from actual student supervision meetings and highlight the most common challenges encountered during the review process. They include not only the 'What do I do?' types of questions but also the 'Why do I do this?' and the 'What are my options?' types of questions. Our answers set out practical approaches to help students deal with these issues. We know that a lot of students turn to the Internet for further resources, so our publishers have designed a purpose-built website (https://study.sagepub.com/doingasystematicreview2e) which contains resources to complement the material in this book; any student can browse our online systematic review materials and search for information that is relevant to their own review. In addition, we have included references to supporting web links and web pages at relevant points throughout this book. Common sense will tell you that these links have a tendency to go out of date quickly – we have tried to reference only well-established organizations, pages and resources, so that if the links no longer work, they can still be accessed via a quick Internet search.

We have drawn on our own extensive experiences of carrying out systematic reviews when writing this book. This means that the book relies heavily on the systematic review of healthcare interventions using quantitative methods. However, the principles covered in this book are also relevant to students in other disciplines, such as social work or education, where there is encouragement to systematically review current research or practice. We know that there is more than quantitative data to review so we have included introductions to reviewing qualitative data and health economics data, both of which are currently exciting, controversial and evolving areas of research. We acknowledge that these two sections only offer students a starting point for their review journey, but hope they will inspire students to read more widely around these methodological areas.

What does this book have to offer you?

We had to make some general assumptions regarding the typical reader of this book. We thought long and hard about the research skills and resources postgraduate students might have at this point in their academic journey. Based on this, we have assumed that you, the typical reader of this book, will:

- be carrying out a systematic review as part of your postgraduate study;
- have access to a computer;
- be able to search the Internet;
- have word-processing skills and not be afraid to use them;
- have your own learning objectives relating to either professional practice or to the research process;
- have a specific research area in mind;
- be working (mainly) independently;
- need to meet a set-in-stone deadline.

As with the first edition, we've tried to make the contents of this book useful and easy to read. We've assumed that you want a no-frills approach and each chapter is written with this in mind. The basics of systematic review methods are delivered in bite-sized chunks so that you are not overwhelmed by the enormity of your project. Students tell us that they are happiest (and most productive) when they are in control of their own research and are not reliant on others for data or direction. This book is therefore written to guide you as you take control of your review. We are confident that it will help you move forward at your own pace, particularly when used in conjunction with the digital materials and resources on our website (https://study.sagepub.com/doingasystematicreview2e). We know that you will want to excel in your studies so, at the end of most chapters, we have also set out a section on what an examiner might be looking for in the final thesis.

What's new in this second edition?

One of the most obvious changes to our second edition is the front cover! In keeping with our journey analogy, we have added a trailer to our much-loved truck. This symbolizes the addition of the many extra tools and resources contained both within this book and within our new website (which we are delighted to say is now hosted by our publishers, Sage Publishing).

Within the book itself, there are several significant changes – thank you to our reviewers and readers for their constructive feedback and suggestions. We have rearranged the structure of the book, and have rewritten certain sections to make them easier to understand. Specifically, we have:

- moved the positioning of the 'Planning and Managing My Review' chapter to much earlier in the book, because feedback on our first edition indicated that students valued the advice and information contained within this chapter and felt that it was far too important to be the final chapter;
- split the 'Developing My Search Strategy and Applying Inclusion Criteria' chapter into two chapters, and have included more 'step-by-step' instructions for each activity so as to make the two activities easier to understand and conduct;
- swapped around the 'Quality Assessment: Where Do I Begin' and the 'Data Extraction: Where Do I Begin' chapters, because we felt that this order better reflects the order in which many students conduct these activities;
- changed the title of the 'Understanding and Synthesizing My Numerical Data' chapter to 'Understanding and Synthesizing Numerical Data from Intervention Studies', and added additional content to help students to better understand the complex principles discussed in this chapter;
- significantly supplemented the 'Reviewing Qualitative Evidence' chapter in order to provide students conducting systematic reviews of qualitative evidence with a more comprehensive starting point;
- added more examples from non-health fields and disciplines in order to illustrate the application of systematic review methodology to a variety of topic areas;
- added a 'Further Reading and Resources' section to each chapter to provide students with a guide to exploring the wider literature base.

There are also several notable additions to this edition, the most significant of which is a new chapter that focuses on dissemination (i.e. the sharing of research findings or ideas through avenues such as publication, conference proceedings or academic social media). In the first edition of this book, aside from some brief recommendations about dissemination in the Epilogue, we only really focused on the processes involved in completing a systematic review as part of a Master's thesis. We realize now that this was an important oversight on our part, so we hope that you enjoy this new addition and that it helps you to recognize the value in disseminating your work.

We pitched the tone of the first edition of this book as an informal, friendly 'advisor'. However, there was inevitably some assumed knowledge, which may have made some sections difficult for the novice reader to understand. We have tried to be mindful of this in our second edition. We haven't changed our tone, as we believe that this is one of the strengths of our approach, but have included a Glossary of terms to give the reader a more in-depth explanation of terms as they arise. Glossary terms appear in bold type at first mention in the text. If you are unfamiliar with the vocabulary of systematic reviewing, then we encourage you to consult this Glossary frequently until you feel able to fully engage with the content of each chapter.

Future partnerships

In the preface to the first edition of this book, we stated that we did not see publication of the book as the end of our work with students; rather, we saw it as the beginning of a partnership. We must reiterate this here as we have received so much valuable feedback from students since the publication of our first edition. We will continue to build on the educational resources we have brought together in this book and add to those we've provided on our website. We intend to use our materials to support students who are interested in the rewards of systematic review methodology. We therefore encourage both you and your supervisors to submit questions to us via our website (https://study.sagepub.com/doingasystematicreview2e), and we look forward to hearing from you about your experiences as systematic reviewers.

Carrying Out a Systematic Review as a Master's Thesis

Rumona Dickson, M. Gemma Cherry and Angela Boland

This chapter will help you to...

- Understand the term 'systematic review'

- Gain an awareness of the historical context and development of systematic reviewing

- Appreciate the learning experience provided through conducting a systematic review

- Become familiar with the methods involved in carrying out a systematic review

Introduction

In this chapter we introduce you to the concept of systematically reviewing literature. First, we discuss what **systematic reviews** are and why we think carrying out a systematic review is a great learning experience. Second, we give you an overview of the evolution of systematic review methodology. Third, we introduce the key steps in the systematic review process and signpost where in the book these are discussed. Finally, we highlight how systematic reviews differ from other types of **literature review**. By the end of the chapter we hope that you will be confident that you have made the right decision to carry out a systematic review and that you are looking forward to starting your research.

What is a systematic review?

A systematic review is a literature review that is designed to locate, appraise and synthesize the best available evidence relating to a specific **research question** in order to provide informative and **evidence-based** answers. This information can then be used in a number of ways. For example, in addition to advancing the field and informing future practice or research, the information can be combined with professional judgement to make decisions about how to deliver interventions or to make changes to policy. Systematic reviews are considered the best ('**gold standard**') way to synthesize the findings of several studies investigating the same questions, whether the evidence comes from healthcare, education or another discipline. Systematic reviews follow well-defined and transparent steps and always require the following: definition of the question or problem, identification and **critical appraisal** of the available evidence, synthesis of the findings and the drawing of relevant conclusions.

A systematic review: a research option for postgraduate students

As a postgraduate student you may be offered the choice of conducting a **primary research** study (e.g. an **observational study**) or a **secondary research** project (e.g. a systematic review) as part of your academic accreditation. There are very good reasons why you are asked to carry out a research project as part of your studies, the most important being that conducting a research project enables you to both understand the research process and gain research skills.

Systematically reviewing the literature has been accepted as a legitimate research methodology since the early 1990s. Many Master's programmes offer instruction in systematic review methods and encourage students to conduct systematic reviews as part of postgraduate study and assessment. It is widely acknowledged that this approach to research allows students to gain an understanding of different research methods and develop skills in identifying, appraising and synthesizing research findings.

Every Master's course and every academic institution is different. For you, this means that the presentation of your thesis as part of postgraduate study must be carried out within the accepted guidelines of the department or university where your thesis is due to be submitted. Your thesis must be an independent and self-directed piece of academic work; it should offer detailed and original arguments in the exploration of a specific research question and it should offer clarity as to how the research question has been addressed.

Let's assume that you are interested in studying issues related to unintended teenage pregnancy. As a researcher, you have a variety of investigational methods open to you. However, the likelihood of being able to pursue these may be impeded by time and resource constraints, as well as by the specific requirements of your academic institution. Table 1.1 illustrates a number of possible project options that may be open to you and the likelihood of you being able to successfully complete your chosen project as part of your postgraduate thesis.

In our experience, students who opt for primary research mainly explore questions relating to current status and/or correlation factors. The main problem with this kind of research is that its **generalizability** is often hampered by small sample sizes and time constraints. Although conducting a systematic review can be just as time-consuming as undertaking primary research, students who form questions that can be addressed using systematic review methodology have the opportunity to work with a variety of different study designs and populations without necessarily needing to worry about the issues commonly faced by researchers carrying out large-scale primary research. Due to the very nature of a systematic review, students are able to work in the realm of existing research findings while developing critical appraisal and research synthesis skills. A systematic review provides an excellent learning opportunity and allows students to identify and set their own learning objectives.

Good research is rarely carried out on an ad hoc basis. From the outset, you need to be clear about why you are carrying out your systematic review. For example, you may want to evaluate the current state of knowledge or belief about a particular topic of interest, contribute to the development of specific theories or the establishment of a new evidence base and/or make recommendations for future research (or you might just want to carry out your review as quickly and as effortlessly as possible to gain your qualification). However, you need to think about what you want to learn from your postgraduate studies. You might find that balancing your learning objectives with the objectives of your review may be challenging at times; this is most likely to be true if you are reviewing a topic of interest in your professional field (as we suggest you do). Discussing your learning objectives with your supervisor and exploring alternatives with your classmates or colleagues can often help you to clarify these objectives. Box 1.1 outlines some of the advantages and disadvantages of conducting a systematic review as part of a Master's thesis.

TABLE 1.1 Example project options for postgraduate students interested in unintended teenage pregnancy

Question	Research options	Type of research	Risk* of not being able to complete this as a Master's student
Relationship questions			
What is the incidence of unintended teenage pregnancy in my practice or region?	Epidemiological survey	Primary	Low
What programmes are available in my practice or region for reducing teenage pregnancy rates?	Survey	Primary	Low
What are the most commonly reported methods used to decrease rates of teenage pregnancy?	Systematic review	Secondary	Low
Correlation questions			
Is there a relationship between education levels and rates of teenage pregnancy in my practice or region?	Survey of existing data	Primary	Moderate
What are pregnant teenagers' views on the importance of sex education?	Focus groups or structured interviews	Primary	Low, with small sample size
What is the reported relationship between education level and rates of teenage pregnancy?	Systematic review	Secondary	Low
Causation questions			
Does the provision of emergency contraception in schools decrease teenage pregnancy rates?	Intervention study	Primary	High
What impact do one-to-one counselling and group meetings have on rates of abortion for teenagers experiencing unintended pregnancy?	Randomized controlled trial	Primary	Very high
What have been shown to be the most effective programmes for decreasing teenage pregnancy rates?	Systematic review	Secondary	Low
Qualitative questions			
What are the views of teenagers on the reasons for high teenage pregnancy rates?	Focus groups	Primary	Moderate, with small sample size
What are the reported views of teenagers on the reasons for high teenage pregnancy rates?	Systematic review	Secondary	Low

* Low = you are in control or have unlimited access to the data that you need; moderate = you may or may not have to go through an ethics committee, you are dependent on other people to give you data or you need to recruit participants; high = your study is likely to be expensive, excessively time-consuming and/or dependent on the interest of others.

Box 1.1

A systematic review as a Master's thesis: advantages and disadvantages

Advantages

- You are in control of your learning objectives and your project
- You can focus on a topic that you're interested in
- You don't have to gain formal ethical approval for your review before you begin
- You don't have to recruit participants
- You can gain understanding of a number of different research methodologies
- You can gain insight into the strengths and limitations of published literature
- You can develop your critical appraisal skills
- The research can fit in, and around, your family (or social) life

Disadvantages

- You don't experience writing and defending an ethics application
- It can be isolating as you are likely to be primarily working on your own
- You don't face the challenges of recruiting participants
- You may not get a sense of the topic area in terms of lived experience
- You are reliant on the quality and quantity of available published information to address your research question
- You may find the process dull or boring at times
- There are no short cuts and the process is time-consuming

Evolution of the systematic review process

There are some common misconceptions about systematic reviewing. Some students (and supervisors) choose primary research projects over systematic reviews because they worry that systematic reviews aren't 'proper research', or that systematic reviews can only be conducted in the field of health. If you are thinking of conducting a systematic review as part of your Master's thesis, then we think that it will set your mind at ease to know a little bit about the history and evolution of the systematic review process and the disciplines in which systematic reviews can be carried out.

It might surprise you to know that the systematic review of **published evidence** is not new. As early as 1753, James Lind brought together data relating to the prevention of scurvy experienced by sailors. He wrote:

As it is no easy matter to root out prejudices ... it became requisite to exhibit a full and impartial view of what had hitherto been published on the scurvy ... by which the sources of these mistakes may be detected. Indeed, before the subject could be set in a clear and proper light, it was necessary to remove a great deal of rubbish. (Chalmers et al., 2002, p. 14)

From Lind's farsightedness we move to the 1970s. Two important events took place that laid the foundations for a revolution in the way that evidence could be used to inform practice in healthcare and other areas. In the UK, a tuberculosis specialist named Archie Cochrane had recognized that healthcare resources would always be finite. To maximize health benefits, Cochrane proposed that any form of health-care used in the UK National Health Service (NHS) must be properly evaluated and shown to be clinically effective before use (Cochrane, 1972). He stressed the impor-tance of using evidence from **randomized controlled trials** (RCTs) to inform the allocation of scarce healthcare resources. At about the same time, in the USA, work by Gene Glass (1976) had led to the development of statistical procedures for combining the results of independent studies. The term '**meta-analysis**' was formally coined to refer to the statistical combination of data from individual stud-ies to draw practical conclusions about **clinical effectiveness**. In years to come, outputs of both research communities would combine to form the basic tenets of systematic review methodology.

In 1979, Archie Cochrane lamented:

It is surely a great criticism of our profession that we have not organized a critical summary, by specialty or subspecialty, adapted periodically, of all relevant randomized controlled trials. (Cochrane, 1979, pp. 1–11)

In response, a group of UK clinicians working in perinatal medicine made every effort to identify all RCTs relating to pregnancy and childbirth. They categorized the studies that they found and then synthesized the evidence from these studies. This work led to the development of the Oxford Database of Perinatal Trials (Chalmers et al., 1986). In addition, their groundbreaking work was published in a two-volume book which detailed the systematic and transparent methods that they had used to search for, and report the results of, all relevant studies (Chalmers et al., 1989). This work was instrumental in laying the foundations for significant developments in systematic review methodology, including the establishment of the **Cochrane Collaboration** in 1992. The Cochrane Collaboration is an international network of more than 37,000 dedicated people from over 130 countries who work together to help healthcare providers, policymakers, and patients and their advocates and carers make well-informed decisions about healthcare. They do so by preparing, updating and promoting the systematic reviews that they conduct; these reviews are known throughout the world as Cochrane Reviews (The Cochrane Collaboration, 2017). Since the development of the Cochrane Collaboration, others have followed suit. The **Campbell Collaboration** was established in 2000 and is focused on reviewing literature to demonstrate the effects of social interventions, particularly in the areas of education, crime and justice (The Campbell Collaboration, 2012). More recently, the Department for International Development (DfID) has used the results of systematic reviews to develop national and international policy in many countries worldwide (DfID, 2012).

Why all the fuss? Why have people spent so much time developing a systematic review process? The answer is quite simple. Given the amount, and complexity, of available information and the limitations of time, there has been a real need to develop and establish a process to provide, in a concise way, a summary of the results of research findings. Most notably, the dramatic increase in the amount of accessible research today makes it impossible for decision makers, policymakers and professionals to keep up to date with advances in their field. Systematic reviews allow concise synthesis of a large body of research and therefore address some of these issues.

Why are we telling you all of this? Well, there are two important points to take away from this historical background. First, we want to convince you that systematic review methodology is accepted as a research methodology in its own right; in light of this, we use the terms **'review question'** and 'research question' interchangeably throughout the book. In fact, most funding bodies require a systematic review of the literature to be performed before they will fund a primary research project. In the UK, systematic reviews form the basis for the **National Institute for Health and Care Excellence** (NICE) guidelines for treatment and clinical practice. Throughout the world, Cochrane Collaboration and Campbell Collaboration publications are viewed as the gold standard in systematic reviews. Literature reviews are also an integral component of any doctoral thesis. While you wouldn't necessarily be expected to produce a review as detailed or as comprehensive as a Cochrane or Campbell review for your thesis, if you follow the systematic review methodology outlined in this book, then you can be confident that not only are you conducting research, you are producing some of the highest quality research possible.

Second, we want to show you that although the systematic review process began, and is common, in the field of healthcare, systematic reviews are being carried out and used to inform decision-making in a variety of disciplines and professions. In fact, if you conduct a quick Internet search combining the terms 'systematic review' with 'education', 'social work', 'veterinary medicine' and so on, you can see for yourself the widespread application of systematic review methodology. Irrespective of the field in which you study, the basic tenets of systematically reviewing the evidence are the same. When researchers or **practitioners** are faced with a problem, they aim to identify, assess and bring together the evidence relating to that problem. This information can then be used to inform changes to policy and/or professional practice.

What are the basic steps in the systematic review process and how can this book help me to follow them?

There are 10 basic steps to be taken when carrying out a systematic review. These are presented in Box 1.2 along with signposts to the chapter(s) of this book in which they are discussed in more detail. These steps are continually referred to and explored throughout this book, so don't worry if you don't recognize all of the terms at this stage. Use the Glossary to help you to become familiar with key terms; we expect that you'll quickly start to understand their relevance to the systematic review process as you read through this book. The authors of a good-quality systematic review will transparently report the methods that were used so that the reader has sufficient information to be able to replicate the review. Additionally, providing details about each step makes it easy for the reader to assess the validity of the review's findings. The remainder of this book provides you with a pragmatic, yet detailed, approach to carrying out each of these steps and we focus our attention on research activities that are essential to the successful completion of your review as part of a postgraduate thesis.

But don't all types of literature review follow these steps?

When we say that we've carried out a systematic review of the literature, this means that we have clearly planned and fully described the review steps that we've taken; all of our actions are transparent; all of the key methodological decisions have been informed by theory and/or pragmatism and are explicitly set out for the reader to judge. Unfortunately, not all reviews that are published have been written with our definition of systematic in mind. You may be familiar with the terms 'literature review', 'systematic review' and '**narrative review**', but you might not know exactly what the different terms mean. To complicate matters, in the published literature, these terms are frequently used interchangeably. Furthermore, researchers are increasingly using adapted systematic review methodology to perform other types of review, such as '**rapid reviews**' and '**scoping reviews**'.

Box 1.2

Ten steps in the systematic review process

Step 1: Planning your review (Chapter 2)

The first step is to plan your review by thinking about how best to use the time and resources available to you.

Step 2: Performing scoping searches, identifying the review question and writing your protocol (Chapter 3)

In this step you carry out **scoping searches** to help you identify background literature that will help you to define and refine your review question and to set your inclusion and **exclusion criteria**. You will also write a **protocol**. The protocol is a written plan ('map' of your journey) that enables you to set out the approach you will use to answer the review question.

Step 3: Literature searching (Chapter 4)

The aim of this step is to identify evidence (published and unpublished), using **bibliographic databases** and other evidence sources that you can use to address your review question.

Step 4: Screening titles and abstracts (Chapter 5)

In this step you read the titles and abstracts of the studies identified by your searches and discard the ones that aren't at all relevant to your review question and keep the ones that may be relevant.

Step 5: Obtaining papers (Chapter 5)

This step involves obtaining the full-text papers of the evidence that you identified in Step 4.

Step 6: Selecting full-text papers (Chapter 5)

This is when you apply your **inclusion criteria** to your full-text papers and ruthlessly exclude ones that don't fit the criteria.

Step 7: Data extraction (Chapter 6)

This is when you identify relevant data from each paper, and summarize these data using forms or tables.

Step 8: Quality assessment (Chapter 7)

In this step you assess each included full-text paper for **methodological quality** using an appropriate **quality assessment tool**.

Step 9: Analysis and synthesis (Chapters 6, 8, 11 and 12)

This is where you scrutinize and synthesize your data, either narratively or through meta-analysis. We discuss how to do this step in Chapter 6 (if you want to undertake a **narrative synthesis**) and Chapter 8 (for those who have appropriate data for meta-analysing). We also discuss how to analyse **qualitative data** in Chapter 11 and **health economics** data in Chapter 12.

Step 10: Writing up, editing and disseminating (Chapters 2, 9, 10, 11 and 12)

This is where you bring all of your hard work together. Step 10 involves writing up your background, methods and results, discussing your findings, drawing conclusions from your review and disseminating your findings. We discuss how to carry out this step in Chapters 2, 9 and 10, and also touch upon it in Chapter 11 and Chapter 12 for those looking at qualitative evidence and **economic evaluations**, respectively.

Literature reviews

The term 'literature review' is often a common catch-all term for any study that assimilates and synthesizes, or describes, the findings of more than one study.

Narrative reviews

Narrative literature reviews were (historically) and are (currently) typically prepared by 'experts' to provide an overview of a specific topic, to raise overlooked issues and/or identify information gaps, and to encourage new research. Authors of narrative reviews do not usually claim that their reviews are comprehensive. Some of the inherent differences between narrative reviews and systematic reviews, in relation to research process, are displayed in Table 1.2.

Rapid reviews

Rapid reviews have emerged due to an ever-increasing need for information within a short time frame. Although their exact methods and approaches are yet to be defined, these reviews are primarily systematic reviews in which researchers take legitimate shortcuts in order to deliver findings rapidly. These shortcuts should always be explicitly stated and justified in the write-up of the review. Examples of shortcuts that may be taken are shown in Table 1.2.

Scoping reviews

Scoping reviews also differ from systematic reviews, though again the precise definition and methods are still developing and there is currently little consensus in the literature as to what constitutes a scoping review. Having said that, most definitions of scoping reviews include the concept of mapping out the evidence base pertaining to a particular research question or topic area (Arksey and O'Malley, 2005; Levac et al., 2010). Scoping reviews can be performed to outline the breadth and type of literature available relating to a specific topic, or to identify any gaps in the literature in question. In some cases, a scoping review can be performed to assess the feasibility of conducting a systematic review on a topic. Scoping reviews follow a similar process to systematic reviews, though the methods employed at each stage vary slightly. Specifically, researchers carrying out scoping reviews often adopt a more iterative approach, and place greater emphasis on consultation with consumers and stakeholders (Table 1.2).

A simple way to illustrate the difference between narrative reviews, systematic reviews, rapid reviews and scoping reviews is shown in Figure 1.1. Essentially, a narrative review considers great breadth of information, but in little depth. A systematic review is usually

TABLE 1.2 Differences in review processes

	Narrative reviews	Systematic reviews	Rapid reviews	Scoping reviews
Defining a question	May or may not be clearly defined	Clearly defined and well-focused Always required	Clearly defined and well-focused Always required	Clearly defined Broader in focus Always required
Writing a protocol	Not usually required	Recommended/essential	Recommended	Recommended
Methodology	Does not follow explicit or rigorous methodology	Follows explicit and rigorous methodology	Follows explicit and rigorous methodology	Follows explicit and rigorous methodology but can be iterative
Searching	No pre-defined search strategy Not necessarily comprehensive Generally relies only on published literature Search strategies may be based on expert experience	Exhaustive and with an appropriate balance of sensitivity and specificity Carried out across a number of bibliographic databases, hand searching of reference lists from relevant papers and high-yield journals and documents/reports Grey (unpublished) literature sometimes searched Comprehensive and explicit searching methods used and reported	Predefined and explicitly stated Possibly limited by: • Search of only one database • Narrow time frame • Reliance on published literature only • No hand searching	Breadth balanced with resource availability Iterative, with additional terms added as a result of identifying key papers (use of citation chaining)
Definition of inclusion and exclusion criteria	Not essential No selection of studies based on study design	Essential Study design can be selected (e.g. only include qualitative data, RCTs or both)	Essential More exclusive than in systematic review	Essential Can be defined post hoc if rationale is reported
Screening titles and abstracts; selecting full-text papers	Generally carried out by one researcher by reading through relevant papers and based on their own experience	Explicit and systematic screening and selection, using predefined method Usually cross-checked by another researcher	Explicit and systematic screening and selection, using predefined method Possibly limited by: • Single person screening • Single person selection	Explicit and systematic screening and selection, using predefined method Usually cross-checked by another researcher

(Continued)

TABLE 1.2 (Continued)

	Narrative reviews	Systematic reviews	Rapid reviews	Scoping reviews
Quality assessment	Not necessarily	Yes	Unlikely	Unlikely
Data extraction	Yes	Yes	Yes Possibly limited by: • Single person extraction • Cross-checked by one person • Limited data extracted	Yes, though can be more iterative
Analysis and synthesis	No clear method of synthesis	Can involve meta-analysis, narrative or qualitative synthesis	Narrative synthesis only	Numerical analysis of extent and nature of studies An analytical framework or thematic analysis can be used to provide an overview of breadth
Application	Any field	Any field	Any field	Any field
Timescale	May be carried out relatively quickly	Can be time-consuming due to rigour required	Variable but usually shorter than full systematic review	Variable but usually shorter than full systematic review
Replication	Not easily replicable	Explicit methods and therefore replicable	Explicit methods and therefore replicable	Iterative process but explicit methods and therefore replicable

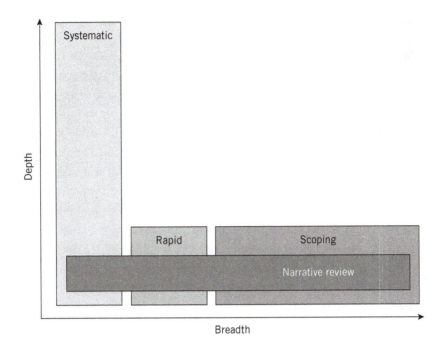

FIGURE 1.1   The depth and breadth of different types of reviews

narrow in the breadth of information considered but it looks at the data in great depth. A rapid review is as narrow, or maybe narrower, than a systematic review but due to time constraints does not look at the evidence in as much depth. Scoping reviews are broader in scope than rapid reviews but do not go into as much depth as systematic reviews.

Other types of review

Integrative reviews

'**Integrative reviews**' are a recent development and were first carried out by researchers in response to the criticism that many systematic reviews only use evidence from RCTs and that the value of systematic reviews is limited in areas where there is little, or no, trial evidence. To be more inclusive, the term integrative review was coined to reflect a literature review that included both quantitative and qualitative evidence (Sandelowski et al., 2007). We believe that, with an appropriately stated research question, a single systematic review can include both qualitative and quantitative evidence (and not just evidence from RCTs). A word of warning though, we believe that students should not be advised to conduct an integrative review as part of their postgraduate study unless they are experienced systematic reviewers. The approach is new and methods for use are evolving.

Realist reviews

This approach is often called realist synthesis and was developed by Pawson and colleagues (2005) as a means of determining what works for whom, in what circumstances, in what respects and how. **Realist reviews** differ from systematic reviews in a number of ways. Notably, realist reviewers aim to use existing theory to understand and explain how and why different outcomes were observed in a sample of empirical studies. Reviewers first develop a set of 'programme theories' by making assumptions about how an intervention is expected to work and the impact that it is expected to have. Relevant empirical data are then systematically identified and used to populate the theoretical framework. By considering the context in which an intervention is delivered, the mechanisms by which change occurs (or not), and the outcomes of the intervention, programme theories are supported, refuted or modified until a final theory, or set of theories, is identified. Realist reviews can be especially useful for policymakers and decision makers, as their findings are rich and detailed and can be used to further understanding of complex interventions in a way that systematic review methodology may not permit. However, due to its complexity, we wouldn't recommend this type of review as an option for postgraduate students new to systematic reviewing.

Evidence maps

Evidence-mapping is an emerging method of evidence synthesis that shares some commonalities with scoping reviews. There is currently no published guidance on how to carry out evidence-mapping, or on what constitutes an **evidence map**. Miake-Lye and colleagues (2016) concluded, from a systematic review of self-styled evidence maps, that 'the implied decision (...) of what constitutes an evidence map is a systematic search of a broad field to identify gaps in knowledge and/or future research needs that presents results in a user-friendly format, often a visual figure or graph, or a searchable database' (p. 18). As with integrative reviews, this approach is new and methods for its use will likely evolve as further research is published. Until then, we don't recommend that postgraduate students carry out this type of review as part of their thesis.

A few thoughts before you begin your systematic review

We like to think of the systematic review process as a journey. Experience has taught us that systematic reviewing can be challenging – especially when you don't have a good plan (protocol) to guide you. We know that untoward conditions mean that you might have to divert from your chosen route (e.g. uncommunicative authors, missing papers, poor-quality studies). Experienced systematic reviewers learn to anticipate what is going to happen next. Whether you are travelling on a busy motorway or on a rural lane, it is a good idea to pay attention to your journey time (time management) and plan what to do if your vehicle breaks down (contact your supervisor). Collective experience has taught us how to overcome the most common road hazards and we'd like to share our knowledge with you. In this book, we offer a broad range of tips and strategies to help you begin your journey and reach your final destination.

This chapter has introduced the notion of carrying out a systematic review as part of your Master's thesis. In the next chapter, we discuss practical tips to help you plan and manage your review. In Chapters 3 to 9, we talk you through the individual steps involved in conducting a systematic review. In Chapter 10, we lead you through ways to disseminate your review to wider audiences. Finally, Chapters 11 and 12 focus on how to carry out systematic reviews of specific types of evidence: qualitative evidence and economic evaluations, respectively. We recognize that systematic reviews can be 'bitty' in that you might start a new step before the current one is fully finished; this might occur, for example, if you are waiting for papers to arrive in the post or for input from others. As such, the advantage of this book is that it hasn't been set out like a novel (i.e. written for you to read cover to cover once). Instead, each chapter is designed to stand alone. We hope that you will start by reading the whole book in chapter order, but we then expect that you will dip in and out of chapters at appropriate points in your research journey. As we mentioned earlier, some of the concepts explored in the book will seem unfamiliar to you on first reading, which is why we have included a Glossary of key terms for you to refer to as and when needed.

Frequently Asked Questions

Question 1: Is a systematic review 'real research'?

This is a valid and common question posed by Master's students. There are some researchers and academics who argue that carrying out a systematic review is not 'real research'. We believe that they are wrong. Submitting a systematic review as a research project for a Master's thesis, or as part of a doctoral thesis, has become commonplace in many universities and across a variety of different disciplines. We believe that the many learning opportunities that are derived from the systematic review process can help students to achieve academic goals and can equip them with the skills that are required to meet the needs of research communities and to enhance their continuing professional development and practice. Indeed, systematic reviews are now regarded as legitimate outputs for the periodic assessments of research conducted within universities worldwide, particularly in the UK and North America.

Question 2: Am I taking the easy option by carrying out a systematic review?

No, definitely not. Systematic reviewing can be a difficult, time-consuming and solitary activity. It's not for the faint-hearted. While you don't (usually) have to go through the ethics process (which can take time and be fraught with difficulties), there are other challenges to face, such as coping with thousands of possible research reports or government documents or, worse yet, finding none. However, the rewards in terms of outputs and learning opportunities make carrying out a systematic review an excellent choice of project for your thesis. For example, it offers an opportunity to display rigorous and reflective practice in your write-up and the examiner will acknowledge this effort when marking your thesis.

Question 3: Can a systematic review form part of a doctorate as well as a Master's thesis?

Yes, but it is worth bearing in mind that the focus of the review may differ. Master's students typically need to answer a single specific question, but doctoral students tend to use systematic review methodology to describe the literature and/or theory base that informs their primary research. If you are planning to carry out a systematic review to inform a doctorate then you may well find yourself conducting a series of mini systematic reviews rather than one single review that aims to answer a defined and specific question. Alternatively, you might conduct a single systematic review on a very tightly defined topic and go on to conduct a wide-ranging narrative review to situate the results of your systematic review.

Question 4: Should I conduct a systematic or a narrative review for my thesis?

We are often asked this question by students who believe that narrative reviews are somehow easier, or less time-consuming, than systematic reviews, and our answer is always the same: we advocate that students should, where possible, conduct a systematic rather than a narrative review for their Master's thesis. Students are often surprised when we tell them that a lot of the steps involved in systematic and narrative reviews overlap, so there isn't usually a lot of difference in workload between the two methods. However, systematic reviews have a number of advantages over narrative reviews. For example, systematic reviews are less open to **bias** than narrative reviews, as they represent a synthesis of the available evidence pertaining to a specific review question. As such, they can help to advance knowledge, and are often easier to publish than narrative reviews. Students often find the transparent and rigorous nature of systematic review methodology helpful too, as it gives structure to the review process and minimizes the chances of missing any potentially relevant papers. Students also tell us that it can be reassuring to be able to 'check' the quality of their review against a **standardized systematic review checklist** (see Chapter 7 for more information). Having said that, some topics lend themselves better to narrative rather than systematic reviews (e.g. reviews of conceptual issues or reviews in which the primary aim is to give a broad overview of a diverse topic area). As such, we recommend that you speak to your supervisor and choose the most appropriate methodological approach for your topic area.

Question 5: I'm studying for a Master's in a non-health discipline – can I still conduct a systematic review?

The short answer is: yes, you can! Although the process of systematically reviewing the literature originated in healthcare, systematic reviews are now considered best practice across a range of disciplines and topic areas, including criminology, transport, housing, environmental studies, politics and history. A good-quality systematic review has the potential to advance a field of enquiry regardless of discipline, so please don't rule out conducting a systematic review solely because you are studying for a Master's in a non-health discipline. To further illustrate the widespread application and value of systematic review methodology, we have endeavoured to use case examples from systematic reviews conducted across a range of disciplines throughout this book.

Question 6: Are there any ethical considerations that I need to think about if I decide to conduct a systematic review as my Master's thesis?

This is a good question, and one that is commonly overlooked by Master's students. It's rare to have to seek ethical approval to conduct a systematic review, as it's commonly assumed that each study included in the review will have been subject to ethical review already. However, that does not mean that there aren't potential ethical issues that may arise during the conduct of a systematic review (Vergnes et al., 2010). For example, systematic review methodology does not explicitly prevent the inclusion of 'unethical' studies, although this is something that would likely be picked up on during **quality assessment** (see Chapter 7). Furthermore, if participants have given informed consent for their data to be included in the primary research studies included in the review, this consent may not stretch to secondary analysis of these data in the form of a systematic review or meta-analysis. It's unlikely that these issues will arise, but it's important to be mindful of the potential for this, and to discuss these issues with your supervisor if and when you come across them.

Question 7: Can I ask other people to help me with review activities or do I need to work on my own?

We strongly believe that the best way to conduct a high-quality systematic review is through teamwork, as working independently can be seen as a limitation of the review process. In particular, if you are planning on publishing your work (see Chapter 10), then collaboration on some specific review activities is essential (e.g. **searching**, **screening** and selecting studies, **data extraction** and quality assessment). However, you must be aware that, as with any assessed assignment, your review is expected to be your own work. Make sure that you check your institutions' guidelines, and take advice from your supervisor *before* involving anyone else in any part of your review. If this isn't permitted by your institution, then it's important to ensure that your work is thorough and that you act as your own colleague (e.g. by **cross-checking** your own data extraction or quality assessment – see Chapters 6 and 7 for more information). We also believe that you should acknowledge this as a limitation when writing up your work. If your final review is good enough, then you may always have the option of getting a potential co-author to perform the cross-checking necessary for publication after your review has been assessed.

Further Reading and Resources

Borrego, M., Foster, M. and Froyd, J. (2014) 'Systematic literature reviews in engineering education and other developing interdisciplinary fields', *Journal of Engineering Education*, 103: 45–76.

Gough, D., Oliver, S. and Thomas, J. (2013) *Learning from Research: Systematic Reviews for Informing Policy Decisions: A Quick Guide*. A paper for the Alliance for Useful Evidence. London: Nesta.

Langer, L. and Stewart, R. (2014) 'What have we learned from the application of systematic review methodology in international development? – A thematic overview', *Journal of Development Effectiveness,* 6(3): 236–48.

Pickering, C. and Byrne, J. (2014) 'The benefits of publishing systematic quantitative literature reviews for PhD candidates and other early-career researchers', *Higher Education Research and Development,* 33(3): 534–48.

Pickering, C., Grignon, J., Steven, R., Guitart, D. and Byrne, J. (2015) 'Publishing not perishing: How research students transition from novice to knowledgeable using systematic quantitative literature reviews', *Studies in Higher Education,* 40(10): 1756–69.

Pooley, N., Olariu, E. and Floyd, D. (2016) 'When is the use of a systematic literature review appropriate? A comparison of systematic, rapid, and scoping reviews and their application to the HTA process', *Value in Health,* 19(7): A396.

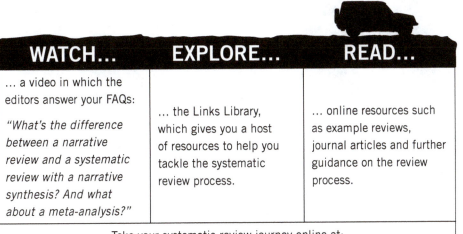

WATCH...	EXPLORE...	READ...
... a video in which the editors answer your FAQs: *"What's the difference between a narrative review and a systematic review with a narrative synthesis? And what about a meta-analysis?"*	... the Links Library, which gives you a host of resources to help you tackle the systematic review process.	... online resources such as example reviews, journal articles and further guidance on the review process.

Take your systematic review journey online at:
https://study.sagepub.com/doingasystematicreview2e

Planning and Managing My Review

Gerlinde Pilkington and Juliet Hounsome

2

This chapter will help you to...

- Plan and make appropriate use of the resources available to you

- Co-ordinate your research activities

- Feel confident managing all aspects of the systematic review from start to finish

- Write your thesis document and submit your thesis on time

Introduction

This chapter focuses on how you can co-ordinate your review activities, and suggests how you can employ the resources at your disposal to maximize the chances that the review will progress smoothly. We start by helping you to consider the key resources available to you before you start your review. We then discuss hints and tips for successful time and resource management that you can use as your review progresses. Some of the points considered in this chapter will also be addressed in other chapters, but we feel it's necessary to highlight their importance in this chapter too.

Help: where do I start?

Welcome to the world of systematic reviewing. You may be feeling both apprehensive and excited, and you may have many questions regarding the research process and be wondering what lies ahead. Be assured that you are not alone! This chapter has been designed to help by offering you advice on how to successfully manage each stage of your research project.

Don't just think of the review process as one distinct entity; break it down into bite-sized chunks – macromanaging the whole journey and micromanaging the individual stops along the way. Planning ahead and thinking about each stage at the outset can help save time later. Organization and planning are the key factors to successfully completing a systematic review, so take a deep breath, get out your pen and paper (or keyboard, tablet, laptop or smartphone) and get started. Put a plan in place now for the research activities you need to undertake. However, be aware that plans don't always go as intended, and as a researcher you need to learn to be pragmatic and flexible, and to adjust your timetable as necessary.

The first thing that you need to think about is the submission deadline for your thesis. As a student, it is likely that you will be working to a tight time schedule. Think about when your thesis is due to be submitted and plan backwards from then. Whether you are looking at months or weeks, you will find that the review process will expand to fill the time that you have available.

The next thing that we recommend that you do is to write a review protocol (a summary of the methods that you are planning to follow during the review process). Students often worry about how to do this, but don't panic. We discuss this further in Chapter 3, and, in addition, most of the chapters in this book contain a list of points to consider when writing your review protocol. Their aim is to provide you with key information that you can use to guide the development of your review protocol.

Writing a review protocol makes you think about the overall review process and therefore allows realistic goals to be set at the start of the project. It is likely that only you and your supervisor will ever read your protocol, unless you choose to register it online (more about this in Chapter 10), so you don't need to worry too much about structure or style; your supervisor will prefer you to concentrate on the content. You don't have to write a protocol, but we encourage you to do so! Take a look at our website for examples of published protocols that we've used to guide our systematic reviews (https://study.sagepub.com/doingasystematicreview2e).

You also need to consider the potential scale of your review. You probably won't know this yet, but hopefully you will have a better idea once you have completed your scoping searches and formulated a protocol (see Chapters 3 and 4). The results of your scoping searches should give you an idea of the volume and type of relevant studies available. If your review is likely to include a small number of studies (i.e. fewer than five), then spending time setting up systems and learning how to use new software may not be time well spent. However, if you are likely to include more than five studies in your review, then the use of, for example, **bibliographic software** may save you time and effort in the long run. The design of your included studies also affects how you manage your review. For example, quantitative and qualitative studies are likely to require different analysis packages. Having a clear idea, from the outset, of the direction of your review allows you plenty of time to investigate the available data management and analysis options.

If we liken the systematic review process to a journey, planning the route is essential. You need to know how long you have to reach your destination (when do you submit?), what type of route you are going to take (qualitative/quantitative?) and what to pack for your journey (what resources?). The rest of this chapter focuses on how you can co-ordinate your activities. We suggest how you can use the resources at your disposal to ensure that your review continues moving forward without too many disruptions.

What types of resources are available?

Time

As a student you will be very aware that your project has a deadline – an often inflexible one that is set by your academic institution. Careful planning, efficient project management and realistic expectations of what is achievable will enable you to make the most of your time. You will make life much easier for yourself if you overestimate, rather than underestimate, the time it takes to complete key tasks.

People

During the review process other people (e.g. supervisor, peers and/or family) may be available to contribute to review activities. These activities include cross-checking your extracted data and quality assessment exercise, or proofreading text. More importantly, don't forget to call on the help of other reviewers, **information specialists** and/or statisticians if you need them – they can help you to choose the most effective review methods, search for evidence, locate references and analyse your data appropriately. Throughout the book, we highlight areas where we feel your review may benefit from the help of others. A word of warning though: you need to speak to your supervisor to find out how much of a contribution from others is allowed, as some academic courses demand that every piece of work that you produce is entirely your own. In our view, having somebody to assist you with, for example, study selection does not violate this principle any more than asking your supervisor for guidance. However, you must check before asking others for help with your review.

Tools

We assume that, as a student, you are using a computer and have Internet access. We also assume that you are using a word-processing package to write up the different stages of your review. There is an array of tools available to help you manage your research. These include software packages that can assist with data management, data storage and structured thesis template examples. The companion website has resources to help you decide which is the most appropriate software and gives guidance on cost (some are free!) and compatibility.

In particular, think about the advantages and disadvantages of using a bibliographic software package to manage your studies (e.g. EndNote or RefWorks). Be creative. Look for technology that can help you conduct your review, chat to other students about the tools that they have used, or will be using, and listen to your supervisor's advice. Also, check what resources are available to you via your institution as they are likely to be free (or discounted) and may come with additional support that explains how to use the software/application appropriately.

Managing your time and co-ordinating activities

Figure 2.1 lists all of the individual steps in the systematic review process that are discussed throughout this book, which hopefully will soon become familiar to you. It can be used as a checklist of the different stages that you will inevitably go through when completing your review. You can use it as you make plans to start your journey, building in some scheduled stops before arriving on time at your final destination.

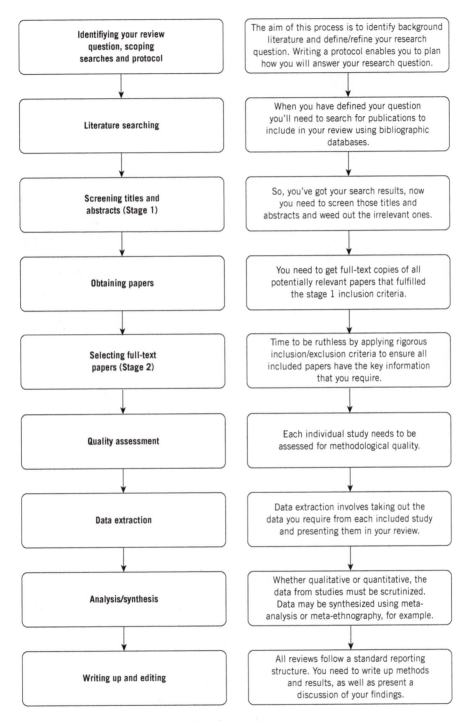

FIGURE 2.1   Key steps in the systematic review process

Time is probably the most crucial resource you have so it's a good idea to plan now for what lies ahead. You need to make sure you meet your timelines, whether self-imposed or supervisor-driven. Start by managing your review project as you mean to go on. Be calm, organized and efficient. Unfortunately, we can't tell you how much time to allocate to the individual stages of your review. In our experience, data extraction almost always takes more time than you anticipate, and almost every-one underestimates how long it takes to reflect on their results and write up the discussion. Furthermore, systematic reviews of qualitative evidence tend to be more iterative than those of quantitative evidence, and so the processes of extracting and synthesizing data may be more time-consuming. Having said that, each review (and reviewer) is different and, with so many unforeseeable factors at play, the best advice we can give you is that, inevitably, some deadlines will be missed. Just make sure that you know your final submission deadline and that you meet it!

When it comes to systematic reviewing, you will never find that you have spare time on your hands – even if you might want (need) some. While some tasks may seem tedious (or perhaps you may just put off doing a task because you don't think you have time to complete it before you have to go out), you can always find a differ-ent task to be getting on with. You'll soon learn that you can start a task and then put it on hold while you make progress with another task. As you get on with your review you will be working on distinct, yet overlapping, activities. You might find that while some tasks are ongoing (such as waiting for the arrival of the full-text papers that you have ordered) you can get on with something else (such as reading the papers that you already have).

Peers, friends and/or family are often quite willing to help out with some basic tasks. For example, when screening and applying inclusion criteria (Chapter 5), your supervisor or peer could cross-check all or some of your decisions. This helps to ensure you are not dismissing potentially relevant studies. From an editing perspec-tive, your supervisor should take a periodic look at drafts of your work and provide feedback. How this will be done, and when, needs to be negotiated in advance with your supervisor to ensure that you are both aware of when you will send drafts and receive feedback. We all have friends and family who are great at spotting mistakes; you can ask them to read chapters of your work and to do their best to find typ-ing errors or half-written sentences. Just make sure you (and your collaborator(s)) are clear on expectations and timelines before you begin, particularly if you plan to publish your review (more about this in Chapter 10).

Another way to make best use of your time is to make sure that your work, from ini-tial drafting of your protocol to final editing of your thesis, is consistent. Establishing consistency across all aspects of the review process early on can save precious time and effort later. You might wonder why this is important at such an early stage and perhaps you are thinking, 'Surely I can go back and change minor things later?' The short answer to this is that 'minor' things can end up as 'major' things. It is likely that you will end up spending hours and hours editing sections of text in your document because you didn't carefully consider consistency (in formatting, data extraction, analysis and so on) at the beginning of your research. We suggest that you consider the following advice as you conduct your review:

- Throughout your project, be consistent with use of terminology. For example, some authors will discuss health status, treatments and patient groups, while other authors will talk about health outcomes, interventions and populations. You need to choose the terms that you want to use and stick with them.
- If your review topic refers to terms or concepts that are interchangeable, it's often useful to pick the most commonly used/preferred term and stick with it to avoid confusion for the reader; for example, 'social interactions' and 'social relations' could be interchangeable, but also mean different things in different contexts.
- Think carefully before using abbreviations, but if you have to use an abbreviation then be consistent; for example, if you want to abbreviate the phrase 'cardiovascular disease' don't use both CD and CVD.
- It will save time if you're consistent with how you spell words or phrases. Think about capitalization and hyphenation; for example, would you use Actor-Network Theory or actor network theory?
- Always list the included studies in your tables in the same way (alphabetically or chronologically) – be consistent throughout your document.

Managing your review: employing the right resources for the job

Now that we've discussed time-saving tips and highlighted potential pitfalls, it's time to consider how other resources can be used to make the review process easier for you to manage.

Managing your record keeping

Make record keeping a priority! Record keeping is a basic and required step in project management and allows you to keep an up-to-date and accurate account of what you have achieved at different stages of the review. It also helps you to outline and plan future activities. Unfortunately, it is an activity that is all too often neglected during the review process. Inevitably, the reviewer ends up questioning his/her own actions: Why did I leave out that study? Did I search that bibliographic database? How many duplicate references did I have? The best way to avoid such unnecessary stress is to take note of everything you do as you carry out day-to-day review activities. There are many ways to keep records, from paper and pen notes written chronologically to the use of electronic database systems tailored to suit your review. Choose the method that you prefer. From our experience, electronic record keeping is more efficient than the pen and paper method, especially when it comes to searching for information, and it is satisfyingly time-saving if you are dealing with a large number of included studies.

Table 2.1 gives an example of record keeping. Keeping thorough and accurate records in this way allows you to review the decisions you have made, and having the information to hand can help you to defend and justify your decision-making. For example, if you are asked why a specific paper was not included in your review, you can easily check your records and determine whether it was included in your search results and, if it was, the reason for its subsequent exclusion (Chapter 5).

TABLE 2.1   Example of record keeping

Reference	Included at screening?	Obtained paper	Included at selection?	Reason for exclusion
Anderton (2002)	Yes	Electronic	No	Inappropriate population
Apple (2013)	Yes	Paper	Yes	Not applicable
Brent (2002)	Yes	Still to get		
Bryan (2002)	No	Not applicable		
Clyde (2003)	Yes	Paper	Yes	Not applicable

In addition, we suggest that you keep a research activity journal (again, electronic or paper) on a daily or weekly (as appropriate) basis. The purpose of this journal is to allow you to look back and reflect, at regular intervals, on your more general research activities. This will enable you to monitor progress and highlight issues that you might want to return to at a later date. Often, conducting a systematic review is a steep learning curve during which you will be developing and refining many new skills, so it's a good plan to keep track – especially for your CV.

Managing your files (paper or electronic)

The term 'managing files' (electronic and/or paper) relates to systems for storing information, backing up information and keeping files in order so that you are always working on the most up-to-date version of your document.

Storing information

During the review process, organized storage of information is essential. The storage of information is comparable to packing for a journey: you need to have more than enough space in your car as you know that you will be picking up more passengers along the way.

However small you think your project is, you will soon be engulfed in piles of papers, information, data and different versions of reports and tables. Before you even start your review you need to think about how you will keep track and store your electronic and non-electronic data. Clearly ordered information storage systems accompanied by good record keeping and unique labelling of studies will help you to quickly access information as and when required by your review.

When storing files electronically, the use of folders and subfolders can be a considerable help. It is a good idea to set up folders to allow you to save files in a logical manner. An example of how to organize all the information and data you might gather during the review process is shown in Figure 2.2.

This organizational system is by no means exhaustive, and perhaps small reviews might adopt a simpler system. However, note how many of the folders and subfolders match with the key stages of the review process shown in Figure 2.1.

Backing up information

The ideal electronic system has automatic, built-in backup facilities but if this isn't a feature of your computer, make sure you back up your work regularly. You could use a removable memory stick, external hard drive or web-based storage to keep copies – get into good habits early on and it will save you time and effort later in the review. For example, make sure that, on a regular basis, you back up your work to your computer, leave an electronic copy with a friend or colleague, send the latest version to yourself via email as well as backing up to your academic institution's file storage. This might sound a little excessive but you can never have too many backups!

Keeping files in order

You also need to consider version control. You need to make sure that you are always working on the most up-to-date copy of your work, be it **data extraction tables**, report writing or referencing. One way of managing this is to include the date in the name of a file (e.g. introduction_25_nov_2017). It is then important to change the date with each substantive update of your work. As can be seen in Figure 2.2, to avoid confusion, older versions of your files can be moved into an archive folder.

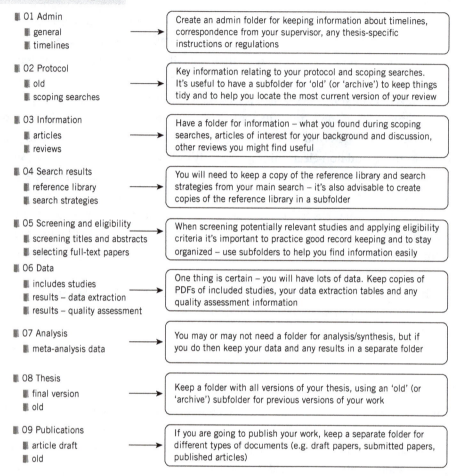

FIGURE 2.2 Useful folder and subfolder headings

Unique labelling of studies used in your thesis (e.g. as part of background information or included studies) should be assigned consistently. For example, use of first
author and year of publication (e.g. Brown_2016) is a simple way to identify studies
and is easy to remember; if the author has published multiple studies in a single year,
include the journal title as well (e.g. Brown_BMJ_2016) or add 'a', 'b', and so on to
the year (e.g. Brown_2016a).

Managing your data extraction (Chapter 6)

Planning how you are going to manage your data is critical to the quality of your
review; it is important that you are clear about the data you need, how you are going

to use the data and what format the data need to be in. Furthermore, you need to know all of this before you begin to extract data from your included studies.

Not all study authors will report the data that interest you in the same way. You need to try to make the data that you are extracting as uniform as possible so that they can be used as planned when it comes to **data synthesis**. For example, when extracting data on participant characteristics, authors can choose to record age as a mean value (65 years of age), median value (62 years of age) or present a range of ages (58 to 70 years of age). For your review, you should extract data on participant age in such a way that you can compare age across your included studies. Designing and piloting a structured **data extraction form** or data extraction table(s) and thinking carefully about how each required field should be completed (and therefore reported in your thesis) will go a long way to ensuring that the data you extract can be used as you had originally planned (see Chapter 6 for more information). The content of the data extraction form must always be considered in relation to the **data tables** that you plan to use in your thesis (e.g. participant characteristics, study characteristics and study results tables).

Managing your references

We recommend that students use some form of bibliographic software package to facilitate storage and use of references. If you do not have access to such a program through your academic institution there are several open-access (free) programs available on the Internet.

The main purpose of bibliographic software is to help you to organize, annotate and integrate required references into your work. As a systematic reviewer, this type of software offers you the following benefits:

- automatic download of reference details (titles, abstracts, **keywords**, etc.) from bibliographic databases (e.g. Web of Science, formally known as Web of Knowledge);
- electronic storage of all reference information, including notes, images and PDFs;
- ability to group and organize studies using keywords (e.g. background, included studies, excluded studies);
- the function of adding and formatting in-text **citations** and bibliographies (e.g. **Harvard** or **Vancouver** referencing style).

Although extremely useful, bibliographic software is not infallible. It is necessary to check that automatically downloaded references have been imported correctly from each bibliographic database. It is also important to check for spelling mistakes and capitalization, particularly if you have entered references by hand, and that in-text citations and bibliographies are formatted correctly. Remember, if you are manually typing references into your reference library, each field (such as 'journal title' or 'authors') may have to be entered in a specific way.

It is worth noting that examiners often check the accuracy of the referencing in a thesis to allow them to form an overall assessment of the student's attention to detail. Bibliographic software, appropriately used, helps you to make a good impression without having to make too much effort.

Practical applications: choosing the right software

Table 2.2 lists different types of software packages that you might think about using during your systematic review. It gives practical advice on how and when you might use these packages, and further details of specific software options are available from our website (https://study.sagepub.com/doingasystematicreview2e). Our view of the pros and cons of the different packages will hopefully help you to make an informed choice when it comes to identifying the most appropriate software package(s) for your review. The right tools for the right job make everything go smoothly – why walk to the next town when you can hitch a ride with a friend?

Remember, the Internet can help you to decide which software to use, how to get the best from it and how it can benefit your project. Search for instructional **blogs**, video tutorials and 'how to' guides. Audio-visual material (with step-by-step software instructions) can be a fantastic help, especially if you learn by watching and doing rather than reading. Ask your supervisor if there are staff or students who are experienced software users within your institution, ask the librarian for help with bibliographic software and check your institution's web pages for resources that may be useful. You never know, there may be a free course or workshop that has all the right answers!

Writing your thesis document

You will need to obtain (and follow) a copy of your academic institution's thesis submission guidelines. Read this document thoroughly, boring as this may be, before you even begin your systematic review. Key things to look for are: required thesis structure and length, and recommended referencing system. What we present here stems from our experiences of building documents that require consistent presentation of text, headings, tables, figures and references. Remember, word-processing packages make it

TABLE 2.2   Software packages available and their pros and cons

Software package	What can I do with it?	Advantages	Disadvantages
Word-processing software	Keep records of: Time management Progress made Search results Reference lists and unique identifiers Which studies are included Create forms for: Inclusion/exclusion Data extraction Quality assessment Writing up and editing Also: Create templates and use pre-set styles	A word-processing package is very useful for all stages of the review, not just writing up. You will be able to look back and reflect on decisions made – justification and accountability are crucial in a viva voce situation.	Compared with spreadsheets and database software, word-processing packages have less functionality when it comes to creating and manipulating tables. Additionally, they are not always the best choice when dealing with complex numeric data – they are more suited to text.
Spreadsheet software	Keep records of: Time management Progress made Reference lists and unique identifiers Which studies are included Create forms for: Inclusion/exclusion Data extraction Quality assessment Manipulation of numerical data Also: Create tables, graphs and charts	Excellent for numerical data and can be used throughout the review process. Better than a word-processing package for creating tables through use of filter and sort tools. Each workbook can contain multiple sheets. Most packages have a function that allows data to be imported and exported (e.g. into a word-processing or statistical package), the same data can then be presented in different formats.	Not so useful if the majority of data is qualitative in nature. Make sure you know the basics before setting something up. Spreadsheets are often misused or data input incorrectly into inconsistently formatted cells. This can alter values and skew results.
Database software	Keep records of: Time management Progress made Search results Reference lists and unique identifiers Which studies are included Create forms for: Inclusion/exclusion Data extraction Quality assessment	Excellent for use in reviews with vast quantities of data. Can be used for everything other than statistical analysis, referencing and writing up your report. Databases are usually intuitive and user-friendly with lots of useful functions. Each database has the capability to store multiple forms and tables that can be interlinked, and this avoids having several documents clogging up your folders.	If you have never used a database before you might find it time-consuming to learn. If you've fewer than five studies included then setting up a database probably isn't worthwhile. A few hours spent learning how to get the best from software is time well spent in a bigger or more complex review.

(Continued)

TABLE 2.2   (Continued)

Software package	What can I do with it?	Advantages	Disadvantages
	Also: Create tables, charts and graphs	Most packages have the function to import/export data (e.g. to word processor, spreadsheet or statistical package), which enables the same data to be presented in different formats and ensures that the data are input accurately.	
Specialist software (e.g. statistical, qualitative)	Conduct statistical analyses Directly extract data into the package Create graphs and charts Code data Prepare data for analysis	Can perform analyses for you and produce graphs, tables and figures.	If you don't know very much about statistics then you might be analysing your data inappropriately. If you are keen to use a statistical package then we suggest you take some time to look at the different packages available and, in consultation with an expert, decide how you might utilize them. It can take a significant period of time to learn how to use specialist packages.
Reviewing software	Conduct all stages of the review using just one package	There are numerous packages, both free and paid, which cover all aspects of the review process from screening titles and abstracts, data extraction, producing tables and forest plots, to writing up.	As they are designed for generic reviews and have pre-defined functions, they may not allow enough flexibility for certain reviews.
Bibliographic software	Store references De-duplicate multiple references Generate unique identifier for individual studies Use custom fields and grouping feature Insert references in-text and create bibliographies Attach PDFs and images to the correct reference	Most online databases allow you to save citations to a bibliographic software package. Use this software to create bibliographies and insert the correct references into a document – this function can save a significant amount of time. Multiple fields allow for adding notes, grouping and organizing references (i.e. background, included studies, excluded studies).	Software may not be freely available via your institution; however, you can access free/online versions. It can be time-consuming to learn to use. However, the likelihood is that you will spend more time referencing manually. You must check that the word-processing package and bibliographic software that you choose are compatible, otherwise you will not be able to insert in-text citations.

easy for you when it comes to writing up your thesis. Not only do they have set styles for headings, subheadings, regular text and bullet lists, they can even create your table of contents. As you become familiar with the software you will find all sorts of helpful features that will allow you to manage your review efficiently and effectively. Don't forget to make full use of the search facility and the electronic thesaurus. Take time to 'play' around with the programs you have chosen and discover the useful functions they offer.

Write as you go along, or at the very least keep bullet points that you can expand on later. We suggest that you structure your thesis as soon as you can so that you can write the straightforward sections, such as background information or research rationale, long before you start to write up your results. For information, we have included a suggested thesis document structure (Box 2.1). This structure has generic headings that you might find helpful as you plan how to write up your review as a

Box 2.1

Suggested thesis document structure

- Title page and preface (don't forget to include your name, date and acknowledgements, etc.)
- Glossary and definitions
- Table of contents
- Abstract or summary (a brief synopsis of all included chapters or sections)
- Background
- Research question
- Methods

  o   **Search strategy**
  o   Inclusion and exclusion criteria
  o   Screening and selection
  o   Data extraction and quality assessment
  o   Methods of synthesis/analysis

- Results
- Discussion (including principal findings, strengths and limitations, and relevant factors)
- Conclusion
- References
- Appendices

postgraduate thesis, and gives subheading detail for what should be reported in the methods section. It would also be useful to look at other published systematic reviews or theses for inspiration.

Importantly, it's all an issue of style. Does your institution have a set format for word-processed documents? Will you lose marks if you use the wrong style? For example, you could be asked to write using the Times New Roman typeface with the font size at 11 pts and the spacing set to double, perhaps with a large margin. Does your subject area or institution have preferred styles of writing? Can you use abbreviations? How should you reference? We always recommend starting as you mean to go on by using the correct styles from day one.

As soon as you start to write up your review you will realize that it is extremely important for you to manage your references appropriately. You could find yourself writing text such as 'Three studies were set in Japan' or '16 studies used valid outcome measures'. You need to make sure that the reader can identify the studies to which you refer. To do this you need to add references to your text. In this book we have not always included references when using illustrative or suggested text. However, you must! You need to plan ahead and think about how to make your review easy to read. Take, for example, the sentence: 'Three studies were set in Japan.' Using Vancouver formatting, this sentence would look like this: 'Three studies[1,2,6] were set in Japan.' Using Harvard formatting, the same sentence would look like this: 'Three studies (Brown, 1999; Smith, 2000; Jones, 2012) were set in Japan.' Some reference formats are more conducive than others to the reporting of systematic reviews. However, you must follow the reporting guidelines set by your institution. Referencing is made easier with bibliographic software because it allows for the formatting of in-text references and bibliographies in a variety of predefined styles at the touch of a button. This comes in handy if you want to publish your review in a peer-reviewed journal that requires a different referencing style (see Chapter 10).

Also, as we mention in Chapter 7, don't forget that you can use a systematic review quality assessment checklist on your own review. Using a checklist is a win–win situation. You can identify areas where you think your thesis is weak (and you can make changes before submission) or, more likely, you can reassure yourself that you have done a good job.

Final thoughts

So, now you have a better idea about how to make use of your time and how to co-ordinate your research activities, using the appropriate resources for each job. But we know that you're a beginner, and that this all might still seem very bewildering. We think it is a good idea for you to keep the lessons you've learnt from this chapter at the back of your mind as you work through your review – treat this chapter as a practical guide that you have to hand.

Here are our key messages:

- Organization is key to a successful review
- Plan ahead but be prepared to be flexible
- Identify the resources you have available to you
- Plan your file storage system at the beginning of the project so you know where information is to be stored
- Back up files regularly
- Keep detailed records of the tasks that you've done
- Use a bibliographic software package
- Check institution style guides for thesis submission
- Larger or more complex reviews may benefit from the use of specialist software packages
- Speak to your supervisor and/or experts for help and advice

Key points to think about when writing your protocol

Well-designed protocols reflect most of the headings in Box 2.1 with the exception of results and discussion. Protocols usually include a section on project timelines – use the information in this chapter to help plan your time

What an examiner is looking for in your thesis

- A well-structured document that adheres to institutional submission guide-lines
- Academic style with appropriate use of language and with no (or very few) spelling mistakes and typing errors – if this is an area where you are weak (e.g. if English is not your first language), then seek assistance
- Appropriately formatted (and correct) references and a similarly correct **reference list** – don't throw away marks by skimping on this aspect of your thesis

Frequently Asked Questions

Question 1: As well as studying I work full time, so how can I manage my time?

Many of the tasks, such as Stage 1 screening (Chapter 5) and data extraction (Chapter 6), can be carried out in short time slots. Make the most of the time that you do have available. For example, if you have an hour free, scan-read some titles. An important thing to remember is that, with certain non-critical tasks, it is okay to start a new task before you have completed a current one. Be flexible, co-ordinate your activities to reflect the time available on any given day, but remember that you need to block out some dedicated time for writing up (and **dissemination**).

Question 2: What do I do if an article that I ordered arrives later than planned?

It depends. If the article arrives on the day that you are due to submit your thesis, then you can acknowledge its existence without incorporating it into your review. You might state, 'The following study was received too late for incorporation in the review. However, future updates should examine its eligibility and implications.' If it arrives the week before you are due to submit, and you are confident that inclusion will not change your conclusions, you could state, 'The following study was received too late for incorporation in the review; however, a cursory examination suggests that the results of the current review would not be sensitive to its findings.' If it arrives the week before you are due to submit, and you believe that inclusion will change your review findings, then you need to discuss what to do about it with your supervisor and make a pragmatic decision based on what you can realistically achieve during the week before submission.

Question 3: I don't know what to do about the statistical aspects of my review – what are statistical software packages, and will they help me?

Statistical software packages are specialized computer programs for combining numerical data. It is possible that, at some point in your review, you will need to use a statistical package to conduct statistical analyses and/or produce graphs and tables. If you are not familiar with statistical software packages, then you are probably not very familiar with statistics either. This means that you really should get statistical advice from an expert.

Question 4: Should I use a spreadsheet (e.g. Microsoft Excel) or a database (e.g. Microsoft Access) to help me manage my review?

The tasks that can be achieved using spreadsheets and databases are similar – both systems use tables to store data. However, while there is an overlap in functionality, they are designed to carry out different jobs. In short, spreadsheets are essentially large tables (or several tables) that have the ability to run formulae and analyses, and produce summaries and reports of data. Databases are large tables that can store vast amounts of data in various formats; tables can be interlinked and manipulated. There isn't a right or wrong choice; your choice will be based on what software you think best fits the needs of your review.

Question 5: How can I get the most out of my chosen software?

If you know what you want to achieve with specific software, but don't quite know what steps you need to take, then we recommend that you take advantage of all that the Internet has to offer. Be assured – there are people who are knowledgeable when it comes to making software do what they want, from basics to more complex functions, and they are more than happy to share their skills online, for free, to help others. Part of the research journey (for us at least) is often figuring out how to do something new, how to solve a problem; this might include carrying out multiple Internet searches for inspiration, followed by a bit of trial and error, and then the joy of walking into a colleague's office and celebrating success (and then sharing the new-found knowledge)!

Question 6: Are there any checklists available to help me structure my write-up?

Yes, there are many checklists available to help you structure your write-up. Looking at other systematic reviews, you will find that a common feature is the inclusion of a PRISMA flow diagram (Figure 2.3). PRISMA stands for Preferred Reporting Items for Systematic Reviews and Meta-Analyses (Liberati et al., 2009; Moher et al., 2009). The PRISMA flow diagram represents a standardized approach to reporting how many studies were identified for inclusion in your review, and what happened to these studies as your review progressed (i.e. how many were excluded from your review, why and when?). You can also visit the EQUATOR Network (www.equator-network.org) for more information about reporting guidelines for systematic reviews.

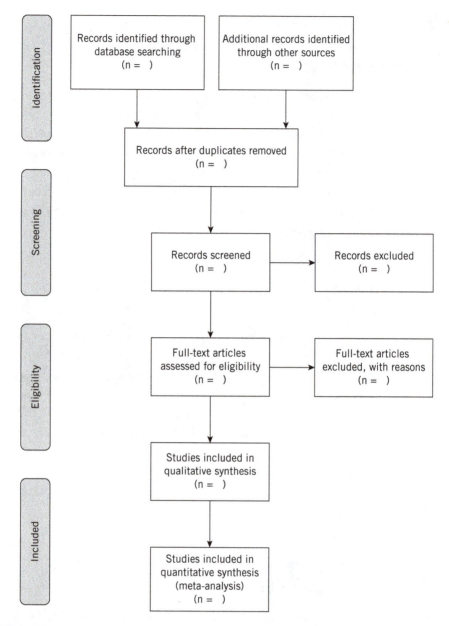

FIGURE 2.3   The PRISMA flow diagram for use in systematic reviews of quantitative evidence

Source: Liberati et al., 2009; Moher et al., 2009.

Further Reading and Resources

Booth, A., Papaioannou, D. and Sutton, A. (2016) *Systematic Approaches to a Successful Literature Review*. 2nd edn. London: SAGE.

Gough, D., Oliver, S. and Thomas, J. (eds) (2012) *An Introduction to Systematic Reviews*. London: SAGE.

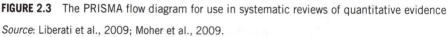

Higgins, J.P.T. and Green, S. (2011) Cochrane Handbook for Systematic Reviews of Interventions. (www.handbook.cochrane.org). (Last accessed February 2017).

Joanna Briggs Institute (2014) Reviewers' Manual. (www.joannabriggs.org). (Last accessed February 2017).

Pears, R. and Shields, G. (2010) *Cite Them Right: The Essential Referencing Guide*. 8th edn. Basingstoke: Palgrave Macmillan.

Petticrew, M. and Roberts, H. (2008) *Systematic Reviews in the Social Sciences*. 2nd edn. Oxford: Blackwell.

WATCH...	EXPLORE...	READ...
... a video in which the editors answer your FAQ: *"How do I decide if it is worth the time to learn how to use a new software package to manage references in my review?"*	... the Links Library, which gives you a host of resources to help you tackle the systematic review process.	... online resources such as example reviews, journal articles and further guidance on the review process.

Take your systematic review journey online at:

https://study.sagepub.com/doingasystematicreview2e

3

Defining My Review Question and Identifying Inclusion and Exclusion Criteria

M. Gemma Cherry and Rumona Dickson

This chapter will help you to...

- Understand the importance of taking the time to develop, refine and clarify your review question

- Become aware of the pitfalls and challenges related to the development of a good review question

- Identify inclusion and exclusion criteria

- Appreciate the value of writing a review protocol

- Deal with challenges, for example, if your review question or inclusion and exclusion criteria need to change during the review process

Introduction

In this chapter, we lead you through the process of formulating a clearly structured review question using six practical steps. These steps will help you to focus your systematic review topic. We introduce the role of scoping searches and highlight the importance of discussing your topic with others. The chapter then provides guidance on translating your chosen topic area into a valid and manageable review question, and a set of inclusion and exclusion criteria. Finally, we include practical advice on how to write your protocol.

Be prepared: good preparation leads to good performance

When embarking upon a research project, two key components are required to ensure a successful and smooth journey: your review question (which tells you your destination) and your review protocol (which details your proposed route and research activities).

The development and refinement of the question is the most important phase of any research project. When carrying out a systematic review, the review question and the review protocol are what you come back to when you are in the middle of the research and feel a bit overwhelmed or confused – which you almost certainly will be at some point during your systematic review journey. The review question, therefore, needs to be clear, well defined, appropriate, manageable and relevant to the outcomes that you are seeking. Be aware that defining your review question and writing your review protocol may take longer than you think. However, we can assure you that it is a vital investment on your part, as it will save you time and energy as your project proceeds.

How do I develop my review question?

Box 3.1

Developing a review question

Step 1: Identify a topic area of interest to you

Step 2: Carry out early scoping searches

Step 3: Focus your ideas to define the scope of the review

Step 4: Finalize your review question and develop your inclusion and exclusion criteria

Step 5: Consider contacting experts in the topic area

Step 6: Write a review protocol

We recommend that you follow six steps when developing your review question. These six steps are presented in Box 3.1.

Step 1: Identify a topic area of interest to you

It is important to identify a review question in a topic area that interests you. You will be working on your review for some time and you will need this interest to help you maintain motivation for the duration of the project. Your topic may be informed by external forces (e.g. requirements of your professional practice or your supervisor's research interests); however, the specifics of your research question are likely to be under your control.

Unfortunately, you might have your heart set on addressing a review question only to discover unexpected challenges. For example, someone else may have already published a review addressing your specific question, or there may be very limited research available on your chosen topic, or there may already be a massive amount of published research. To manage these challenges, we recommend that you keep your topic area broad and remain open-minded when initially looking at the available evidence.

Step 2: Carry out early scoping searches

Once you have identified your potential topic area(s), the next step is to conduct preliminary literature searches. These are frequently called scoping searches, and are discussed more fully in Chapter 4. These are not as comprehensive as the **main search** that you will use later to identify studies, reports or documents for inclusion in your review, but rather are performed to determine whether your topic area is suitable for a review by giving you a snapshot of the volume and type of evidence available for synthesis. You can choose to search a range of bibliographic databases (see Table 4.2 in Chapter 4, which shows many of the most commonly searched databases available), including Google Scholar. Don't forget to also search **PROSPERO**, which is an international prospective register of systematic reviews held by the University of York's **Centre for Reviews and Dissemination** (CRD), to check what reviews are currently under way in your topic area.

The results of your scoping searches will quickly let you know if the review that you want to carry out has already been published. If this is the case then don't panic, just be glad that you have discovered it at this early stage rather than midway through your write-up. Look closely at the published review that you have found to check what question was actually addressed. Is it exactly the same as your question and did the authors use appropriate systematic review methods? When was it published? Has there been research published on the topic since it was published? If so, then there may be a rationale for updating the existing published review. If not and/or you see too much overlap, then you will need to reformulate or adapt your review question. Think of it like planning an alternative route because of a road closure – it's a nuisance but far better to re-route before you set off.

Scoping searches also allow you to identify the individuals or groups of researchers who are leaders in your topic area of interest. The results may also highlight a variety of (perhaps disparate) viewpoints. Published research studies frequently contain a section that outlines future research directions; it can be useful to read these to see if your proposed review question is mentioned or if authors have called for a synthesis of available evidence before more primary research is conducted. If this is the case, then it is a good sign that there is a gap in the research evidence that your review could fill.

The results of scoping searches also tell you how much published literature and information are available in your topic area. For example, from the results of your scoping searches you will know whether there is little or no published research in your topic area, a common fear raised by many of the students we supervise. When we are asked, 'How little is too little?' the answer that we give is that this depends on the purpose of your review. For example, if the purpose of your review is to demonstrate to your examiners that you are able to identify, synthesize and critically appraise literature, then including zero papers in your review would be inappropriate. You might then think about expanding your review question to include wider groups of participants, more interventions or different outcomes (see Frequently Asked Questions at the end of this chapter). However, if you are carrying out a review to inform your own professional practice, then you may want to continue with your original question, particularly if you are thinking of applying for a grant to fund primary research. Many funders make it a requirement that a systematic review is carried out prior to funding approval to show that there is a need for the research. If there is no published evidence, it is generally appropriate to use results of the (rather thin) review to demonstrate that your research has identified a gap in knowledge.

On the other hand, we are often asked, 'How much is too much?' Some students find that their scoping searches end up returning hundreds of published papers or documents. If this happens, you might want to think about narrowing your review question or changing the focus of your review. For example, perhaps choose a more specific population, comparator, intervention, phenomena, **perspective**, outcome or setting. You can look at some of the published papers in the topic area to get a sense of how to narrow your review question. For example, if your interest is in adolescent pregnancy, you may want to consider the lived experiences of pregnant adolescents. Is there a certain stage of pregnancy in which you are interested? Are you only interested in pregnant adolescents in a specific country? Considering different perspectives will help you to focus your question and will yield a more manageable and homogeneous set of evidence.

Do not be disheartened if, at this stage, you have to modify, expand or reject a topic area or review question because your scoping searches identify an evidence base that is different to the one that you expected (or hoped) to find – this is very common. The aim of scoping searches is to give you an idea of the current state of knowledge relating to your topic. It is like studying a map before starting a journey so that you get the lay of the land and are able to explore different travel options.

Step 3: Focus your ideas to define the scope of the review

Once you have identified a topic area and conducted early scoping searches to determine the volume and type of literature available and the important current issues, the next stage is to focus on the direction that you want your review to take. At this stage, it is important to produce a short summary of your ideas (no more than one side of A4 paper), and explore these ideas with your supervisor and/or peers to solicit their views. If possible, it may also be worthwhile attending a live or online conference in the topic area to get a sense of the current research issues relating to your chosen topic. A **mind map** of the results of your earlier scoping searches can be a useful way to summarize your ideas and may highlight key issues that you had not previously considered. You can either mind map by hand, or take advantage of the many free mind-mapping websites available on the Internet.

Figure 3.1 provides an example of how mind-mapping can help to focus a topic area. The example shown in Figure 3.1 is typical of the refinement of a research question relating to fever in children. You can see that there are a number of different ways to approach such a broad topic area of interest, and that there are also a number of potential review questions. For example, you could consider current guidelines for treating fever in children and systematically review them; you could take a qualitative approach and systematically review research reporting parents' views on treating fever in children; or you could consider the best method or time to treat fever (e.g. when first presented or after 12 hours). Each review question requires its own specific methods of searching for evidence and synthesizing data (see Chapter 4) so it's important to consider all of the options before finalizing your review question (see Box 3.2 for more detail).

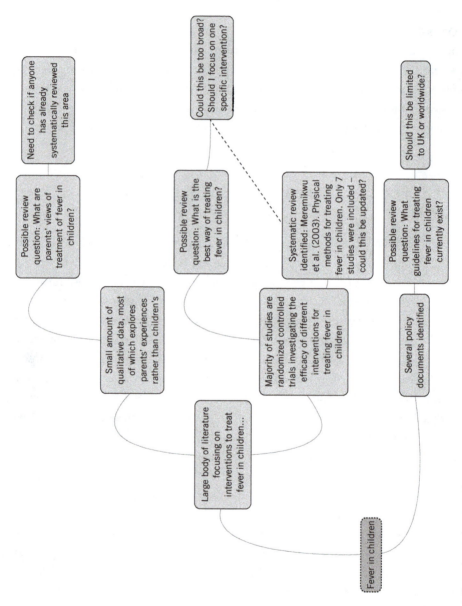

FIGURE 3.1 Evolution of a review question

Box 3.2

Evolution from general idea to final review question

Qualitative or quantitative evidence?

Students often ask, 'Should my systematic review include qualitative or quantitative evidence, or both?' The answer to this lies with your review question. You must choose the evidence that best helps you to answer that question. Consider again the fever in children example. Figure 3.1 displayed a number of possible ways that you could choose to systematically review the research in this area.

1. When is the best time to treat fever in children?

This approach lends itself best to quantitative evidence. The variable of interest is a quantifiable concept (time) and therefore the outcome that you are interested in would be efficacy of treatment at a certain time point after the initial onset of fever. Doctors' or parents' views on the best time to treat fever would not be very useful in this case.

2. What is the best way of treating fever in children?

This too is a quantitative question. You may be interested in the clinical effectiveness of a new drug for lowering fever. Does it work quickly? Does it have side effects?

3. What are parents' views on treatment of fever in children?

In this case you are interested in considering parents' views on the best way to treat fever in children and qualitative research findings would provide a rich source of data.

4. What guidelines for treating fever in children currently exist?

This question can only be answered by quantitative evidence and can be addressed through a review of existing guidelines for, perhaps, healthcare workers or parents.

By this stage, you may have spent a lot of time and invested a great deal of energy in your chosen topic area and the thought of starting again or changing your approach might not be welcome. However, it is important to consult and consider the views of others, especially your supervisor. It is far better for your topic area to change or evolve at this stage rather than after the review is under way. It might require a little more reading or literature searching, but consideration of the opinions and ideas raised in your discussions with your supervisor, peers and/or professional colleagues is time well spent.

Step 4: Finalize your review question and develop your inclusion and exclusion criteria

Now it is time to finalize your review question and develop your inclusion and exclusion criteria. Up until now you have approached your systematic review as a topic area that interests you. It is only now that this abstract concept will begin to take shape as a review question. Your review question is a formal statement of the intention of your systematic review. It is a statement that develops from what you know (as identified through the examination of available evidence) to what it is that you want to know, or know more, about. A good systematic review question should be motivating and spark your own thoughts and interests, be researchable (i.e. can be completed to a high standard within the timelines set and resources available), be neither too broad nor too narrow, and have a focus on information that is both available (i.e. published or **grey literature**) and accessible (i.e. available to you).

A review question is different from a hypothesis because a hypothesis states the probable direction of a relationship between variables, whereas a systematic review question always ends with a question mark and is always connected to a body of existing knowledge. A systematic review question can be descriptive (presenting a concept), normative (exploring preferences about what should happen), observational or relational (investigating a relationship between two or more variables), causal (investigating the effect of one or more independent variables on one or more outcome variables) or theoretical (exploring factors that cause a condition, event or process). Examples of review questions relating to infection control in hospitals are displayed in Table 3.1.

Inclusion and exclusion criteria

At this stage, it's also important to define your inclusion and exclusion criteria. Inclusion criteria describe the specific attributes that a study must have if it is to be included in your review; they are sometimes known as eligibility criteria. Exclusion criteria describe the specific attributes that *disqualify* a study from inclusion in your review. Inclusion and exclusion criteria are often mutually exclusive, but not always. For example, study design, date of publication, language of publication and publication type may all form exclusion criteria but may not be explicitly stated in your inclusion criteria.

TABLE 3.1   Different types of review question

Type	Example review question
Descriptive	What are the trends in hospital-acquired infections over the past 10 years in the UK?
Normative	How do healthcare professionals perceive the care delivery issues relating to allocation of scarce infection control resources in rural hospitals?
Observational/relational	Is there a relationship between hospital-acquired infections and death rates in hospitals?
Causal	Do structured educational interventions have an impact on the number of hospital-acquired infections?
Theoretical	What reasons do healthcare professionals give for non-compliance with infection-control policies in hospitals?

Inclusion and exclusion criteria should clearly map onto your review question and contain sufficient detail and clarity to enable you to accurately and appropriately include and exclude studies from your review. Development of your inclusion/exclusion criteria and review question often occur in parallel, and should be seen as complementary rather than separate tasks; to some extent your review question defines your inclusion/exclusion criteria, but thinking specifically about inclusion/exclusion criteria can also help you to identify review questions that are ambiguous or too specific, broad or narrow, and can help you to focus your review question accordingly.

There are several ways to define your inclusion and exclusion criteria. One way to develop inclusion criteria, used predominantly in systematic reviews of effectiveness, is to generate a **PICO** table. PICO stands for population, intervention, comparator and outcome. Occasionally people also include study design and setting, therefore turning PICO into **PICOSS**. An example of a PICOSS table assessing the evidence for reading as an intervention is shown in Table 3.2.

TABLE 3.2   A detailed and comprehensive PICOSS table

Review question	What is the evidence for reading aloud and group reading as therapeutic interventions to improve the health and well-being of patients with neurological disorders in clinical and long-term care settings?
Population	Adults and children with any neurological disease or insult, progressive or traumatic.
Intervention	Individual reading; reading aloud; reading in groups. Any form of reading used either as a therapeutic intervention or as an activity to identify therapeutic benefit and/or improve health or well-being.
Comparator	The stated interventions compared with each other or no intervention.
Outcomes	Any positive or adverse health-based outcome, any objective health-based clinical outcome measure. Any subjective outcome, whether it be identified through thematic analysis or quantitative data collection methods.
Study design	All.
Setting	Hospital wards, rehabilitation centres, nursing and residential homes, respite centres and hospices. Outpatient and community settings.

The PICOSS table shown in Table 3.2 is detailed and clearly states relevant inclusion criteria pertaining to the key components of the research question. However, some people find it helpful to replace PICO/PICOSS with a more general table or summary paragraph outlining the key parameters and variables of interest, particularly if they aren't focusing on intervention research. An example of a detailed summary paragraph is presented in Box 3.3. If you plan to systematically review qualitative evidence, then please see Chapter 11 for further guidance on how to develop your inclusion and exclusion criteria.

Box 3.3

A comprehensive summary paragraph detailing inclusion/exclusion criteria

Review question

'Is there a relationship between shame and criticism in family carers of people with long-term mental health difficulties?'

Inclusion/exclusion criteria

Studies will be included if they: a) are published in English or have an English-language abstract available; b) report data from family carers aged 18 years or over who provide at least 10 hours of face-to-face care to relative(s) aged 18 years or over with long-term mental health difficulties; and c) report **quantitative data** sufficient for computation of **effect size**(s) regarding the relationship between shame and criticism. In keeping with relevant literature in this area, the term 'long-term mental health difficulty' will be defined as any non-organic mental health difficulty of ≥6 months' duration. Studies will be excluded if they are published prior to 1975.

Irrespective of *how* you define your inclusion and exclusion criteria, it's important to pay careful consideration to this step, regardless of whether the evidence considered as part of the review is qualitative, quantitative or both. This will help you to avoid nasty surprises later on in the review process. It's also important to think about whether you will introduce bias into your review by stipulating specific inclusion and exclusion criteria (e.g. by only including studies published in a certain language). We recommend that you pay particular attention to **language bias**, **publication bias** and bias that may arise as a result of only including studies reported in a particular format. Language bias occurs because studies that report positive findings are most likely to be published in English-language journals, and studies with null or negative findings are more likely to be published in non-English-language journals. You therefore need to consider the implications of including only English-language papers in your review. Publication bias occurs because studies that report positive findings are more likely to be submitted and selected for publication in a peer-reviewed journal than studies that report null findings. It's important to bear this in mind when deciding what type of evidence you plan to include in your review (see Chapter 4 for more information). Finally, if you choose to only include evidence that is reported in full-text format, you may miss out on the most up-to-date evidence. An example of this would be the results of studies that have recently been reported at a conference, which may be available in abstract format only. However, if you do include abstract-only evidence, then you need to acknowledge the limitations of this type of evidence in your thesis (e.g. limited information available and the fact that early results do not always match final results).

You may, at this stage, realize that you need to carry out further work before you can finalize your review question and/or inclusion and exclusion criteria. If this is the case, then please don't get disheartened – it's essential to get this right before progressing to the next stage.

Step 5: Consider contacting experts in the topic area

At this point you should have a well-developed and well-defined review question and inclusion and exclusion criteria, and should feel confident that your review question is unique and has not previously been considered. At this stage, you may wish to contact experts in your topic area for reassurance. The purpose of the contact would be to ensure that your question is relevant and that you are indeed on the right track in relation to currently accepted practice. If you choose to contact experts, then we suggest you should be well versed in your topic area before you approach them and be very clear about what it is you want from them. As you would expect, a generic email saying you are a Master's student doing a review and want their help is unlikely to receive a response. However, a well-thought-out email (as shown in Box 3.4), explaining your review question and its importance to your professional practice, and containing a set of well-defined questions, has a good chance of receiving a response.

Box 3.4

Example of a well-thought-out email

Dear Professor Smith

Re: Systematic review of non-pharmacological treatments for the management of agitation in patients with psychotic illness

I would be very grateful if you could advise me on an aspect of the review that I am currently conducting as part of my Master's studies at the University of Liverpool. The preliminary aim of the review is to examine the efficacy of non-pharmacological treatments for the management of agitation in patients with psychotic illness. I've completed my scoping searches and have identified several relevant systematic reviews in the area (please see attached). As a published expert in this clinical area, please could you have a quick read through this list and let me know if you are aware of any pertinent systematic reviews that I may have missed during my searches and/or if you know of any ongoing reviews that are due to be published in the next 3 months? This will help me to ensure that I am addressing a novel question, which has not previously been addressed.

Thank you very much for your help.

Yours sincerely
Student

If you are conducting the review to inform your professional practice, you may also wish to consider key stakeholders' perspectives, a process which in healthcare is commonly referred to as '**patient and public involvement**', or PPI. For example, if you are interested in investigating the effectiveness of interventions designed to target chronic pain, changes in pain levels may seem an appropriate outcome from a clinical point of view. However, people living with chronic pain may view this differently, and instead consider psychological well-being, irrespective of pain levels, to be a more appropriate outcome. Consideration of the views of patients and the public may therefore help to ensure that your review question has both practical and theoretical relevance.

Step 6: Write a review protocol

Good news – you are almost ready to begin your review! You have a research question (the destination); now you need to write a review protocol (which explains how you will get there). This is a very important stage and should not be skipped. Every piece of quality research is guided by a research protocol. No researcher would consider conducting a randomized controlled trial without a protocol, and your systematic review is just as important a piece of research as any other and one which deserves to have an overall plan. A well-thought-out protocol describes the current evidence base, identifies the question that the review will address and outlines the methods that will be used to answer the question. Table 3.3 provides a guide to the sections you may want to consider including in your review protocol. These suggestions do not need to be followed exactly but writing a clear protocol based on them will help you set out your work plan and will also serve as a guide that you can return to during the research process.

TABLE 3.3 Example of a protocol structure

Title	Content
Background, including summary of existing literature	This section can be developed from the results of your scoping search. It should provide a context for your review, and should include a discussion of relevant literature. However, it should generally not make specific reference to any of the studies that you are likely to include in your review. This section should end with a rationale explaining why your review question is important and why it needs to be addressed. This text can eventually form the background section of your thesis.
Research question	You should present your research question in as much detail as possible.

Methods
  Search strategy
  Inclusion and exclusion criteria
  Screening and selection
  Data extraction
  Quality assessment
  Data analysis
  Patient and public involvement
  Dissemination plan
	This is the section where you detail what you will do during the review process and how long you think each task will take. Under the heading of search strategy, we recommend that you describe the resources that you want to search and give summary details of how you will look for published literature (e.g. journal articles and conference proceedings) and, if appropriate, unpublished or grey literature (e.g. registry data and government reports). In a protocol, you don't have to list all the specific search terms you used; however, it is good practice to provide one example search strategy in an appendix. It should then clearly state your inclusion and exclusion criteria; it can also be helpful to reproduce your PICO/PICOSS table, if appropriate, in your protocol. Finally, this section should go on to describe what data will be extracted, how data will be quality assessed, who will do each task and how the data will be analysed. If you plan to carry out a meta-analysis then you need to think about subgroups and heterogeneity in advance. It's also helpful to outline your plans for PPI (if relevant) in your protocol, together with details of how you plan to disseminate the findings of your review.

Time frame	You should include a plan of how long you anticipate that each important review activity will take. Chapter 2 may help you to set realistic timelines for your review.

When writing your protocol, we recommend that you also make use of the 'Key points to think about when writing your protocol' and 'What an examiner is looking for in your thesis' sections that are provided at the end of most chapters. There are also some example protocols on our website (https://study.sagepub.com/doingasystematicreview2e).

Begin your review

You are now ready to begin searching for evidence. If you've taken our advice, your review question will be well focused, and you will have clearly stated inclusion and exclusion criteria and a clearly written protocol.

Key points to think about when writing your protocol

- Results of scoping searches can help you to describe the quality and quantity of relevant evidence available
- It is important to make a case for why your review question is important and needs to be addressed
- Clearly stated inclusion and exclusion criteria are essential to the successful completion of your review

---

What an examiner is looking for in your thesis

- Evidence of scoping searches
- A well-set-out systematic review question – this lets the examiner know you have carefully considered the different components of the question
- An explicit statement of your inclusion and exclusion criteria

---

Frequently Asked Questions

Question 1: How long will it take to develop my review question and inclusion and exclusion criteria, and produce my protocol?

This is a valid and common question asked by Master's students and unfortunately the answer is 'How long is a piece of string?' It will depend on the topic area, your experience in the topic area, the amount of published research available, the clarity of the original idea, the length of time it takes to hear back from your supervisor and others involved in your review, the amount of time you can dedicate to it (i.e. will you be studying full time or part time?) and many other variables. At this point, you will likely consider different options and this will take time, but remember 'failing to prepare means preparing to fail'. Whatever time is spent on this activity will be time saved later because you will have a clear question and a plan that you will be able to use to guide your review.

Question 2: What if I can't define my inclusion and exclusion criteria?

It is our experience that students often fail to clearly define aspects of their inclusion and exclusion criteria. For example, the population might be very broad – such as adults with diabetes. It might be necessary to define the population more specifically as 'adults with newly diagnosed diabetes' – which would identify a population that is totally different from people diagnosed with diabetes in childhood. If you are finding it difficult to define your inclusion and exclusion criteria at an early stage, then you will most definitely struggle when it comes to putting searches together and/or deciding which papers are relevant. Clearly defined inclusion and exclusion criteria will save you time and reduce stress later in the review process. If you're struggling to define yours, then we recommend that you revisit your review question to see whether it requires some modification. It may also be helpful to discuss this with your supervisor, as they may be able to provide a more objective viewpoint.

Question 3: What if I lose interest in the topic halfway through the review?

Unfortunately, this is something that sometimes happens to students and often can't be helped, particularly as you will be investing a lot of time and energy in the review. This is why we strongly encourage you to pick a topic area that interests you. For example, we often suggest that students carry out reviews in topic areas that are of interest to the health and/or welfare of a family member, or that will be used as part of their professional practice. However, as you will likely be conducting a relatively short-term research project, we hope that you will stay motivated throughout the research process. It is worth knowing that all researchers, at some point in a research project, will wonder why they ever began the project.

Question 4: Can I refine or change my review question?

This is a question that is commonly asked by Master's students at various points in their systematic review journey. In our experience, students' most commonly cited reasons for wanting to refine or change their review questions relate to bore-dom or lack of interest, having an unrealistic initial topic idea or question, and/or being faced with unforeseen developments in the field (such as someone publishing a very similar review). We tell students that, unfortunately, losing interest in a topic is not a good reason to refine or change a review question. However, if, after conducting your scoping searches, you realize that your initial review question is too broad, narrow or unrealistic, then by all means refine or change it. Again, if a very similar review to yours is published while you are still in the planning stages, it might be advisable to refine or alter your review question so as to avoid duplication. If this happens much later in the review process, however, then we would advise you to think carefully before abandoning your review question completely. Can you reflect upon this publication in your discussion? Is your review exactly the same, or can the results of your work still make a contribution to your discipline? Try to view this challenge as a learning opportunity rather than a barrier to your success.

Question 5: Do I have to write a review protocol?

Simply put, it is good practice to write, and then refer to, a review protocol. Having a protocol makes your research journey easier and will help you to plan research activities, guide your decision-making and show what progress you have made. However, it is not essential.

Further Reading and Resources

Booth, A., Papaioannou, D. and Sutton, A. (2016) *Systematic Approaches to a Successful Literature Review*. 2nd edn. London: SAGE.

Gough, D., Oliver, S. and Thomas, J. (eds) (2012) *An Introduction to Systematic Reviews*. London: SAGE.

Higgins, J.P.T. and Green, S. (2011) Cochrane Handbook for Systematic Reviews of Interventions. (www.handbook.cochrane.org). (Last accessed February 2017).

Joanna Briggs Institute (2014) Reviewers' Manual. (www.joannabriggs.org). (Last accessed February 2017).

Petticrew, M. and Roberts, H. (2008) *Systematic Reviews in the Social Sciences*. 2nd edn. Oxford: Blackwell.

WATCH...	EXPLORE...	READ...
... a video in which the editors answer your FAQs: *"Do I have to write a protocol for my systematic review? What if I make a mistake?"*	... the Links Library, which gives you a host of resources to help you tackle the systematic review process.	... online resources such as example reviews, journal articles and further guidance on the review process.

Take your systematic review journey online at:
https://study.sagepub.com/doingasystematicreview2e

4

Developing My Search Strategy

Yenal Dundar and Nigel Fleeman

Introduction

This chapter guides you through the processes of identifying evidence of relevance to your review question. We begin by discussing scoping searches, and then provide guidance on how to carry out the main search for evidence of relevance to your review question. Finally, we discuss how best to report these methods in your protocol and thesis.

What is meant by searching and where do I start?

Searching is an umbrella term that is used to describe the many methods by which you can identify evidence of relevance to your review question. Potential sources from which you may be able to identify relevant evidence include bibliographic databases, volumes of specialist journals, reference lists from retrieved articles, research registers, government databases, newspapers and experts in your particular field. In this chapter, we focus on two related yet distinct modes of searching: scoping searches and your main search for evidence. As discussed in Chapter 3, scoping searches are used to inform the development and refinement of your review question and inclusion/exclusion criteria. In contrast, your main search for evidence is the one that identifies relevant evidence for inclusion in your review. We will explain how you might carry out each of these searches in more detail later in this chapter, but before you start, it's important to remember that, no matter what you are doing, it is always good to have help. As such, we recommend that you first take some time to think about the help available to you before you begin to search for evidence. This advice might feel frustrating, particularly if you are keen to start searching immediately. However, seeking help at this stage may save you time in the long run, so it's time well spent.

When it comes to searching, a helping hand can come from an information specialist or librarian who is used to searching bibliographic databases (more on these later!). These experts have professional knowledge of the information that is kept and indexed electronically, and have a good idea of how to interrogate specialist bibliographic databases efficiently. When you take your preliminary or final research question to specialists you may be surprised (pleasantly, we hope) that they can offer a different perspective and help you to explore your question more fully. We are often amazed at the different perspectives brought by colleagues who see things through a different kaleidoscope from our own.

As discussed in Chapter 2, help can also come in the form of bibliographic software packages such as EndNote or RefWorks. Such software packages not only allow for direct exportation of citations (and their abstracts) from the Internet and bibliographic databases, but they also have tools that enable you to easily identify (and then delete) duplicate records (a process that is explained in Chapter 5). Bibliographic software packages are also extremely useful when extracting data, synthesizing results and writing up your thesis. For example, these packages allow you to sort references into relevant groups, such as all included studies, or all studies with the same endpoint. Furthermore, bibliographic software packages enable you to directly insert references into your thesis and in the referencing style (e.g. Harvard or Vancouver) required by your academic institution.

Finally, your supervisor is also a valuable source of help and advice. S/he may be able to quickly identify key papers in your topic area that you can use as a starting point when developing your main search. S/he will also be able to advise you about how much evidence you need to find, where to search for it and who in your institution may be able to help you carry out this important task. We recommend that you speak to your supervisor before going any further.

Scoping searches

As discussed in Chapter 3, scoping searches should be the first searches that you conduct. Scoping searches differ from the main search that you carry out in your systematic review as they use simple **search terms** and are designed to provide an overview of literature of relevance to your review question or topic area. Scoping searches can help you to locate a sufficient number of key references quickly (e.g. studies and other reviews published on your research topic), give you a clearer understanding of the key issues related to your topic area and provide an estimate of how many studies you are likely to find when you carry out your main search. The results of scoping searches can therefore help you to determine the direction of your review, develop and refine your review question, and develop your main search.

Scoping searches need to be carried out at the start of your project, prior to finalizing your review question and writing your review protocol. You may, or may not, need to report the details of your scoping searches in your thesis. Ask your supervisor if there is a departmental preference or, to be on the safe side, include details in an appendix. Scoping searches may sound time-consuming, but it's time well spent. It's also important to remember that, when carrying out scoping searches, you don't need to search every available resource – a couple of relevant and up-to-date data sources will likely suffice. Similarly, you don't necessarily need to read through hundreds of full-text papers at this stage – often the titles and abstracts of potentially relevant studies will give you an idea of the type and breadth of available evidence.

Planning your main search and designing your search strategies

Once you have carried out your scoping searches, focused your research question and inclusion/exclusion criteria, and written your protocol, the next step is to plan your main search and design your search strategies. For clarity, we use the terms 'main search' and 'search' interchangeably throughout this book to refer to a global approach to searching, and the term 'search strategy' to refer to specific and structured search syntax for individual bibliographic databases.

Box 4.1 summarizes the key steps to consider when planning your main search. Although we present these as sequential steps, we often find that searching is an iterative process and therefore you may find that you work through these steps in a non-linear fashion, returning to a step more than once.

Box 4.1

Key steps to consider when planning your main search

Step 1: Think about how comprehensive your search needs to be

Step 2: Consider the different types of evidence available to you

Step 3: Identify the specific bibliographic databases that you will search for evidence

Step 4: Identify and refine your key search terms

Step 5: Search bibliographic databases using your final search strategies and collate citations

Step 6: Consider complementary searching activities

Step 1: Think about how comprehensive your search needs to be

The first thing to do is to think about exactly how comprehensive your search needs to be in light of your review question and your topic area. Some argue that it is essential that you find all available evidence relevant to your review question, no matter how long it takes. The counterargument is that it is not worth spending long periods of time conducting lots of different searches that only find one additional obscure piece of evidence which includes information that will not, in all probability, change the overall results of the review. As a student, you will likely have time and resource constraints placed upon you and, therefore, we recommend a pragmatic approach to searching. That's not to say that we discourage thoroughness (quite the opposite!), but recommend that you ensure that your main search is adequately balanced in terms of specificity (it identifies the relevant evidence) and sensitivity (it does not identify too many irrelevant sources or pieces of evidence).

Step 2: Consider the different types of evidence available to you

Once you have reflected on how comprehensive your search needs to be, it is important to consider the different types of evidence available to you. Broadly speaking, there are two main types of evidence. Evidence from commercial publishers is commonly referred to as 'published literature'. Common examples of published literature include peer-reviewed journal articles or academic books. The main sources of published litera-ture include bibliographic databases, volumes of specialist journals, reference lists from already retrieved articles and newspaper archives. In contrast, the term 'grey literature' is commonly used to refer to the vast array of evidence *not* controlled by commer-cial publishers. Common sources of grey literature include legislation, government documents or databases, annual reports, bulletins, statistics, dissertations or theses, **conference proceedings** and research registers of ongoing or unpublished studies.

TABLE 4.1   Strengths and limitations of searching for published and grey literature

	Published literature	Grey literature
Pros	• Easier to locate • Easier to systematically and transparently search • Easier to clearly report results in thesis • Easier to transfer results of search to reference management software • Usually peer reviewed	• Allows access to diverse evidence sources • Reduces risk of publication bias • Often not limited by restricted word count • Searches can identify ongoing or unpublished studies
Cons	• Data might be limited • Risk of publication bias	• Harder to locate • Peer-review status is often unclear, and therefore evidence may be more likely to be biased • Harder to search systematically and transparently • Harder to store results of searches • Harder to clearly report methods in thesis

It is a common misconception that systematic reviews should only include published literature. While it is true that some topics lend themselves more to the inclusion of published literature (such as systematic reviews of clinical effectiveness of healthcare interventions), others do not (such as systematic reviews of changes in governmental legislation). When choosing what type of evidence to search for, our advice is to think carefully about the most relevant evidence for your review question, together with the strengths and limitations of searching for published and grey literature (see Table 4.1).

Step 3: Identify the specific bibliographic databases that you will search for evidence

Once you have decided whether to search for published and/or grey literature, you must next identify how you plan to search for this evidence. The majority of systematic reviews rely on bibliographic databases as their primary data source. Bibliographic databases are available electronically or via the Internet, and contain records of published and grey literature, including journal articles, theses and dissertations, books, government and legal reports, newspaper articles, conference abstracts and patents. These records, as a minimum, include a title, author(s) and a source (e.g. journal article). The structure in which these databases are accessed is commonly referred to as a platform or **interface**. Most bibliographic databases relate to a particular discipline, although some are multidisciplinary in content. While some bibliographic databases can be accessed without charge by the general public via the Internet, the majority are available on a subscription-only basis. Your institution should have access to a range of bibliographic databases. If, however, you cannot access a particular bibliographic database through your institution, speak to a librarian or information specialist who might be able to get you temporary access.

Examples of some common databases are presented (by discipline) in Table 4.2, although it must be noted that this list is not exhaustive but rather is intended as a guide.

It is likely that you will need to search more than one bibliographic database in order to identify relevant evidence for inclusion in your review. However, make sure that you search only those that are most relevant to your review question and topic area. For example, if the aim of your research is to derive a theory to explain a particular phenomenon, then you will need to consider the different research approaches that exist to derive theories (e.g. **grounded theory**), and you will require a wide range, as opposed to an exhaustive amount, of evidence. As such, a broad search across several bibliographic databases is likely to be required. However, if the aim of your research is to examine the clinical effectiveness of a particular healthcare intervention, then your search would likely be focused solely on a smaller number of specific healthcare databases.

TABLE 4.2   Databases and other sources of information by discipline

Database	Platform/interface
Multidisciplinary	
British Library Archives	http://searcharchives.bl.uk
Copac*	http://copac.ac.uk/
Google Scholar*	scholar.google.com/
JSTOR	www.jstor.org/
Library of Congress Catalogue	https://catalog.loc.gov/vwebv/searchBrowse
ProQuest Dissertations & Theses (PQDT)	ProQuest
Scopus	SciVerse
Web of Science (formally Web of Knowledge)	Thomson Reuters
Zetoc*	http://zetoc.mimas.ac.uk
Criminal justice	
The Home Office (UK Government)*	www.homeoffice.gov.uk/
National Criminal Justice	EBSCO Host
The US NCJRS (National Criminal Justice Reference Service) Abstracts Database*	www.ncjrs.gov/App/AbstractDB/AbstractDBSearch.aspx
Economics	
EconLit	EBSCO Host
HEED (Health Economic Evaluation Database)	Wiley Online Library
Research Papers in Economics (RePEc)	www.repec.org
Education	
EPPI Centre (The Evidence for Policy and Practice Information and Co-ordinating Centre)*	http://eppi.ioe.ac.uk/cms/
ERIC	EBSCO Host
Educational Research Abstracts Online	Ingenta
Health	
CINAHL	EBSCO Host
ClinicalTrials.gov	www.clinicaltrials.gov
Cochrane Library* (including DARE, HTA, NHS, EED)	http://onlinelibrary.wiley.com/o/cochrane/cochrane_clcentral_articles_fs.html
EMBASE	Ovid
EU Clinical Trials Register	https://www.clinicaltrialsregister.eu/
HTA database*	www.crd.york.ac.uk/CRDWeb/SearchPage.asp
MEDLINE	Ovid, EBSCO Host
PROSPERO	www.crd.york.ac.uk/NIHR_PROSPERO
PubMed*	www.ncbi.nlm.nih.gov/pubmedhealth/
UK Economic and Social Research Council's research catalogue	http://researchcatalogue.esrc.ac.uk/

(Continued)

TABLE 4.2   (Continued)

Database	Platform/interface
History and humanities	
America: History & Life	EBSCO Host
British Humanities Index	ProQuest
British Periodicals	ProQuest
ProQuest Historical Newspapers	ProQuest
Social sciences	
ASSIA (Applied Social Sciences Index and Abstracts)	ProQuest
Campbell Collaboration Library of Systematic Reviews	www.campbellcollaboration.org/library.php
CORDIS*	http://cordis.europa.eu/newsearch/index.cfm?page=advSearch
PsycINFO	www.apa.org/pubs/databases/psycinfo/index.aspx
Sociological Abstracts	ProQuest
Social Sciences Index	Thomson Reuters

* Free to access without the need for subscription

Step 4: Identify and refine your key search terms

Once you have identified which bibliographic databases you plan to search, you need to choose key search terms and refine these until you arrive at a final search strategy (or search syntax) for each database. This may sound easy, as no doubt you are familiar with searching the Internet via search engines such as Google or Google Scholar, where you type in a number of search terms relevant to whatever it is you are trying to find. However, you will probably be less familiar with searching specialist bibliographic databases, which can make devising search strategies more challenging. Indeed, we must stress that designing an optimal search strategy for a specific bibliographic database can take time and is likely to be an iterative process. It is highly unlikely that you will identify the optimal search terms to use on your first attempt (and if you think you have, it will be worth double-checking your terms with an information specialist).

The majority of bibliographic databases allow you to be more precise and use more advanced and complex searches than those you would use when searching the Internet. This is because most bibliographic databases have more than just one box (i.e. field) in which to add text terms. You can also combine the terms entered in each box by using 'AND', 'OR' and 'NOT', also known as **Boolean operators** (see Table 4.3).

TABLE 4.3   Use of Boolean operators when searching for evidence

Boolean operator	Function	Examples
AND	Combines terms and therefore narrows the search and identifies references containing all of the words entered	(education AND university) This search retrieves records containing both the words 'education' and 'university'
OR	Broadens the search and identifies references containing *any* of the words entered	(education OR university) This search retrieves records containing either the word 'education' or the word 'university'
NOT	Used to exclude something and therefore narrows search and identifies references that *do not* contain the term following it	(education NOT university) This search retrieves records containing the word 'education' but excludes those which also contain the word 'university'

Most bibliographic databases also allow you to search specific fields, such as author, title or year of publication, to limit your searches and to specify search parameters, for example, by year or language. Furthermore, most bibliographic databases allow you to search for and combine both **free-text words**, and **subject headings/index terms**. Free-text words are words located anywhere in the title, abstract or main text of the article. In addition to whole words such as 'cancer', most bibliographic databases offer you the option of using 'wildcards' (commonly a question mark (?), an asterisk (*) or a symbol such as '$') when searching for free-text words. These enable you to:

- search for part of a word (e.g. 'wom?n' will find 'woman' and 'women'; 'psychiatr*' will find 'psychiatrist', 'psychiatry' or 'psychiatric');
- search for a whole word that may have different spellings (e.g. 'behavi*r' will find 'behavior' and 'behaviour');
- include a search term and its plural (e.g. 'trial$' will identify 'trial' and 'trials').

Subject headings/index terms are used to index the content of bibliographic databases. Most databases have their own list of particular subject headings/index terms. For example, **Medical Subject Headings (MeSH)** are a list of subject headings used for indexing articles for MEDLINE and PubMed. MeSH terms allow you to consistently retrieve information even when authors use different terms to refer to the same concept. To illustrate, all qualitative research articles should be indexed in MEDLINE and PubMed under the term 'Qualitative Research', even if they use different methodologies (e.g. **interpretative phenomenological analysis**, or grounded theory), and therefore using the MeSH term 'Qualitative Research' may help to improve the accuracy of your search. When conducting a MEDLINE search via PubMed, free-text words are automatically mapped to the corresponding MeSH terms, making the searching of databases easier. You can refer to the United States National Library of Medicine Website for further information on MeSH terms (www.nlm.nih.gov/mesh/).

When devising a search strategy for use within a particular bibliographic database, students often tell us that it can be difficult to decide how many free-text words or subject headings/index terms to use, together with how best to combine them. In our opinion, using a combination of free-text words (e.g. breast cancer OR breast tumour OR breast neoplasm OR breast carcinoma) and appropriate subject headings or index terms (e.g. 'Breast Neoplasms') in your search strategy is considered good practice and should improve the accuracy of your search results. However, the exact number of terms to use depends on your review question and inclusion and exclusion criteria.

When deciding on your search terms, it is often helpful to identify the database record for a study that you have already identified as being important, check what keywords were used to index it and then use the same keywords to begin your main search. Keywords are words assigned to publications to highlight the important topics or subjects being discussed (e.g. a randomized controlled trial, a specific type of exposure or particular group of participants), and they appear in a separate field in the database. Looking at the keywords of a number of relevant pre-identified references can help you to build up the key terms for your search, and can be a useful starting point when building a search strategy. It may also be helpful to revisit your inclusion and exclusion criteria at this point, as they may provide some direction (e.g. if you plan to only include studies that focus on people with psychosis, then the term 'psychosis' may be a useful starting point). Don't forget that there are often UK spellings (e.g. tumour) and US spellings (e.g. tumor) of the same word, as well as technical terms (e.g. neoplasm) and lay terms (e.g. cancer). Don't worry if you need to include multiple search terms for one concept or keyword either – it's better to be comprehensive than to miss potentially relevant studies.

Adapting a search strategy to fit a different database

It is likely that you will search more than one bibliographic database. Remember, one size does not fit all when it comes to searching and you may need to develop different searches for different databases. Most databases offer online user guides, which contain all of the information that you will need to tailor your search strategy to a specific database. Don't be afraid to use these guides! When searching several resources, information specialists can also advise you on how to tweak your key search terms to ensure that your searches are capable of identifying the data that you need. This is one of the reasons that we recommend that you work with information specialists – they are familiar with the unique features of different databases and can help you to identify appropriate search terms for each database.

Step 5: Search bibliographic databases using your final search strategies and collate citations

Once you think that you have finalized your search strategies, run them and remember to check that the key studies you identified from your scoping searches are among the results – if not, go back and revise your search strategies until these studies are identified. When you are happy with your final search strategies, it's time to search your chosen databases and collate all of the identified citations. As previously stated, most bibliographic databases allow you to export citations directly into bibliographic software (revisit Chapter 2 for more information). We recommend that you take advantage of this facility where possible, as it can save a lot of time and effort. However, make sure that you make a note of the number of citations retrieved for each database before exporting them to your reference management software, as you will need to report this information in the 'Results' section of your thesis. It's also a good idea at this stage to copy and paste your search strategies into a separate electronic file so that you know exactly how your search strategies were configured, as you'll need to include this in your 'Methods' section. Some platforms will also allow you to save your search strategies so that you can rerun them at a later date to check for newly published evidence (see the Frequently Asked Questions at the end of this chapter). We recommend that you take advantage of this facility when time allows.

Step 6: Consider complementary searching activities

In addition to searching bibliographic databases, you may also wish to consider complementary searching activities such as **hand searching**, **citation chaining** and contacting relevant researchers in the field. If these activities result in the identification of new references, then make sure that you add these to your reference management software.

Hand searching

The concept of hand searching has evolved over time. In the early days of conducting systematic reviews (up to around the 1990s), researchers did not have access to extensive bibliographic databases that listed both past, current and upcoming publications. It was therefore necessary to go to the library and literally hand search the journals of interest to identify relevant studies (and then make photocopies of potentially eligible papers).

While literal hand searches may still be undertaken, increasingly the term 'hand searching' is used to refer to manual searches of electronic tables of contents of key journals or conference proceedings to identify potential articles of interest. Hand searches of this nature are often carried out to supplement bibliographic database searches but can be time-consuming, so it's important to reflect on the potential added value of this approach before beginning.

In contrast, literal hand searching might be of particular value if your review takes a historical perspective and you need to examine specific documents held in specialist libraries or document storage areas. Having said this, resources that are available electronically change almost daily. For example, the British Library (British Library Archives, 2013) and the Library of Congress (Library of Congress, 2013) now have excellent online archives of British and US newspapers, so it's worth seeing what is available electronically before considering literal hand searching!

Citation chaining

Citation chaining, sometimes referred to as snowballing, is the practice of looking at the **bibliography** of one article to find other, related articles. The effectiveness of citation chaining at identifying citations makes it best practice in systematic reviews despite being a time-consuming task. There are two main types of citation chaining. If you have a key reference, you can look at its bibliography to find other relevant research that your search may have missed – this process is known as **backward searching**. Alternatively, you can see which papers have subsequently cited the key reference by using a database such as Web of Science (using the 'Cited Reference Search') or a search engine such as Google Scholar (using the 'Cited By [# results]' link) – this process is known as **forward searching**.

Contacting relevant researchers

If you plan to include unpublished literature in your review, including studies in progress, it is also good practice to contact relevant researchers in the field (e.g. people who publish widely in your topic area) to see whether they are aware of any unpublished or recently submitted data of relevance to your review question.

Reporting the methods of your search for evidence

It is important to keep detailed records of the methods that you used to search for studies. Having this information available means that you (and others) can rerun and update the searches at a later date if you need to. It should also make life easier for you when it comes to writing the 'Methods' section (i.e. how you searched for studies) of your thesis. You therefore need to make sure that you record the following information as you go along, and then include it in the 'Methods' section of your thesis:

- the date that each search was carried out (including scoping searches, if any);
- the version of each bibliographic database searched (e.g. MEDLINE 1946 to Present);
- the interface used for each bibliographic database searched (e.g. Ovid or Dialog, which can both be used to access MEDLINE);
- all of the search terms used for each specific search (note: your institution may require you to report only the full search syntax for one bibliographic database in your 'Methods' section, and include the remainder in an appendix, so it's best to check);
- any complementary search activities, such as contacting experts or performing hand searching or citation chaining;
- the bibliographic software that was used to store and manage the results of your searches.

We recommend that you consult Box 4.2 as it contains an example of how to write up the conduct of your search strategy in the 'Methods' section of your thesis.

Box 4.2

How to report your search strategy in your 'Methods' section

This case study is taken from a real systematic review conducted by Cherry et al. (2017), which examined the relationships between guilt, shame, emotional over-involvement and critical comments/hostility in carers of people with long-term mental health difficulties.

Search strategy

The conduct and reporting of this review adhere to the general principles recommended by the Centre for Reviews and Dissemination (CRD, 2009) and the **Meta-Analysis of Observational Studies in Epidemiology (MOOSE) guidelines** (Stroup et al., 2000). After several scoping searches, five bibliographic databases (MEDLINE, CINAHL, Scopus, PsycINFO and ProQuest) were searched for relevant published and unpublished literature from their inception until October 2015.

(Continued)

(Continued)

Searches were devised in collaboration with an information specialist and contained no methodological search **filters** or disorder-specific keywords that would limit results to specific study designs or diagnostic groups. Table 4.4 details the search syntax used for each database. Conference proceedings and the authors' own files were then examined for additional relevant literature, followed by the reference lists of both included full-text studies and relevant systematic reviews. Finally, corresponding authors of included papers were contacted for information regarding studies in progress and unpublished research. Searches were repeated in October 2016 to identify any relevant new publications.

TABLE 4.4   Search syntax

Database	Syntax
Medline and PsycINFO	(Expressed Emotion/ OR Hostility/ OR (critic* or hostile* or ((emotion* adj3 (express* or over-involv*)) or (critic* adj2 comment*)).tw.)) AND (Caregivers/ or Family/ OR (carer* or caregive* or famil* or relative* or relation* or caring).tw.) AND (Guilt/ OR Shame/ OR ((shame* or guilt* or self-blame*) OR ((self-conscious* or selfconscious or "self conscious") adj2 emotion) OR ((shame* or guilt*) adj2 pron*) OR (shame-pron* or guilt-pron*)).tw.)
CINAHL	(Expressed Emotion/ OR Hostility/ OR (critic* or hostile* or ((emotion* n3 (express* or over-involv*)) or (critic* n2 comment*)).tw.)) AND (Caregivers/ or Family/ OR (carer* or caregive* or famil* or relative* or relation* or caring).tw.) AND (Guilt/ OR Shame/ OR ((shame* or guilt* or self-blame*) OR ((self-conscious* or selfconscious or "self conscious") n2 emotion) OR ((shame* or guilt*) n2 pron*) OR (shame-pron* or guilt-pron*)).tw.)
Scopus	(Expressed Emotion/ OR Hostility/ OR (critic* or hostile* or ((emotion* w/3 (express* or over-involv*)) or (critic* w/2 comment*)).tw.)) AND (Caregivers/ or Family/ OR (carer* or caregive* or famil* or relative* or relation* or caring).tw.) AND (Guilt/ OR Shame/ OR ((shame* or guilt* or self-blame*) OR ((self-conscious* or selfconscious or "self conscious") w/2 emotion) OR ((shame* or guilt*) w/2 pron*) OR (shame-pron* or guilt-pron*)).tw.)
ProQuest Dissertations and Theses	Ab,ti((emotion* NEAR/3 (express* OR over-involv*)) OR (critic* NEAR/2 comment*)) AND (carer* OR caregiver* OR family* OR relative* OR relation* OR caring) AND ((sham* OR guil* OR self-blame*) OR ((self-conscious* OR selfconscious OR "self conscious") NEAR/2 emotion) OR ((shame* OR guilt*) NEAR/2 pron*) OR (shame-pron* OR guilt-pron*))

Final thoughts

We hope that, after reading this chapter, you understand the difference between scoping searches and a main search for evidence, feel sufficiently confident to be able to plan, execute and report the methods of your search for evidence, and know who to ask for help with these tasks. It's now time to see what you've found!

> ## Key points to think about when writing your protocol
>
> - Summary details of your scoping searches and results are useful to the reader
> - List the databases (and any other resources) you plan to use for your main search
> - A sample search strategy in an appendix to your protocol is helpful; for example, you could outline the search terms you plan to use for a particular database

> ## What an examiner is looking for in your thesis
>
> - A clear, comprehensive and well-planned search, which has an adequate balance of sensitivity and specificity
> - Sufficient detail about your search so that it could, at least in theory, be replicated by another person (see Box 4.2)

Frequently Asked Questions

Question 1: What if I don't have access to a librarian or information specialist?

Input from a librarian or information specialist will help you to identify which resources to search and how you can most effectively search them. If you do not have access to experts, do not panic. You may find you already have sufficient experience of using the bibliographic database that you plan to use and your supervisor may also be able to help. It is also useful to identify systematic reviews in similar topic areas so that you can determine which sources of data the authors searched and the search terms that they used. Also, there are many educational resources that can help you with your searching – from online tutorials to library information sheets (for details see https://study.sagepub.com/doingasystematicreview2e).

Question 2: Can I search multiple bibliographic databases in the same interface?

The short answer is yes. In an interface such as Ovid you can search multiple bibliographic databases separately, or simultaneously, by selecting the bibliographic databases that you wish to search. However, your search strategies will likely differ slightly between bibliographic databases, so it may be advisable to search each bibliographic database separately.

Question 3: What is the difference between MEDLINE and PubMed?

The MEDLINE database can be searched directly from the National Library of Medicine as a subset of the PubMed database, as well as through other numerous search services that license the data (such as Ovid). Perhaps the main advantage of MEDLINE over PubMed is that it is easier to build a search strategy in steps, using multiple combinations of MeSH terms and keywords. However, you may find PubMed more user-friendly, particularly when you want quick results (e.g. scoping searches). PubMed is also useful when you are looking for articles that have been recently published but have not yet been indexed with MeSH terms, and/or articles submitted by publishers ahead of print.

Question 4: Do I need to run my searches again prior to submitting my thesis? If so, is it easy to do?

It's best practice to rerun your electronic searches prior to submitting your thesis, particularly if several months have passed since the searches were originally conducted. It's possible to create accounts and update your search strategies with some interfaces (e.g. Ovid). You may find this useful when you are near the end of your thesis, as this will enable you to easily check for relevant papers that may have been recently published in the period after running your searches. It will be harder to update searches of other sources of information, such as grey literature, as you will need to manually rerun your searches in order to be certain that no additional relevant evidence has been recently published. This final step may not be compulsory for your Master's thesis, but may be required should you choose to publish your thesis at a later date (see Chapter 10 for more information).

Question 5: What if I miss relevant papers or don't have time to conduct complementary searching activities?

This is a common worry faced by Master's students given the time pressures that they are often under. It is likely that, in the time you have available, you may not be able to be exhaustive in your searching, and even if you are, it's impossible to be 100 per cent certain that you have identified all of the relevant papers. The important thing is that you can demonstrate that you have searched the key resources, used appropriate methods to identify relevant studies and consulted with others who can help, such as an information specialist, librarian or your supervisor. If you realize that you have missed a key study later down the line (e.g. when you are writing your 'Discussion' section), you must address the fact that your review may not include all available information, and outline how this might affect the conclusions that you draw and the recommendations that you make (discussed further in Chapter 9).

Question 6: Should my bibliographic database search find all of the available evidence?

Not necessarily. When devising your bibliographic database search strategies, you should strive for an adequate balance of sensitivity and specificity – you don't want to have to trawl through thousands of irrelevant citations, but equally, you don't want your bibliographic database searches to return only 25 papers either. We can't advise on the optimum number of citations to aim for, but we advise you to be comprehensive rather than exhaustive when searching bibliographic databases. If you are concerned that your electronic bibliographic database search is missing a lot of potentially relevant papers, then speak to an information specialist and/or revisit the steps outlined in this chapter.

Further Reading and Resources

Centre for Reviews and Dissemination (2009) Systematic Reviews: CRD's Guidance for Undertaking Reviews in Health Care. University of York: Centre for Reviews and Dissemination (https://www.york.ac.uk/media/crd/Systematic_Reviews.pdf). (Last accessed February 2017).

Glanville, J., Bayliss, S., Booth, A., Dundar, Y., Fernandes, H., Fleeman, N.D., Foster, L., Fraser, C., Fry-Smith, A., Golder, S., Lefebvre, C., Miller, C., Paisley, S., Payne, L., Price, A. and Welch, K (2008) 'So many filters, so little time: The development of a Search Filter Appraisal Checklist', *Journal of the Medical Library Association,* 96(4): 356–61.

Lefebvre, C., Manheimer, E. and Glanville, J. on behalf of the Cochrane Information Retrieval Methods Group (2011) 'Searching for Studies', in J.P.T. Higgins and S. Green (eds), *Cochrane Handbook for Systematic Reviews of Interventions* (http://handbook.cochrane.org). (Last accessed February 2017).

Petticrew, M. and Roberts, H. (2008) *Systematic Reviews in the Social Sciences.* 2nd edn. Oxford: Blackwell.

Primary Health Care Research and Information Service (2016) Getting Started Guide: Grey Literature (http://www.phcris.org.au/guides/grey_literature.php). (Last accessed February 2017).

Royle, P. and Waugh, N. (2003) 'Literature searching for clinical and cost-effectiveness studies used in health technology assessment reports carried out for the National Institute for Clinical Excellence appraisal system', *Health Technology Assessment,* 7(34): 1–51.

WATCH...	EXPLORE...	READ...
... a video in which the editors answer your FAQs: *"What are 'scoping searches' and why should I do them? Do I have to find all of the studies that are out there?"*	... the Links Library, which gives you a host of resources to help you tackle the systematic review process.	... online resources such as example reviews, journal articles and further guidance on the review process.

Take your systematic review journey online at:
https://study.sagepub.com/doingasystematicreview2e

5

Applying Inclusion and Exclusion Criteria

Yenal Dundar and Nigel Fleeman

This chapter will help you to...

- Screen the titles and abstracts of potentially eligible studies against your inclusion and exclusion criteria

- Select full-text papers for inclusion in your review

- Report the results of your search for evidence

Introduction

This chapter guides you through the processes of screening and selecting studies for inclusion in your review. We first provide guidance on how the results of your search should be screened using your inclusion and exclusion criteria, and how to determine whether individual papers should be included in your systematic review. We then suggest different options for reporting the results of these activities in the 'Results' section of your thesis.

Choosing your included studies

Congratulations – by now, you should have finalized and conducted your main search (Chapter 4), and should hopefully be ready to press ahead and screen studies against your inclusion and exclusion criteria in order to determine their eligibility for inclusion in your review. This whole process is commonly referred to as 'screening and selection' and is usually conducted in two stages (Stage 1 = screening titles and abstracts; Stage 2 = screening and selecting full-text papers). Box 5.1 outlines the key steps involved in screening and selection.

Box 5.1

Key steps to consider when choosing your included studies

Step 1: **De-duplicate** references

Step 2: Develop and pilot your **screening and selection tool**

Step 3: Screen all titles and abstracts identified via searches against your inclusion and exclusion criteria (Stage 1)

Step 4: Obtain the full-text papers of all potentially eligible references

Step 5: Use your screening and selection tool to help you identify full-text papers for inclusion in review (Stage 2)

Step 1: De-duplicate references

Before you apply your inclusion and exclusion criteria to your long list of potentially relevant studies, you first need to de-duplicate your references. This simply involves identifying and deleting any duplicate references from your main search results. Duplicates are almost inevitable if you have searched more than one resource. If you have stored your references using bibliographic software, it should be possible to merge search results from different databases and then easily remove any duplicates automatically. However, you may also need to remove some duplicate references manually, because minor differences in how a reference is indexed in different databases will result in some duplicates being missed (e.g. if an author is indexed as J.W. Rigby in one database and J Rigby in another). It is important to stress that duplicates are the only references you should ever delete. You should always know how many references your search identified and how many references were duplicates.

Step 2: Develop and pilot your screening and selection tool

Up to this point, your inclusion and exclusion criteria (the criteria against which you judge the relevance and suitability of studies for inclusion in your review) will have been used to refine and shape your review question, and will probably take the form of a series of statements or bullet points. We now recommend that you use these criteria to create an electronic or paper screening and selection 'tool'. You can use this tool to easily screen potentially relevant full-text papers against your inclusion and exclusion criteria, and ultimately to select only those that are of relevance to your review question. An example of a screening and selection tool is shown in Table 5.1.

You should then pilot your tool before going any further. Ideally, you and a fellow researcher (maybe your supervisor or a fellow student, if permitted by your institution) should independently screen a few of the titles and abstracts of the studies identified by your main search, and then meet up to compare and discuss which references each of you have identified as being relevant to the review question. This is to ensure that you both fully understand the type of studies to be included in the review. If there are discrepancies in your results, you should discuss these discordant opinions and identify reasons for them. This pilot testing reduces the chances of regular disagreements later in the review about what studies should or should not be included, and allows you to identify and correct any problems with your screening and selection tool. As for the number of references to look at during the pilot exercise, this will depend on the number of citations you have identified. It is not uncommon for your search strategy to have identified hundreds, if not thousands, of citations, particularly in the early stages of searching. It may therefore be sensible to pilot your screening and selection tool on around 30 titles and abstracts.

TABLE 5.1   An example of a bespoke screening and selection tool

Review question: What is the clinical effectiveness of different regimens of first-line chemotherapy in addition to radiotherapy for adult patients with locally advanced non-small cell lung cancer?

Inclusion criteria (based on PICOSS):

Population = adult patients aged 18 years or over) with non-small cell lung cancer

Intervention = any chemotherapy + radiotherapy regimen

Comparator = any other chemotherapy + radiotherapy regimen

Outcomes = overall survival, progression-free survival, time to progression, death, adverse events and/or quality of life

Setting = any

Study design = randomized controlled trials (RCTs) only

CHEMOTHERAPY + RADIOTHERAPY SCREENING AND SELECTION TOOL

Reviewer name:		**Date:**
Author name/Study ID:		**Year:**
Title:		**Journal:**
Patient population	**Include**	**Exclude**
	☐ Adult patients aged 18 years or over with non-small cell lung cancer	☐ Adults aged 18 years or under with other cancers ☐ Patients aged under 18 years
Interventions	**Include**	**Exclude**
	☐ Chemotherapy + radiotherapy regimen	☐ Chemotherapy only ☐ Radiotherapy only
Comparators	**Include**	**Exclude**
	☐ Chemotherapy + radiotherapy regimen	☐ Chemotherapy only ☐ Radiotherapy only
Outcomes	**Include if one of more of:**	**Exclude**
	☐ Overall survival ☐ Progression-free survival ☐ Time to progression ☐ Death ☐ Adverse events ☐ Quality of life	☐ Does not report any outcome specified in inclusion criteria
Study design	**Include** ☐ RCT	**Exclude** Any study design other than RCT
Overall decision	☐ **INCLUDED**	☐ **EXCLUDED**
Notes		

Step 3: Screen all titles and abstracts identified via searches against your inclusion and exclusion criteria (Stage 1)

The next step is to screen the titles and abstracts of all the studies identified via your search against your inclusion and exclusion criteria, using your screening and selection tool to guide your decision-making. This stage is called Stage 1 screening, and simply entails applying your inclusion and exclusion criteria to the title and abstract in order to determine whether the study appears relevant to your review question, and appears to fit your inclusion criteria. For example, you might decide to include only studies examining domestic violence and so you may look for these keywords, or related synonyms, in the title and abstract. You do need to scan every reference identified by your searches and this task can be time-consuming; it can take days or even weeks if you have hundreds or thousands to look at. However, although it's a good idea to have your screening and selection tool to hand as you read through titles and abstracts and make decisions about the potential eligibility of individual studies, it's not necessary at this stage to actually complete the form for each individual reference. If you have any doubts about whether a reference should be included at this stage (in particular, if it is unclear whether the study meets all of your inclusion criteria), it is always safest to include it.

If you are working electronically, you can export your titles and abstracts into a word-processing package and then use the 'find' function to highlight relevant keywords (as bold text and/or in a different colour). For example, if you are only looking for **cohort studies**, then you can find and highlight 'cohort', or if you are only looking for studies that include patients with low self-esteem, then you can find and highlight 'self-esteem'; this simple activity makes potentially relevant articles easier to spot. However, you will need to be creative and think outside the box about how these concepts may be described in the text in order to reduce the chance of excluding relevant articles by accident – electronic scanning may speed up the screening process but should never take the place of manual scanning of titles and abstracts.

During this process, it is worthwhile making a note of any references that are useful and that can be used to inform the 'Introduction' or 'Discussion' sections of your thesis. If there has been some delay between your scoping searches and your main search, then before you start to scan your references, it may also be prudent to check whether your main search results include any relevant recently published systematic reviews that have addressed your review question. An easy way to check is to search for the words 'systematic review' in your main search results and then to scan all of the titles and abstracts where this term appears. Such a search may be possible within your bibliographic software package or by exporting all the titles and abstracts into a word-processing package (and again highlighting the keyword term 'systematic review'). If you are extremely unlucky and a review addressing your research question has just been published, then revisit Chapter 3 for tips on what to do next.

A word of caution before you begin: ideally, each reference should be dual screened – that is, you and a fellow researcher should each independently consider the suitability of each citation for inclusion in your review, discussing and resolving any discordant opinions as they arise. This reduces bias and helps to make your review more robust. However, don't worry if this isn't possible or permitted. If you are working alone, simply screen your titles and abstracts, put the results to one side, and repeat this process a few days (or weeks) later, reflecting upon and resolving any discrepancies. Alternatively, see whether a peer or your supervisor may be willing to screen a random sample (say, 10 per cent) of your identified citations, or 'cross-check' all or some of your screening (i.e. see whether they agree with the decisions that you have made). This may be a more practicable solution, particularly if your search has retrieved a large number of citations.

Step 4: Obtain the full-text papers of all potentially eligible references

Once you have completed screening of titles and abstracts, you then need to obtain copies of the papers you marked for possible inclusion in the review. You need to have the full text of each potentially eligible reference in front of you – either electronically or in paper format. While an increasing number of full-text papers are available online, it is probable that some relevant papers are not. Your institution is likely to have an inter-library loans system and, if so, this is an obvious route for obtaining your selected papers when they are not available electronically or held in your institution's libraries. This option costs money though, so make sure that this cost is covered by your institution's budget before ordering papers. Alternatively, you can try to contact authors and ask them to send or email you a copy of their publications, or search the Internet to see whether the authors have made the publication freely available via, for example, academic social media. If, having tried all of these routes, you have been unable to obtain the full-text versions of the papers that you need, then, when you write your thesis, you should clearly identify which references you have been unable to obtain, as this is a limitation of your review (see Chapter 9).

Step 5: Use your screening and selection tool to help you identify full-text papers for inclusion in the review (Stage 2)

Having obtained the full-text papers, the next step is to determine whether these papers really do meet your inclusion criteria. You should carefully read each full-text paper, and complete your screening and selection form for each. If you decide that a paper is not eligible for inclusion in your review, then it is important to note the reason you excluded the paper at this stage. You should note your reason for exclusion and keep a record of which studies are to be included or excluded using a database (e.g. the bibliographic software package in which your references are stored), word-processing package or spreadsheet (see Chapter 2 for more information). When you produce your full list of included studies you may find it helpful to list all of your excluded references, together with reasons for exclusion, in a table that can be placed in an appendix to your thesis.

At this stage, you will likely be grateful for your exclusion criteria, as they may provide you with a speedy way of excluding records without having to review the papers in detail. For example, you might decide to exclude all studies that include pharmaceutical interventions and include studies only looking at public health interventions. If use of pharmaceutical interventions is listed as an exclusion criterion, you can exclude these types of papers immediately without reading through the text looking for public health interventions.

Ideally, you should collaborate with a peer, colleague or supervisor on this exercise, and meet up to discuss your findings. However, if you are working alone, then follow the same procedure as you did when screening titles and abstracts. Once you think that you have a 'final' set of included papers, it may be worth emailing experts in the topic area to check that you haven't missed any relevant studies. We recommend that you are very clear in your email about what you want from them and include a set of well-defined questions to maximize your chances of a response (see Box 5.2).

Box 5.2

Example of a well-thought-out email

Dear Dr Paton

Re: Systematic review of the effectiveness of metacognitive therapy for anxiety and depression in cancer survivors

I am currently conducting a systematic review as part of my Master's studies at the University of Liverpool. I have attached my protocol to this email, which contains more information about the aims of this review and the planned methodology. After completing my searching and applying my inclusion and exclusion criteria, I have identified several studies for inclusion in my review (please see attached). I would be grateful if, after having a quick read through this list, you could let me know of any other relevant studies that I may have missed during my searches and/or of any ongoing studies that are due to be published in the next 3 months?

Thank you very much for your help.

Yours sincerely
Student

How to report the results of your searching, screening and selection exercises

The methods by which you screened and selected studies are always reported in the 'Methods' section of your thesis, just after the text that reports the methods that you used to search for evidence. In this section, you should report the following information:

- inclusion and exclusion criteria;
- detail on the methods by which these were applied to identified citations, and by whom;
- detail on how disagreements, if any, were resolved between reviewers.

In contrast, the results of your searching, screening and selection are always reported in the 'Results' section of your thesis. In this section, you need to make sure that you record the following information:

- number of references identified by each search;
- number of duplicates removed;
- number of references you looked at when screening titles and abstracts;
- number of references you looked at when selecting full-text papers;
- number of references you excluded at Stage 2 and the reasons for exclusion.

An example of how you might report the methods and results of your searching, screening and selection in the 'Methods' and 'Results' sections of your thesis is provided in Box 5.3. As discussed in Chapter 2, you may find it useful to consult the Preferred Reporting Items for Systematic Reviews and Meta-Analyses **(PRISMA) statement** (Liberati et al., 2009; Moher et al., 2009) before you start writing up the 'Results' section of your review – forewarned is forearmed. PRISMA is an evidence-based minimum set of items that aims to help reviewers improve the reporting of systematic reviews and meta-analyses. The main PRISMA tool is a 27-item checklist and a four-phase flow diagram that outlines all aspects of the conduct of a systematic review (Liberati et al., 2009). Take a look at the PRISMA website (www.prisma-statement.org); you'll find discussion documents as well as the current version of the PRISMA Statement. A template of the flow diagram, which maps out the number of records identified, included and excluded, and the reasons for exclusion, is available from the website as a PDF and also as a word-processing document. A flow diagram similar to the PRISMA flow diagram shown in Chapter 2 should be included in the 'Results' section of your thesis, and is essential if you plan to publish your review in a **peer-reviewed academic journal** (see Chapter 10 for more information).

Box 5.3

How to report the application of your inclusion and exclusion criteria in your 'Methods' and 'Results' sections

In the 'Methods' section of your thesis, a description of how you applied your inclusion and exclusion criteria comes immediately after a description of your search methods (see Chapter 4).

Methods

Inclusion and exclusion criteria

Two reviewers independently screened all titles and abstracts. Full-text papers of any titles and abstracts that were considered relevant by either reviewer were obtained where possible. The relevance of each study was assessed according to the inclusion criteria stated in Table 5.2. Studies that did not meet the criteria were excluded and their bibliographic details were listed in an appendix alongside reasons for their exclusion. Any discrepancies were resolved by consensus.

TABLE 5.2   Inclusion criteria

Population(s)	Females aged 18 years or over with a diagnosis of post-natal depression
Intervention(s)	Cognitive behavioural therapy
Comparators	Wait-list control
Outcomes	Any validated self-report measure of psychological distress and/or well-being
Study design	Any comparative study
Setting	Any

Results

Quantity of research available

Electronic and hand searches identified 2228 citations, which, once duplicates were removed, left 2000 unique citations to be screened for inclusion (Figure 5.1).

(Continued)

(Continued)

Their titles and abstracts were assessed for their relevance to the review (Stage 1 screening), resulting in 20 potential citations being retained. The full texts of all but four of these citations were obtained. After applying inclusion criteria to the remaining 16 full-text papers (Stage 2 selection), 12 citations were excluded; 4 did not examine the appropriate intervention and 8 reported data from the wrong patient population. One additional citation was identified following contact with an expert in the field. As such, five citations were included in the systematic review.

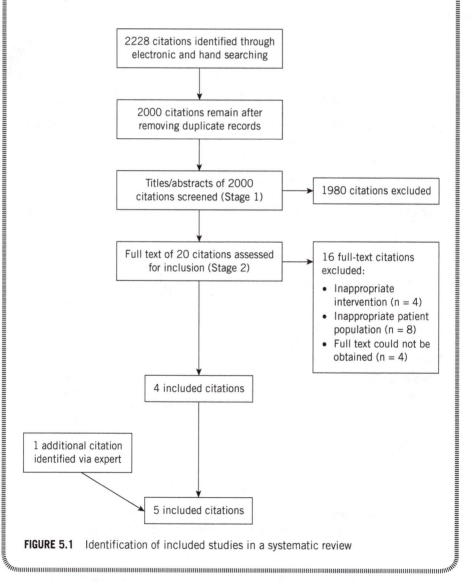

FIGURE 5.1   Identification of included studies in a systematic review

Final thoughts

We hope that, after reading this chapter, you feel sufficiently confident to be able to de-duplicate the results of your final search, develop and pilot a screening and selection tool, screen titles and abstracts, and select the final papers for inclusion in your review. You should now be in possession of the studies that will help you to answer your review question, and hopefully feel ready to take the next step – extracting relevant data from these studies.

Key points to think about when writing your protocol

- Clearly report how you will include or exclude studies, that is, how you will screen and select the studies (and how many people will conduct these tasks)
- Importantly, you should include a table detailing your inclusion and exclusion criteria
- Set a deadline for obtaining the full-text papers of potentially relevant studies

What an examiner is looking for in your thesis

- Inclusion of a flow diagram similar to the PRISMA diagram in your 'Results' section
- A brief explanation of why you excluded studies at Stage 2

Frequently Asked Questions

Question 1: What if there are too many or too few studies that match my inclusion criteria?

If you think that too many studies match your inclusion criteria, then you may want to refine your inclusion and exclusion criteria and/or your review question. You may also wish to consider how you can limit your search results further, such as by year, language or publication type (e.g. include only journal articles, books or letters). On the other hand, if you have only identified a small number of studies that meet your inclusion criteria, then your search terms may be too specific and you may wish to expand them. Alternatively, you may be able to determine, from the reasons you listed when you excluded studies, whether you need to change your inclusion and exclusion criteria (e.g. were the majority of studies excluded because of the study design? If so, do you want to broaden the types of included studies?).

Many credible systematic reviews have included only one study and it may be that only one study really does address your research question. Often, the lack of studies can be considered an important finding in itself, as this would identify important gaps in the evidence base where further research is required. However, identifying only one study may not allow you to fully demonstrate your systematic review skills to your examiner and you may wish to broaden your review question. If you do not identify any studies at all, then we suggest that you go back and modify your review question; you might also find it helpful to reread Chapter 3.

Question 2: What happens if I find a useful paper that has an English abstract but the full-text paper is written in a different language?

The first step is to determine whether the useful paper meets your inclusion criteria – typically you would look for any relevant information that is stated in the abstract. You might also think about using translation software to help you understand the 'Methods' section and any tables and figures. Assuming that the abstract contains potentially relevant information, you have three possible options. The first is to find somebody who can translate the paper or at the very least can extract the data that you need (perhaps a fellow student). The second is to use the data from the abstract and any tables and figures that you can, noting this limitation when writing up your review. The third is to exclude this reference altogether and acknowledge this when writing the limitations of your system-atic review. This last option may not be ideal, particularly if you had not stated 'English language' to be an inclusion criterion in your protocol.

Question 3: My friend included 40 papers but I've only found 5 of relevance to my review question – am I doing something wrong?

This is a difficult question to answer. There is no 'perfect' number of papers to include in your systematic review (although we discuss the potential difficulties associated with having very few (or no!) relevant papers in Question 1). If your searching, screening and selection processes have been sufficiently rigorous, then you should feel confident that you have identified all relevant evidence for inclusion in your review. Try not to compare your review with others; every review is different.

Further Reading and Resources

Centre for Reviews and Dissemination (2009) Systematic Reviews: CRD's Guidance for Undertaking Reviews in Health Care. University of York: Centre for Reviews and Dissemination (https://www.york.ac.uk/media/crd/Systematic_Reviews.pdf). (Last accessed February 2017).

Higgins, J.P.T. and Deeks, J.J. (2011) 'Selecting studies and collecting data', in J.P.T. Higgins and S. Green (eds), Cochrane Handbook for Systematic Reviews of Interventions (http://handbook.cochrane.org). (Last accessed February 2017).

Liberati, A., Altman, D.G., Tetzlaff, J., Mulrow, C., Gøtzsche, P.C, Ioannidis, J.P.A., Clarke, M., Devereaux, P.J, Kleijnen, J. and Moher, D. (2009) 'The PRISMA statement for reporting systematic reviews and meta-analyses of studies that evaluate healthcare interventions: Explanation and elaboration', British Medical Journal, 339: b2700.

Moher, D., Liberati, A., Tetzlaff, J. and Altman, D.G. (2009) 'Preferred reporting items for systematic reviews and meta-analyses: The PRISMA statement', British Medical Journal, 339: b2535.

WATCH...	EXPLORE...	READ...
... a video in which the editors answer your FAQs: *"What do I do if I identify too many studies for inclusion? What if there are too few? And what can I do about studies published in different langauges?"*	... the Links Library, which gives you a host of resources to help you tackle the systematic review process.	... online resources such as example reviews, journal articles and further guidance on the review process.

Take your systematic review journey online at:
https://study.sagepub.com/doingasystematicreview2e

6

Data Extraction: Where Do I Begin?

Nigel Fleeman and Yenal Dundar

This chapter will help you to...

- Understand the purpose of data extraction

- Decide when and how to undertake your data extraction

- Store the data you have extracted

- Feel confident about reporting the results of your data extraction

Introduction

This chapter has been written to guide you through the process of data extraction and to encourage you to think about the links between data extraction, data presentation and data synthesis. In this chapter, we provide guidance on which data to extract, and how and where data could be stored. We discuss the best time to complete the data extraction exercise, and conclude the chapter by describing how to report the results of your data extraction exercise in your thesis.

What do we mean by data extraction?

By this stage in the review process, you will already have identified which papers contain evidence to help you answer your review question, and, as a result of the screening and selection process, you are probably becoming familiar with the data within your included studies. Your next step is to identify, and then extract, relevant data from each individual study. Data extraction is the process whereby relevant data are taken from your included papers and stored in one single format – usually a data extraction form or data extraction table (see Box 6.1). Data are then presented in data tables in your thesis. The process of extracting and presenting relevant data allows you (and the reader of your thesis) to make sense of the data, both descriptively and analytically.

Box 6.1

What is the difference between data extraction forms, data extraction tables and data tables?

A data extraction form is a form into which you can extract and record relevant data from a particular study. You will therefore have one form for each study included in your review.

Data extraction tables are tables which allow you to store extracted data from one or all of your studies in one place.

Data tables are tables that describe and summarize your extracted data in your thesis.

Examples of data extraction forms and data extraction tables designed for use in systematic reviews are available from our website (https://study.sagepub.com/doingasystematicreview2e).

Before you start...

Whether or not you extract data before, during or after quality assessment (Chapter 7) is up to you – as is the order in which you describe what you have done in the 'Methods' section of your thesis. It is sometimes recommended that data extraction takes place after the methodological quality assessment of your included studies has been carried out; this is imperative if you are planning to exclude poor-quality studies from your review (we talk about this further in Chapters 7 and 11, and discuss it in relation to meta-analysis in Chapter 8). Not only does this save time by preventing needless extraction of data you do not require but it can also reduce bias, since having extracted data, you may be more or less inclined to include or exclude a particular study if it contains data that appear to support or refute your thesis hypothesis. However, some people prefer to extract data before they assess the quality of their included studies. The choice is yours.

Extracting and reporting data from included studies

Box 6.2 outlines the key steps involved in extracting and reporting data from your included studies.

Box 6.2

Key steps to consider when extracting and reporting data from studies

Step 1: Identify the data that you want to extract

Step 2: Build and pilot your data extraction form or data extraction table(s)

Step 3: Extract relevant data

Step 4: Complete the data tables for your thesis

Step 5: Report your extracted data in your thesis

Step 1: Identify the data that you want to extract

The first thing to consider is *which* data to extract. When carrying out a systematic review you are primarily interested in two types of data: **descriptive data** (e.g. study characteristics) and **analytical data** (e.g. outcomes). Each of your included studies will contain relevant descriptive and analytical data. However, it is likely that each paper will also contain a lot of *irrelevant* data. It's important to ensure that you only extract data that are likely to be useful and will help you to address your research question. For example, while data on the sex of the participants in a study may be useful to answer some review questions (such as 'What factors explain differences in educational attainment in 16- to 18-year-olds?'), such data may not be relevant to other review questions (such as 'Are there differences in health outcomes for pregnant women who have hospital or home births?').

We recommend that you compile a list of all of the data that you *think* will help you to summarize, describe and interpret the results of your included studies, both as individual studies and as a collection of studies. When doing so, it may be helpful to reread your review question and protocol, and re-familiarize yourself with the data extraction plan included in your protocol, as you will hopefully already have given data extraction some thought earlier in the review process. It's also a good idea to skim-read all of your included papers at this stage, as this will allow you to gain a sense of the data within the studies. You might also want to have a look at published studies or reviews in the same topic area as your review to help you identify specific data that you want to extract. Don't worry if your final list is extensive – it's a good idea to err on the side of caution and plan to extract more, rather than less data. It's far easier to delete data than go back to studies later to collect more data.

Step 2: Build and pilot your data extraction form or data extraction table(s)

Once you have decided on the data that you want to extract, you can start to put together your data extraction form or data extraction table(s). We use the term 'or' because some people prefer to record their extracted data on a series of forms (usually one per study), which they can then collate. Others prefer to store their extracted data by entering it straight into a table or series of tables. The choice is yours! Similarly, whether you choose to complete your data extraction form/table(s) using a software package or plain, old-fashioned paper is up to you. However, using a software package can be more convenient when it comes to producing the final data tables for your thesis, and may reduce the risk of data-entry errors.

If you have a well-designed data extraction form/table(s), then you are less likely to have to keep returning to the source paper(s) of each individual study during the review process, which will save you valuable time and energy. 'Top tips' for designing your data extraction form/table(s) are presented in Box 6.3.

Box 6.3

'Top tips' for designing your data extraction form/table(s)

- At a minimum, record the study's authors (e.g. the first named author) and year of publication.
- If the study has been published in a peer-reviewed academic journal, you should record whether it has been published as a full-text paper or only as an abstract.
- Having a unique identification number for each study and paper is a good idea, particularly where there are many studies by the same authors.
- If a study has linked publications, record information about these (e.g. study author, year of publication, journal or other source where published), even if you do not extract data from these papers.
- Extract study characteristics data, including:

  o   study design;
  o   where and when the study was conducted;
  o   the study's inclusion and exclusion criteria;
  o   number of participants (including any dropouts);
  o   intervention(s) and comparator(s), if appropriate;
  o   study outcomes (including which were primary outcomes and which were secondary outcomes, and which were pre-specified);
  o   analyses;
  o   number of participants included in analyses;
  o   length of follow-up (if appropriate);
  o   study sponsorship.

- Extract participants' demographic information. This may vary depending on your review question, but should include, as a minimum, participants' age, sex and ethnicity. Specific demographic characteristics may also be required; for example, participants' religion, educational level, socio-economic status or mental or physical health diagnoses.
- For certain study designs (such as randomized controlled trials), you should extract baseline participant data (e.g. if your review investigates the effects of an educational intervention on participants' reading ability, then it will be important to know pre-intervention reading proficiency).
- Leave plenty of space to make additional notes.

It's a good idea to pilot your data extraction form/table(s) using at least two or three of your included studies. As with other stages in the systematic review process, piloting your data extraction form/table(s) can save a lot of time and energy if done early on.

The aims of the pilot exercise are twofold: first, to ascertain how easy it is to extract the data; and, second, to check whether all the necessary data are being captured. Piloting should prevent problems such as making the late discovery that important data have not been extracted. You may find that, at the piloting stage, you need to add or remove variables from your form/table(s). You may also find, at this stage, that having started to pilot data extraction with a form, the use of tables is going to be better for your purposes, or vice versa.

If more than one person is extracting data (more on this later), then piloting your data extraction form/table(s) will include a check on whether both reviewers share the same understanding of both the form/table(s) and the data that need to be collected. For example, age is likely to be an important variable for most studies; when extracting data on age, you need to ensure that you explicitly state whether you are referring to mean or median, standard deviation or range, and so on. You can either state this explicitly on your form/table(s), or design an accompanying crib sheet with detailed instructions. Even if you are not working with another person, such a crib sheet can be useful to ensure consistency with your data extraction, particularly where you find there are relatively large periods of time between extracting data.

Step 3: Extract relevant data

The next step is to actually extract relevant data. You can do this electronically, or you can extract data by hand. If you are extracting data from an electronic copy of a study (such as a PDF), then it is likely that you will simply copy and paste relevant sections or chunks of data into your data extraction forms. This approach not only saves time but reduces the chances of making data-entry errors. In addition, storing data electronically enables you to make, and save, backups of your work and may also make your life simpler when it comes to data synthesis. For example, some software packages enable you to analyse your data qualitatively (e.g. the use of a word processor or specialist software such as **NVivo** to move and code data) or quantitatively (e.g. the use of a spreadsheet package to carry out mathematical and statistical tasks). Chapter 2 outlines the advantages and disadvantages of using different software packages for storing data. Your choice will depend, to some extent, on the amount of data you need to collect and also on your own competence and familiarity with different software packages. Whether you extract data electronically or by hand, it's a good idea to record where in the full-text paper the extracted data are located. One way to do this is to highlight the extracted data in the original study (electronic or paper version). It's also important to be aware of potential stylistic differences between papers. For example, a mean and standard deviation may be presented as '64 (12)' in one paper and '64 ± 12' in another. You need to decide how you want to record these data in your data extraction form/table(s), as you can save yourself a great deal of time and effort by being stylistically consistent from the outset.

Ideally, two people would independently carry out data extraction, and then meet to discuss any discordant opinions. This is generally considered to be the most robust approach, as it can help to minimize data extraction errors. Alternatively, you may ask a second person to 'cross-check' all or some of your data extraction. There may be occasions when you and your fellow reviewer do not agree about the data you have extracted. Hopefully, most disagreements can be resolved through discussion. Most simply, you may find one of you has made a transcription error (data-entry error) when extracting the data. You may, however, disagree because the data in the original study are misleading; for example, data contained in a figure or table do not appear to match that quoted in the text. If this is the case, then we recommend that you contact authors for clarity.

Where similar issues recur for the same variable in more than one study, the disagreement may highlight issues about your research question or inclusion and exclusion criteria that need addressing; for example, are your aims and objectives clear? Alternatively, disagreement may occur simply because a poorly designed data extraction form/table(s) results in a lack of clarity about which data need to be extracted, therefore indicating the need for further piloting. In some situations, you and the second reviewer may not be able to agree on which data should be extracted from the paper. In this case, we recommend that you obtain the opinion of a third person (perhaps your supervisor, if they are not the second reviewer), who is familiar with systematic reviews and is fully aware of the aims of your review.

If you are working independently, you need to be creative and identify ways to ensure that the data you have extracted are accurate and complete. For example, you may be able to ask your supervisor to cross-check a random sample (as opposed to all) of your data extraction. Or, you might have to put your data aside for a week or so and then redo your data extraction, cross-checking that both sets of extracted data are the same. The latter approach can be tedious but might help you to identify data extraction errors or inconsistencies.

Whether you are working with others or working independently, you'll hopefully be thankful that you took our advice and highlighted data in your source papers as it should be easy to identify precisely from where you have extracted data. This will allow discrepancies to be quickly and easily rectified.

Contacting study authors for missing or additional data

Where appropriate, contacting authors for further information and clarification can improve the quality of your review. However you should check that there are no other publications that might have been missed during your search, and which might contain the data you are looking for – perhaps, for example, a study was published after your search was completed. When requesting data from authors, it is important to be as clear as possible about the nature of the data you require. For example, is it a mean or median value you need? Or, is it both? It is a good idea to send the relevant part(s) of the data extraction form/table(s) to the author for him/her to complete. Finally, you should prepare yourself for the fact that not all authors will respond to your data requests. It is acceptable to re-contact authors who do not respond to your first contact. It is also a good idea to log all correspondence so that when writing up your review, you can detail where you contacted an author but did not receive a response.

Step 4: Complete the data tables for your thesis

After you have extracted your data, you need to think about how you will describe and summarize your extracted data in your thesis. All of the data discussed in your thesis are likely to be presented in tables. To avoid confusion with data extraction tables, we refer to the tables within your thesis as 'data tables'. We cannot tell you exactly how to build your data tables, but we can suggest that you try to include tables with the following headings and variables:

- 'Study Characteristics' table (e.g. study name, date of publication, study design, study population, country, follow-up, outcomes, study sponsorship/funder(s));
- 'Participant Characteristics' table (e.g. mean age, sex, specific participant characteristics of interest);
- 'Study Results' table (e.g. primary outcomes, secondary outcomes and statistical analyses; see Chapter 8 for a more detailed discussion of the use of numerical data in your review).

Remember, a well-designed data extraction form/table(s) will make it easy to produce these final data tables. Again, it's a good idea to look at published systematic reviews in a similar topic area to get ideas about what you should include in your data tables.

Step 5: Report your extracted data in your thesis

Having extracted your data and built your data tables, the next task is to report and make sense of the data. You need to report them in such a way that the reader can understand and follow your train of thought. The term 'narrative synthesis' is used to describe this process. Narrative synthesis simply refers to any presentation of results using words only (with reference to your data tables). However, there is no point in simply repeating the data from your data tables in your text – don't waste your words, and more importantly, don't annoy your examiner through repetition of data. Always use the data tables to present data from individual studies and use the text to report the overall findings. All discussion and interpretation of the data (including links with wider literature) should take place in the 'Discussion' and 'Conclusions' sections of your review. Don't feel that you have to comment on everything; data tables may include data not described in the accompanying text, but which nevertheless help the reader to interpret individual study results and compare and contrast the included studies.

It is common practice to begin by presenting a summary of descriptive data for all of the included studies in a series of tables. As mentioned previously, the usual practice is to split the descriptive data over two data tables: the 'Study Characteristics' table and the 'Participant Characteristics' table. However, to some extent, this will depend on the number of variables of relevance to the review question; some reviews amalgamate this information into one table, whereas others present it in three or four separate tables. You can then go on to present the results of your included studies, commonly in a 'Study Results' table.

All data presented in your data tables should be accompanied by explanatory summary text. It is important to check that what you write in the text corresponds exactly with the information that you present in the tables. Let's assume that Table 6.1 shows the study characteristics of five hypothetical studies that can be used to assess the impact of a new fast food restaurant (belonging to the hypothetical Acme Corporation) on the local economy.

TABLE 6.1   Example of a 'Study Characteristics' table

Study	When study conducted	Country	General study focus	Source of funding for study
Clarke (1993)	1990	USA	Local work force	Funded by Acme Corporation
Jones (1996)	1992–1993	France	Local economy in general	Grant from European Union
Radebe (2005)	2001–2002	UK	Local work force	Not stated
Strummer (1996)	1993–1994	France	Local restaurants	Not stated
Yeboah (1998)	1995–1996	UK	Local work force	Funded by Acme Corporation

The study characteristics data table might be accompanied by the following explanatory summary text:

The five studies were carried out between 1990 and 2002. The publication dates ranged from 1993 to 2005. The studies were conducted in various countries: one in the USA, two in France and two in the UK. Three studies focused on the impact of the new Acme Corporation restaurant on the local work force, one focused on the impact on local restaurants, and the other on the impact on the local economy in general (i.e. taking into account the impact on both the local workforce and local restaurants). The source of funding for the study was acknowledged in three of the five studies; in two instances the studies were sponsored by Acme Corporation.

Let's assume that Table 6.2 presents the results of four hypothetical studies that assessed the clinical effectiveness of different chemotherapy treatments (Treatments X and Y) for patients with non-small cell lung cancer.

TABLE 6.2   Example of a 'Study Results' table

Study	Outcome (survival)	Treatments	Summary of findings (adjusted HR)
Bremner (2010)	Time from registration to death from any cause	X vs Y	HR = 1.15; 95% CI: 0.78 to 1.61; p = 0.32
Charles (2009)	Time from surgery to death from any cause	X vs Y	HR = 1.75; 95% CI: 0.78 to 3.51; p = 0.11
Strachan (1992)	Time from registration to death from any cause	X vs Y	HR = 1.39; 95% CI: 0.93 to 2.26; p = 0.22
Springsteen (2006)	Time from diagnosis to death or last contact	X vs Y	HR = 0.79; 95% CI: 0.42 to 1.71; p = 0.51

HR = hazard ratio; CI = confidence interval

In this instance, results are presented as **hazard ratios** (HR) and the upper and lower **confidence intervals** (CIs). (Don't worry if you don't understand what these terms mean just yet – Chapter 8 provides a comprehensive introduction to understanding and synthesizing numerical data from **intervention studies**. The purpose of this example is to illustrate how to summarize these data textually.) Your explanatory text should highlight any key differences in values reported by different studies; this will entail examining your data tables for similarities and differences, both descriptive (e.g. similar proportions of males and females) and analytical (e.g. differences in magnitude or direction of reported outcomes). Thus, the data presented in Table 6.2 might be accompanied by the following explanatory text:

> None of the studies reported statistically significant differences in survival between treatments. However, while three of the studies presented a hazard ratio suggesting a slight increase in survival for those treated with Y when compared with X (Bremner, 2010; Charles, 2009; Strachan, 1992), the remaining study suggested an improved outcome for X when compared with Y (Springsteen, 2006). All studies had similar cohort characteristics in terms of median age, the proportion of males and previous treatment received.

Beyond narrative synthesis

As previously mentioned, narrative synthesis refers to any write-up of results using words only (with reference to data in data tables). However, after examining your data, you might also want to investigate your data using quantitative synthesis (e.g. meta-analysis, which in the example cited in Table 6.2 could be considered for the Bremner (2010) and Strachan (1992) studies); if so, please read Chapter 8 for more information. It is important to remember that a narrative synthesis of data is often sufficient. Although we encourage you to consider whether your data lend themselves to meta-analysis, a systematic review does not necessarily require one. Don't be concerned if your data are not appropriate for combination in a meta-analysis; just include an explanation in your thesis that justifies your decision.

Final thoughts

After you have narratively synthesized your data, you should have an idea of the similarities and differences in the results of your included studies and should feel confident about discussing the implications of these results in your 'Discussion' and 'Conclusions' sections. To round off the chapter, we considered it appropriate to give you a few pointers on how to discuss your results in your 'Discussion' section. You may wish to consider one or several of the following questions:

- Were you surprised by the results of the data extraction exercise? Did you find any specific elements of the exercise noteworthy?
- Did any of the results from a single study appear to be different from the majority of the other results and, if so, did you explain why this might have occurred?
- How did you synthesize your study results? Did you carry out a meta-analysis? What were your reasons for or against using such an approach?
- Were you able to answer your review question? Did the data from your included studies have relevance to your target audience?
- Were you able to offer recommendations for future research?

For other ideas on how to integrate and discuss the findings of your review, look at published reviews in your topic area and read Chapter 9.

Key points to think about when writing your protocol

- State how many people will undertake the data extraction
- Where more than one person will undertake the data extraction, describe how disagreements will be resolved
- State the types of data you plan to extract
- Outline your plans for piloting your data extraction form/table(s)
- Discuss your plans for narrative synthesis and, if appropriate, meta-analysis

---

What an examiner is looking for in your thesis

- Expansion of the data extraction methods described in your protocol
- Inclusion of your data extraction form/table(s) in an appendix
- Clearly presented data tables describing key data, including consistent use of headings and informative legends
- Succinct reporting of data from included studies

Frequently Asked Questions

Question 1: When should I design and pilot my data extraction form/table(s)?

Data extraction can only take place after you have applied your inclusion and exclusion criteria. However, a draft of your data extraction form/table(s) can be designed very early in the review process. In fact, this may be done in parallel with writing your protocol. You can begin the process by looking at a key study that you have already identified for inclusion and thinking about the types of data you would extract from this study. However, you will likely need to revisit and amend this form as appropriate before extracting any data from your included studies.

Question 2: How many studies should I use when piloting my data extraction form/table(s)?

This will depend largely on the number of studies you have identified. For example, your searches may only have identified four or five studies, in which case you should pilot the data extraction form/table(s) on two studies. However, if you have 15 included studies, you might want to pilot your form/table(s) on four or five studies.

Question 3: When is it too late to modify my data extraction form?

It is *never* too late to modify your data extraction form. If you discover, after completing your data extraction, that an important variable has not been extracted, then you can go back and extract these data from all of your studies. However, it is preferable not to find yourself in this situation as it can be time-consuming to revisit individual studies (remember, you may also want somebody to cross-check all of your additional extraction).

Question 4: If data are recorded as raw numbers and I require percentages, should I calculate these values?

The short answer to this is yes. However, it may be sensible to have space on your form/table(s) to record numbers and percentages, even if you do not describe both when writing up your review. Furthermore, it is sensible to make a note of where you have calculated numbers because they were not reported in the original studies. Be careful – you may make a mistake and therefore misrepresent the data and, remember, you may be challenged at some point about the origin of your numbers.

Question 5: What should I do if a study is reported in more than one publication?

It is not uncommon to discover that a study has been published in multiple publications, often with different outcomes reported in each, or with the same outcomes reported at different time points. When this is the case, it is best practice to consider all of the different sources as one paper and to extract all of the data on the same form or in the same tables. Where the data differ across publications, this should be noted and, if possible, investigated (e.g. by contacting the author(s) for more information).

Further Reading and Resources

Centre for Reviews and Dissemination (2009) Systematic Reviews: CRD's Guidance for Undertaking Reviews in Health Care. University of York: Centre for Reviews and Dissemination (https://www.york.ac.uk/media/crd/Systematic_Reviews.pdf). (Last accessed February 2017).

Duke University Medical Center Library and Archives (2017) Systematic Reviews: The Process: Data Management: Data Extraction tools (http://guides.mclibrary.duke.edu/c.php?g=158155&p=1035832). (Last accessed February 2017).

Higgins, J.P.T. and Deeks, J.J. (2011) 'Selecting studies and collecting data', in J.P.T. Higgins and S. Green (eds), Cochrane Handbook for Systematic Reviews of Interventions (http://handbook.cochrane.org). (Last accessed February 2017).

Petticrew, M. and Roberts, H. (2008) Systematic Reviews in the Social Sciences. 2nd edn. Oxford: Blackwell.

Steingart, K (2010) Data Extraction and Quality Assessment (http://www.teachepi.org/documents/courses/berlin/Steingart_Data_extraction_critical_appraisal_FINAL_12_Nov_2010.pdf). (Last accessed February 2017).

University of Wisconsin (2010) Systematic Reviews, a Guide: Data Extraction (http://researchguides.ebling.library.wisc.edu/systematic-reviews/author/data). (Last accessed February 2017).

WATCH...

... a video in which the editors answer your FAQs:

"Do I have to extract all the data in my included papers? Is it possible to do each stage of the review on my own?"

EXPLORE...

... the Links Library, which gives you a host of resources to help you tackle the systematic review process.

READ...

... online resources such as example reviews, journal articles and further guidance on the review process.

Take your systematic review journey online at:
https://study.sagepub.com/doingasystematicreview2e

Quality Assessment: Where Do I Begin?

Janette Greenhalgh and Tamara Brown

This chapter will help you to...

- Identify quality assessment tool(s) that suit your review

- Carry out quality assessment of individual articles

- Tabulate and summarize the results of your quality assessment

- Think about how your quality assessment results might impact on the conclusions and recommendations of your systematic review

Introduction

This chapter guides you as you set out to assess the quality of the studies included in your systematic review. First, we explore what we mean by quality and discuss the fundamentals of 'quality' common to all studies, regardless of study design or topic area. Second, we encourage you to think about the different types of study design that you might come across during your review, differentiating between randomized designs and non-randomized designs. Third, we emphasize how important it is to allow sufficient time to rigorously assess the quality of your included studies and discuss how the conclusions of your systematic review might be shaped by the findings of the quality assessment exercise. Finally, we encourage you to critically appraise your own systematic review using one of the many validated systematic review checklists that are available.

Before you read any further, it's important to note that this chapter is largely focused on the quality assessment of quantitative evidence. The examples we provide in this chapter are derived from our own experiences of carrying out systematic reviews in a healthcare context. However, the key steps involved in conducting a systematic review (including quality assessment) are also applicable to non-healthcare contexts. This chapter provides you with an introduction to quality assessment, but if your systematic review is of qualitative evidence, we encourage you to also refer to Chapter 11. For practical guidance on managing the review process, including quality assessment, please revisit Chapter 2.

What is quality assessment and why do I need to do it?

By the time you reach this stage of your review you will have already identified the full set of relevant studies for inclusion in your review and may or may not have extracted data from these studies. It's now important to examine the quality of each of these studies. You need to assess whether the studies have been designed, conducted and reported in such a way that they can be considered reliable (i.e. have rigour) and whether or not they provide meaningful answers to your research question (i.e. have relevance).

The meaning of 'quality' depends on the context in which it is used. When it comes to systematic reviewing, we need to distinguish between the quality of each of the included studies and the quality of the systematic review itself. The latter is discussed at the end of this chapter. When used to describe a study included in a systematic review, the term 'quality' refers to:

> The degree to which a study employs measures to minimize bias and error in its design, conduct and analysis. (Khan et al., 2003, p. 39)

In other words, the content of the publication gives you confidence that both its design and conduct are sufficiently robust for the results to be trustworthy and generalizable. For example, in effectiveness studies, you will want to be sure that the study included participants who were relevant to the aims of the study and that sufficient numbers of participants remained in the study to its end. To illustrate, if a study was designed to assess the effects of bibliotherapy on the psychological well-being of adults with anxiety, the results would be of little use if the participants in the study were adults with depression. Similarly, if only 30 out of 100 participants in the study were followed up and their data included in the results, only uncertain conclusions could be reached about the effectiveness (or otherwise) of bibliotherapeutic approaches.

If you have assessed a study as being of good or high quality, then this is the same as saying that you are confident that the findings of the study are credible and are highly likely to be a true representation of the results of the intervention, phenomenon or exposure that is being tested or explored. Remember, it is likely that your included studies will vary in quality. It is often mistakenly assumed that if a study has been published in a peer-reviewed academic journal, then it must be of good quality; this is not always true. Do not take published studies at face value. Always delve deeper and investigate your studies for flaws and inherent weaknesses. Don't be lulled into a false sense of security by a journal's reputation. To illustrate, in our review of chemotherapy treatments for patients with non-small cell lung cancer (Brown et al., 2013), we concluded that the overall quality of the 23 included studies was poor and yet these studies were all randomized controlled trials (RCTs) published in highly regarded journals. Similarly, one of the key points arising from our review of biofeedback for the treatment of hypertension (Greenhalgh et al., 2009) was that the majority of the 36 included RCTs were of such poor quality that we were unable to synthesize the results or draw any firm conclusions from the data available.

The advantages of quality assessing your included studies are numerous. You will develop a greater understanding of your studies and their results, and you will be able to distinguish between good-quality and poor-quality studies. Your review will benefit as you will be more likely to draw meaningful conclusions from the data. On a personal development level, the quality assessment exercise offers you the opportunity to acquire skills in critical appraisal.

When should I assess the quality of the studies in my review?

Before going any further, it's important to stress again that in the context of your review, it is up to you *when* you carry out the quality assessment exercise; you can do it before, during or after data extraction (please see Chapter 6 for further discussion of this and advice on the data extraction process). If you extract study data before you carry out your quality assessment, you will be blind to study quality and your reporting is less likely to be biased. However, if you are intending to exclude poor-quality studies from your review, then you need to carry out your quality assessment before extracting data. Furthermore, if you choose to assess study quality after you have extracted data, your greater familiarity with the study may help you to answer the quality assessment questions.

What are the main elements of quality assessment and what do they mean?

A single quality assessment tool asks a series of questions. To be able to answer the questions, you need to think very carefully about the methods used in the studies and how the results have been reported. You must be confident that the quality assessment tool you are using measures what it purports to measure (that it is 'valid') and provides consistent results (that it is 'reliable'). Quality assessment tools ask questions about bias, and it is a good idea to use tools that have been validated and checked for reliability. Examples of bias might include **selection**, **allocation**, **detection**, **attrition** and **reporting bias**. Common sources of bias, what bias means and the significance of each type of bias in relation to the precision of the results of a study are shown in Table 7.1. We consider that these key elements of bias are relevant to most study designs.

TABLE 7.1   Important elements of quality assessment for healthcare intervention studies

Element	What does this mean?	Significance
Selection bias	Were the individuals selected to participate in the study likely to be representative of the target population? How were the participants selected?	You need to be able to assess how generalizable and transferable the study results are to the target population.
Allocation bias	How were participants allocated to the treatment groups? Could anyone in the study predict or control allocation to treatment groups?	Type of study design determines how participants are allocated to treatment groups; generally, the 'stronger' the study design, the less risk of bias from allocation to treatment.
Performance bias	Were the participants, providers of the intervention or the study investigators aware of the treatment that participants received, or were they blinded?	You need to be able to assess whether there was awareness of treatment received by certain study personnel and whether this could bias study results.
Detection bias	Were the people who measured the study outcomes aware of what treatment participants received or were they blinded?	You need to be able to assess whether there was awareness of treatment received by study personnel and whether this could bias study results.

Element	What does this mean?	Significance
Attrition bias	What proportion of participants in each group stopped having the treatment? Did they stop by themselves (dropouts) or were they stopped by study personnel (withdrawal) for whatever reason (e.g. adverse event, non-compliance, did not meet inclusion criteria).	If a relatively large proportion of dropouts occurred, this could weaken the generalizability of the study and it might also reflect that the intervention is hard to 'stick to' (it might not 'work' or it might have unpleasant side effects in the target/general population). Attrition rates can also give the reader an insight into compliance rates; if withdrawal/dropout rates were unequal between treatment groups, then this may bias the results in favour of one group.
Reporting bias	Were all outcomes stated to be measured actually reported or did the study authors fail to report outcomes that showed no (or a negative) effect? Were some results measured post hoc, that is, was an outcome measured and reported because there seemed to be a beneficial effect or perhaps the data were trawled for an 'effective' outcome?	What reasons were given to explain the failure to report all stated outcomes? The treatment may appear more favourable than it really is if negative results from other outcomes are not reported within the paper.
Confounders	At baseline, were the participant characteristics, such as age, sex or health status, similar across all treatments?	Participants should be equally balanced in terms of variables considered important to study outcomes (e.g. sex, age, health status) otherwise there is a risk that results will be biased in favour of one group/intervention.
Concurrent/ subsequent intervention	Did any of the participants receive other treatments that could have influenced the study outcomes?	Confidence that the study intervention did/did not have an effect is weakened if participants were not all treated in the same way (except for study intervention).
Analysis	Were the data for all participants included in the final analysis (even those participants who withdrew)?	If there are data missing for a number of participants and these are not accounted for, published results will not properly reflect the results of the study.
Funding bias	Who funded the study?	Funders may have a vested interest in demonstrating positive outcomes for one group/intervention.

Bias is a key component of study quality, but there are also other important issues that are linked to study quality. These might relate to the outcome measure employed in the study, or to the intervention itself. A number of key questions could be considered regarding the outcome measure. For example, is the outcome measure appropriate to the study? Is it a validated measure? Is it reliable? When assessing study quality, it is important to consider whether the intervention was standardized across all study participants. A quality assessment tool might question this, or ask whether the intervention was properly defined or described, and whether it was delivered as intended. Were those responsible for implementing the intervention appropriately trained? Finally, it might be important to assess how far the study reflects the realities of the practice being evaluated (generalizability).

Are any 'off-the-shelf' quality assessment tools available?

Don't worry, there are numerous quality assessment tools available – you don't have to design your own. There are tools that have been designed solely for the quality assessment of studies with specific types of design (e.g. RCTs, cohort and **cross-sectional studies**) and some of these are discussed later in this chapter. There are also quality assessment tools that are designed for use with more than one study design, which can be useful if your review includes studies with a variety of designs.

Where do I start? What are the key quality assessment steps?

The six key steps of quality assessment are summarized in Box 7.1. We now talk through each step in detail.

 Box 7.1

Key steps involved in quality assessment

Step 1: Note the design(s) of your included studies

Step 2: Identify the type(s) of quality assessment tool(s) to suit your review

Step 3: Choose the appropriate quality assessment tool(s)

Step 4: Carry out quality assessment using the appropriate tool(s)

Step 5: Tabulate and summarize the results of your quality assessment

Step 6: Think about how the results of your quality assessment exercise might impact on the conclusions and recommendations of your systematic review

Step 1: Note the design(s) of your included studies

Quality assessment tools were initially developed for use in systematic reviews in medicine and healthcare; however, they are now used (sometimes with adaptations) in systematic reviews within many other disciplines. This means that study design, rather than the review topic area, should guide your choice of quality assessment tool. As such, the first step in quality assessment is to identify the design(s) of your included studies so that you can choose the most appropriate quality assessment tool(s).

There are different quality assessment tools available for assessing each study type. In an RCT, participants are randomly assigned to intervention groups. In **non-randomized studies**, participants might be assigned to different groups but not in a random manner, or the study might describe a group (or groups) of people who are either followed up over a period of time or examined at one specific point in time. Table 7.2 provides a guide to the more common study designs that you might encounter when carrying out your systematic review. For more information on how to quality assess qualitative and economic evidence, please see Chapters 11 and 12, respectively.

TABLE 7.2   Common types of study design

Design type	Description	Example
RCT	Participants are randomized to two or more treatment groups using robust methods of randomization.	The study is designed to compare the effectiveness of a new drug treatment for breast cancer with an existing drug treatment. Participants are randomized to receive their treatment via computer-generated random numbers.
Non-RCT	Participants are assigned to two or more treatment groups but randomization methods are not used in the process.	Participants take part in a study to assess whether cognitive behavioural therapy is more effective than drug therapy to treat anxiety. Each new participant is assigned to a treatment based on the assignment of the previous participant.
Cohort study (prospective or **retrospective study)** May or may not include a control group	A group of participants is identified and followed over time to assess specific outcomes. There may, or may not, be a concurrent control group.	A study to assess the effects of anti-epileptic drugs on the pregnancy outcomes of women with epilepsy recruits a sample of women (via ante-natal clinics) with epilepsy who are taking anti-epileptic medication during pregnancy. A control group might be made up of women from an ante-natal clinic who have epilepsy but who are not taking anti-epileptic medication.
Case–control	A group of participants with a particular condition are matched for age and other characteristics with a control group of participants who do not have the condition.	A group of children with asthma are compared with a group of children who don't have asthma. The two groups are compared in terms of birth weight to examine the influence of birth weight on the development of the condition.
Case series	A person (or series of people) who has been given a similar treatment is followed for a specific time period.	Children with autistic spectrum disorder who are given an intervention of applied behaviour analysis are followed up for six months.
Cross-sectional	Data are collected from a number of people or other sources (e.g. a database) at one point in time.	The relationship between intelligence and scientific reasoning in children is examined using questionnaires at one time point.

Step 2: Identify the type(s) of quality assessment tool(s) to suit your review

Once you have identified the design(s) of your included studies, you are ready to identify the type of quality assessment tool(s) to suit your review. Does your systematic review include only studies of a single type of study design, or does it include a mixture of designs? If you only include one type of study, then you can use a design-specific assessment tool. If you include a range of designs, you need to decide whether to use an assessment tool for each design or an all-inclusive tool that can be used across a range of designs. Quality assessment tools can be scales that give a numerical value of the 'quality' of a study, or they can be checklists that generate an overall picture of quality. We prefer to use a checklist rather than a scoring system as we think that a checklist provides more useful information about the quality of a study; a total quality score for a study does not provide any detail about the individual elements of the quality assessment, and some individual elements of quality assessment may be more 'important' than other elements. However, there are no hard and fast rules, and the choice is yours. To read about the advantages and disadvantages of the more commonly used tools, please consult published guidance for undertaking reviews in healthcare (Centre for Reviews and Dissemination, 2009), or the **Cochrane Handbook for Systematic Reviews of Interventions** (Higgins and Green, 2011).

We cannot advise here on specific tools – you will need to choose the most appropriate tool for your own review. Remember, you will need to make it clear in your protocol and thesis document why you have selected the tool that you have used. In making your decision, you might want to consider a number of factors:

- Has the tool been used in similar reviews in your topic area?
- A tool is often (but not always) designed and then piloted by a number of different people to test whether it measures what it is designed to measure. Has the tool been validated?
- How lengthy is the tool and how many studies do you have to quality assess? Some tools contain a considerable number of items. Are all of the items relevant to your studies? If you have included a large number of studies in your review, will you have time to use the tool on all of them?
- It can be difficult to present and succinctly discuss findings if you are using tools with a long list of items, or ones that contain items requiring detailed textual responses. Is the design of the tool such that all the results are easily tabulated and simple to summarize? Will the tabulated results convey your findings efficiently?

Step 3: Choose the appropriate quality assessment tool(s)

Take a look at other systematic reviews in the same topic area to see which quality assessment tools the authors of these reviews have used. Having found some useful examples, you might then ask your supervisor if s/he can help you to determine which tool(s) would be appropriate to use in your review.

In Table 7.3 we list a number of web-accessible sources of quality assessment tools. This list is not exhaustive, but is enough to help you get started. Before embarking on your search for a specific tool it is worth seeking out the recommended reporting guidelines for individual study types. These guidelines are often designed for use by journal editors and take the form of checklists to help guide decisions as to the quality of submitted articles. The Enhancing the Quality and Transparency of Health Research (EQUATOR) network website is a comprehensive source of all guidelines for health research reporting. There are guidelines for a broad range of study types; these are free to download (EQUATOR, 2017). For the social scientist, the American Educational Research Association (AERA) has developed guidance for ensuring high-quality research (AERA, 2013). We also provide a list of quality assessment tools on our website (https://study.sagepub.com/doingasystematicreview2e).

TABLE 7.3   Selected sources of quality assessment tools

Source	Contents	Our thoughts
Health Technology Assessment (HTA) report (Deeks et al., 2003). A systematic review of quality-assessment tools for non-randomized studies. Six tools considered suitable for use in systematic reviews that included non-randomized studies. We note that the authors of the review did not consider any particular tool to be perfect.	Cowley (1995) (covers comparative and uncontrolled case series). 13-item checklist. Downs and Black (1998) (randomized and non-randomized studies). 27-item checklist. Newcastle–Ottawa scale (Wells et al., 2012) (cohort and case–control studies). 8-item checklist. Reisch et al. (1989) (any study design). 34-'key' item checklist. Thomas (no date) (any study design). 21-item checklist. Zaza et al. (2000) (any study design). 22-item checklist.	These tools were considered suitable for use in systematic reviews by the authors of the HTA report.
Critical Appraisal Skills Programme (CASP) (CASP, 2013)	Critical appraisal checklists for RCTs, systematic reviews, cohort studies, case-control studies.	These checklists were designed to help clinicians assess evidence and so some items may not be relevant to your systematic review.

(Continued)

TABLE 7.3   (Continued)

Source	Contents	Our thoughts
The Cochrane Handbook (Higgins and Green, 2011)	The 'risk of bias' tool used for RCTs in Cochrane reviews. The ROBIS I tool for use with non-randomized studies (Sterne et al., 2016).	Detailed approach to quality assessment; time-consuming to use but very informative if applied conscientiously.
Centre for Reviews and Dissemination guidance (Centre for Reviews and Dissemination, 2009)	Guidance for conducting systematic reviews in healthcare.	Contains guides to criteria important in the assessment of studies. We use a slightly modified version of this guidance in many of our reviews.
The Joanna Briggs Institute (Joanna Briggs Institute, 2014)	Guidance for conducting systematic reviews in healthcare.	Contains a set of critical appraisal tools applicable to a range of study designs.
Social Care Institute for Excellence (SCIE) (Social Care Institute for Excellence, 2010)	Guidelines for conducting systematic reviews in social care.	Offers guidelines on the minimum generic criteria for assessing quality of primary research.

Quality assessment of randomized controlled trials

The RCT is considered to be at the top of the evidence hierarchy in terms of design quality. Table 7.4 shows a tool that can be used to quality assess RCTs. We have based this tool on the quality assessment criteria for RCTs recommended by the CRD (2009), but have modified it slightly. Note that the list includes questions relating to the quality criteria previously described in Table 7.1. When using this tool you should complete the checklist for each included study. The responses are limited to Yes/No/Partially/Not stated/Not applicable. You can add further columns to the right-hand side of your table to allow space for all studies included in your review. At the end of the exercise you will be able to visually compare the studies by each item or component of the assessment.

However, as we noted earlier (and as will become apparent later in this chapter), RCTs can be poorly executed and open to the influence of bias. Not all studies can be RCTs. Many areas of research do not lend themselves well to being examined using RCT methodology due to the nature of the research question and/or the intervention of interest. In addition, ethical and/or financial reasons can make it problematic or inappropriate to carry out an RCT.

Quality assessment of non-randomized studies

As noted earlier, many elements of quality assessment are common to all types of study design. Studies other than RCTs are also open to specific types of bias, and

TABLE 7.4   Example tool for quality assessment of randomized controlled trials

---

Reviewer name:

Author name/Study ID:

Quality item

Randomization (check for allocation bias)

Was the method used to assign participants to the treatment groups truly random?

Was the allocation of treatment concealed?

*Was the number of participants randomized stated?

Comparability (check for confounding)

*Were details of baseline comparability presented?

Was baseline comparability achieved?

Eligibility (check for selection bias)

*Were eligibility criteria for study entry specified?

*Were there any co-interventions that may influence outcomes for each group?

Blinding (check for detection bias)

Were outcome assessors blinded to treatment allocation?

Were the individuals who administered the intervention blinded to treatment allocation?

Were participants blinded to treatment allocation?

*Was the success of the blinding procedures assessed?

Withdrawals (check for attrition bias)

*Were $\geq$ 80% of participants randomized included in the final analysis?

*Were reasons for participant withdrawals stated?

Were there any unexpected dropouts in either group?

Was an intention-to-treat analysis included?

Outcomes (check for outcome reporting bias)

Is there evidence that more outcomes were measured than were reported?

---

* Indicates the modifications that we made to the original CRD checklist

so the measure of quality assessment for your review needs to include items to account for these additional concerns. These concerns may include, but are not limited to questions about:

- relevance of the research design to the research question;
- representativeness of the study participants to the research question;
- how participants were recruited;
- whether any comparison groups were utilized;
- how many people started the study and how many remained at the end;
- whether the measurement tools used in the study were valid, reliable and relevant.

In this section we present the Newcastle–Ottawa Scale (NOS) for assessing cohort studies (Wells et al., 2012). This scale is widely used and often modified to suit the needs of individual reviews. For example, colleagues at the University of Liverpool have adapted the NOS to appraise included studies in one of their recent reviews (Pope et al., 2010). There are tailored versions of the NOS for cohort studies (Box 7.2), **case-control** studies, intervention studies and cross-sectional studies.

Box 7.2

Newcastle–Ottawa Quality Assessment Scale: Cohort Studies

Note: The tool uses a 'star system' by which a study is judged on three broad perspectives: the selection of the study groups; the comparability of the groups; and the ascertainment of either the exposure or outcome of interest for case-control or cohort studies, respectively. Stars are pre-awarded in the NOS and are used to indicate quality elements. A study can be awarded a maximum of one star for each numbered item within the Selection and Outcome categories. A maximum of two stars can be given for Comparability. The handbook for interpretation of the NOS is available at www.ohri.ca/programs/clinical_epidemiology/oxford.asp.

Selection:

1) Representativeness of the exposed cohort

   a) truly representative of the average _____ (describe) in the community*

   b) somewhat representative of the average _____ in the community*

   c) selected group of users, for example, nurses, volunteers

   d) no description of the derivation of the cohort

2) Selection of the non-exposed cohort

   a) drawn from the same community as the exposed cohort*

   b) drawn from a different source

   c) no description of the derivation of the non-exposed cohort

3) Ascertainment of exposure

   a) secure record (e.g. surgical records)*

   b) structured interview*

   c) written self-report

   d) no description

4) Demonstration that outcome of interest was not present at start of study

   a) yes*
   b) no

Comparability:

1. Comparability of cohorts on the basis of the design or analysis

   a) study controls for _____ (select the most important factor)*
   b) study controls for any additional factor* (this criterion could be modified
       to indicate specific control for a second important factor)

Outcome:

1) Assessment of outcome

   a) independent **blind assessment***
   b) record linkage*
   c) self-report
   d) no description

2) Was follow-up long enough for outcomes to occur

   a) yes (select an adequate follow-up period for outcome of interest)*
   b) no

3) Adequacy of follow-up of cohorts

   a) complete follow-up – all subjects accounted for*
   b) subjects lost to follow-up unlikely to introduce bias – small number lost
       – > ____ % (select an adequate %) follow-up, or description provided of
       those lost)*
   c) follow-up rate < ____% (select an adequate %) and no description of
       those lost
   d) no statement

Reproduced with permission from Professor George A. Wells, University of Ottawa
Heart Institute.

Step 4: Carry out quality assessment using the appropriate tool(s)

Once you have chosen an appropriate quality assessment tool, it is time to pilot the
tool. Piloting in this context just means testing the tool to see if it 'works' by taking one or two studies and seeing whether you can answer the quality assessment

questions. If you are working with someone else (e.g. a fellow student or supervisor), then you can both be involved in piloting the tool. You must use the quality assessment tool in a consistent way: that is, treat all the studies the same way when assessing quality. When you are confident that you are both using the tool consistently, and in the same way, then you should both (independently) answer the quality assessment questions for each of the studies. Alternatively, one of you can cross-check the quality assessment responses of the other reviewer. We recommend that you keep careful notes about your decisions, and consistently mark the text of the papers where you found information – marking can be carried out on paper or electronically (see Chapter 2). After completing the quality assessment exercise, you need to compare your responses and discuss any discordant opinions. If any issues remain unresolved (despite several cups of coffee!), try to find a third person to resolve the outstanding issues.

As with screening and selection (Chapter 5), and data extraction (Chapter 6), working with a partner on this task is essential if you are planning to publish your review (see Chapter 10 for more information). However, should you find yourself working on your own, it might be useful to compare your quality assessment results with any published critiques of your included studies that are available in the public domain. Do be sure to note in your 'Discussion' section why, and how, the absence of a second reviewer to quality assess your included studies is a limitation of your systematic review. Chapter 9 provides more guidance on this topic.

Step 5: Tabulate and summarize the results of your quality assessment

Now is the time to summarize your quality assessment findings by tabulating the results and describing them in your text. The quality assessment section is typically presented within the 'Results' section of a review, immediately after the text describing the results of your searching, screening and selection, and immediately before data tables that describe study characteristics and participant characteristics.

In Table 7.5 we present an example of a quality assessment table that appears in our systematic review of first-line chemotherapy treatments for non-small cell lung cancer (Brown et al., 2013). The review included 23 RCTs but here, for brevity, we only show the results for the first 15 studies. We order the studies in the table by date, but you can order them in other ways, for example, alphabetically by first author. No matter how you plan to order your studies in your tables, remember to use this order consistently in all of the tables throughout your review.

TABLE 7.5 Example of quality assessment table of randomized controlled trials

Trial	Randomization		Number stated	Baseline comparability		Inclusion criteria specified	Co-interventions identified	Blinding				Withdrawals		Intention to treat	Other outcomes
	Truly random	Allocation concealment		Presented	Achieved			Assessors	Administration	Participants	Procedure assessed	>80% in final analysis	Reasons stated		
Chen (2004)	NS	NS	✓	✓	✓	✓	✓	NS	NS	NS	NS	✓	✓	✓	✗
Chen (2007)	NS	✓	✓	✓	✓	✓	✓	NS	NS	NS	NS	✓	✓	✓	✗
Douillard (2005)	NS	NS	✓	✓✗	NS	✓	✓	NS	NS	NS	NS	✓	✓	✓	✓
Fossella (2003)	NS	✓	✓	✓	✓	✓	✓	✗	✗	✗	NA	✓	✓	✓	✗
Gebbia (2003)	NS	✓	✓	✓	NS	✓	✓	NS	NS	NS	NS	✓	✓	✓	✗
Gridelli (2003)	✓	✓	✓	✓	NS	✓	✓	NS	NS	NS	NS	✓	✓	✓	✗
Helbekkmo (2007)	✓	✓	✓	✓	✓	✓	NS	NS	NS	NS	NS	✓	✓	✓	✓
Kelly (2001)	NS	NS	✓	✓✗	NS	NS	NS	NS	NS	NS	NS	✓	✓	✗	✗
Langer (2007)	✓	NS	✓	✓	NS	NS	NS	NS	NS	NS	NS	✓	✓	✗	✗
Martoni (2005)	NS	NS	✓	✓	NS	✓	✓	NS	NS	NS	NS	✓	✓	✗	✗
Ohe (2007)	✓	✓	✓	✓	NS	✓	✓	NS	NS	NS	NS	✓	✓	✗	✗
Scagliotti (2002)	✓	✓	✓	✓	NS	✓	✓	NS	NS	NS	NS	✓	✓	✗	✗
Schiller (2002)	NS	NS	✓	✓✗	NS	✓	✓✗	NS	NS	NS	NS	✓	✓	✗	✗
Smit (2003)	✓	NS	✓	✓	NS	✓	✓	NS	NS	NS	NS	✓	✓	✗	✗
Thomas (2006)	NS	NS	✓	✓	✓✗	✓	NS	✗	✗	✗	NA	✓	✓	✗	✗

✓ Yes (item adequately addressed); ✗ no (item not adequately addressed); ✓✗ partially (item partially addressed); NS not stated; NA not applicable

The information in Table 7.5 shows that the studies differed in terms of their quality. Even though these were all RCTs published in peer-reviewed journals, 9 of the 15 studies failed to report important information describing the details of the methods used to randomize participants to treatment arms. In addition, 10 of the studies did not state whether the participants in each treatment arm were balanced in terms of their personal characteristics (e.g. similar numbers of males and females in each arm, participants were of a similar age). In the overall summary of the quality of the 23 studies included in our review we concluded that:

> Overall methodological quality of included studies was poor. Only six of the 23 included studies reported sufficient information for them to be assessed as adequately randomized and with adequate concealment of allocation. All studies clearly reported the number of participants randomized. All studies reported inclusion criteria and, with the exception of four studies, all reported details about co-interventions, for example palliative radiotherapy and/or second-line chemotherapy. Six studies were reported as 'open'. Blinding of participants, investigators or outcome assessors was considered to be not stated in 16 out of the 23 included studies. The outcomes of over 80 per cent of patients were assessed in all studies and all studies reported reasons for dropout; 10 trials used an intention to treat approach to assess overall survival. Five of the studies appeared to report fewer outcomes than initially stated. (Brown et al., 2013)

Step 6: Think about how the results of your quality assessment exercise might impact on the conclusions and recommendations of your systematic review

Now that you have tabulated and summarized the results of the quality assessment exercise, you should have a good overview of your included studies. You should now start to think about how the quality of your studies might impact on the credibility of the overall results of your systematic review. Irrespective of which tool you use to assess your studies, you need to summarize the findings in your thesis. You could use previous reviews in the topic area to guide you when you come to write up your quality assessment exercise. To help you, look for any guidance notes that accompany the quality assessment tool that you have used. Think about what you, as a reader, might want to know about the results of the quality assessment. Does the summary allow other readers to reach an informed conclusion about the quality of the studies included in your review? Remember, you should only present the results of your quality assessment exercise in the 'Results' section; save discussion of these findings for the 'Discussion' section of your thesis.

Quality assessing your own systematic review

There are specific quality assessment tools that you can use to quality assess your own systematic review. It may be useful to apply one of these tools to your work as a final check of your report. Your supervisor and/or examiner might also use a tool for this purpose. Table 7.6 shows the **AMSTAR** quality assessment tool, which is suitable for use with systematic reviews (Shea et al., 2007). The AMSTAR checklist and guidance notes are available at http://Amstar.ca/Amstar_Checklist.php.

TABLE 7.6   The AMSTAR tool for the quality assessment of systematic reviews

Reviewer name:
Author name/Study ID:
Quality item
Response: Yes/No/Can't answer/Not applicable
Was an a priori design provided?
Was there duplicate study design and data extraction?
Was a comprehensive literature search performed?
Was the status of publication (i.e. grey literature) used as an inclusion criterion?
Was a list of studies (included and excluded) provided?
Was the scientific quality of the included studies assessed and documented?
Was the scientific quality of the included studies used appropriately in formulating conclusions?
Were the methods used to combine the findings of studies appropriate?
Was the likelihood of publication bias assessed?
Was the conflict of interest included?

There are also several other tools against which you can assess the quality of your systematic review. These include:

- the Preferred Reporting of Items for Systematic Reviews and Meta Analyses (PRISMA) checklist (http://prisma-statement.org/PRISMAStatement/Checklist.aspx);
- the Meta-Analysis of Observational Studies in Epidemiology (MOOSE) guidelines (Stroup et al., 2000).

Although the process of quality assessing your own systematic review can be time-consuming, it will be time well spent. It will help you to identify any areas of weakness in the conduct or reporting of your systematic review prior to submitting your thesis. It may also be beneficial if you are planning to later publish your systematic review in a peer-reviewed journal (see Chapter 10), as most peer-reviewed academic journals will require your manuscript to adhere to the principles set out in the PRISMA statement (or similar).

Final thoughts

We have summarized the key points from this chapter in Box 7.3. We think that you should save discussion of your results for the 'Discussion' section of your thesis. However, we considered it appropriate to finish this chapter with a few questions that may be helpful to reflect upon when writing your 'Methods' and 'Results' section and formulating your discussion:

- Were you surprised by the results of the quality assessment exercise? Did you find any elements of the exercise noteworthy?
- Did any of the results from individual studies appear to be different from the majority of study results? Were there any specific quality issues associated with these studies?
- How should the study results be synthesized? Is it reasonable to 'lump' similar study interventions together if quality differs markedly between studies? If the majority of studies included in your systematic review are assessed as being of poor quality, then you need to consider whether or not to carry out a meta-analysis. If you are planning to meta-analyse study results, should a **sensitivity analysis** of study results based on quality also be undertaken (see Chapter 8)? For example, excluding poor-quality studies may change outliers and effect size and/or confidence intervals around the effect size.
- Did you find any patterns across studies? Can you offer recommendations for future research? For example, did the majority of your included studies fail to describe how participants were selected? A recommendation for future research could then include a statement that any future studies relevant to the topic of your review must improve the reporting of participant selection as this would enable reviewers to assess the generalizability of the study results to the target population.

For other ideas on how to integrate and discuss your quality assessment findings in your review, look at other reviews in your subject area and read Chapter 9.

Box 7.3

'Top tips' for quality assessment

- Quality assessment can be a time-consuming process and should not be left until the last minute.
- Carefully document where in the study you found information relating to each quality assessment question. This can save time later on and prevent you from having to rely on memory if you have to go back and check your reasoning.

- Use footnotes beneath the quality assessment table to clarify your responses where necessary. For example, if the participant characteristics were partially comparable between the groups, you might want to say in a footnote that this was because there were more males in one group than in another. As well as guiding the reader, this will help you when writing up the results.
- Make notes of anything that stands out as 'interesting' or 'quirky' when you quality assess a study, as this can help jog your memory of the study characteristics and help you to make sense of the study results.
- Quality assessing a paper appears to be a straightforward matter of answering a list of questions. However, the task is rarely so black and white. Whatever tool you use, some degree of subjective judgement will be required to enable you to answer some of the questions. This is why it is useful to have a second reviewer to quality assess your studies.
- Reviewer experience, in terms of the topic being studied and familiarity with study design, can influence an individual's ability to quality assess studies. Ideally each included study should be quality assessed by two reviewers independently.
- Keep records of how you came to make your decisions, especially when you were unable to give a clear 'yes' or 'no' response to a question.
- Sometimes it may not be clear to you what a quality assessment question is really asking, even when there is a guide to help you use the tool. If this is the case, discuss your concerns with your peers or supervisor.

Key points to think about when writing your protocol

- Types of studies (e.g. randomized or non-randomized) that you intend to include in your review
- Quality assessment strategy (e.g. what tool will you use, when will you use it and will anyone help you?)
- Length of time you plan to spend on the exercise

What an examiner is looking for in your thesis

- Appropriate use of quality assessment tool(s) and a list of their associated strengths and weaknesses
- Summary and tabulation of the results of your quality assessment exercise
- Detailed reporting of your quality assessment findings
- Clear discussion of how the quality assessment results might link to the review conclusions

Frequently Asked Questions

Question 1: What do I do if I can't find the right tool for my review?

Sometimes formal tools need modifying to suit the purpose of a particular review. Rather than developing a completely new tool, it is probably best to find a validated tool that best matches the studies in your review and modify or add items to that tool. Please note that any changes made will limit the validity of the tool, and the pros and cons of adapting the tool to a specific review should be discussed.

Question 2: How long does quality assessment take?

Key steps include reading the publication(s), reading through the appropriate quality assessment tool, completing the tool, writing up the results in the review and synthesizing your results with the effectiveness data. Usually, it will take *at least* 45 minutes to complete a quality assessment tool for one study publication. Quality assessment is not a quick task. You need to allow sufficient time to carry it out properly.

Question 3: How do I quality assess a study that is reported in more than one paper?

If a study is reported in more than one paper, then you should treat the paper with the key study data as the 'core' paper, using the other papers as supplements. The 'core' paper would be used in the quality assessment exercise. It is advisable for you to read all of the papers relating to the study, especially if you are unclear about any of the study methods. If, for example, you can only answer a question using data presented in a supplement, then you will need to add a footnote to your quality assessment table to explain the source of this information. If, for reasons of time (or finances), you cannot obtain all of the papers, you should acknowledge this as a limitation of your review.

Question 4: How do I (and should I) assess the quality of a study that is only reported in an abstract?

If you have included abstracts in your review (e.g. from a conference, or from a non-English-language paper with an English abstract), these should be quality assessed as far as is possible. It should be made clear in the quality assessment table (using a footnote) and in the summary text that the study data were only available from an abstract. If there is missing or unclear information, the reader will then be aware that the study information was limited rather than assume that it came from a poor-quality study.

Question 5: How do I deal with a very-poor-quality study?

You should highlight any very-poor-quality studies in your write-up of the quality assessment exercise. You should also consider their impact on the overall results of the review. For example, does their inclusion change your review's conclusions dramatically, or do their results fit with the results of other studies? If you are planning to conduct a meta-analysis, consider carrying out a sensitivity analysis (see Chapter 8) in which poor-quality studies are excluded.

Question 6: Why should I bother quality assessing studies?

While quality assessment might seem like a tick-box exercise, it is an important step in any systematic review. The important part is linking the results of the quality assessment with the conclusions of your review. Quality assessment isn't just limited to students undertaking postgraduate theses: many important publications and reports in the field of (public) health now include 'evidence statements' or 'evidence summaries' alongside advice and recommendations. For example, the National Institute for Health and Care Excellence (NICE) uses evidence statements to reflect the strength of the evidence which is derived from a synthesis of the quality, quantity and consistency of the evidence gathered from carrying out reviews (NICE, 2014). Quality assessment results are an important element underpinning the strength of the evidence, and can be used to help experts formulate and prioritize recommendations for practice. Furthermore, the Cochrane Collaboration has recently introduced Summary of Findings (SoF) tables for each systematic review (Higgins and Green, 2011). Similarly to the NICE evidence statements, the purpose of the SoF table is to help improve decision-making and increase the usability of Cochrane Reviews. Like the NICE evidence statements, a key part of the SoF table is quality assessment of the included evidence. These two practical examples show the importance of quality assessment in informing evidence (or study results) that is used to change practice.

Question 7: My systematic review is on a non-health topic. Can I still use this chapter as a guide?

Yes. The components of quality assessment are essentially similar across health and non-health topics. Have a look at other systematic reviews in the same topic area as your review and discuss potentially suitable quality assessment tools with your supervisor.

Question 8: Is identification of study design part of quality assessment?

As the authors note in Chapter 5 of this book, when setting inclusion criteria for a systematic review, researchers often include or exclude studies based on specific study designs. For example, often systematic reviews of the clinical effectiveness of healthcare interventions stipulate that only evidence from RCTs may be considered for inclusion. However, limiting inclusion criteria to specific study designs is not part of quality assessment. Quality assessment goes beyond study design. It allows you to evaluate the validity, reliability and generalizability of the results of each included study.

Question 9: What should I do if I identify relevant systematic reviews in my topic area – should I quality assess them?

If your searches have identified published systematic reviews in your topic area, you may want to use them as a reference tool. First, their reference lists make it easy for you to check that you haven't missed any potentially relevant studies. Second, reading the background and conclusion sections means that you can very quickly identify any important potential issues that you might also wish to consider in your review. In our systematic review of clopidogrel and modified-release dipyridamole for the prevention of occlusive vascular events (Greenhalgh et al., 2011), we found several existing systematic reviews; however, none addressed the specific question of interest in our review. In this case, we used the existing reviews to check for potentially relevant papers and provided a quality assessment of each systematic review in the appendix of our report, to demonstrate that we were aware of their existence.

Question 10: I have included RCTs, cohort studies and non-randomized intervention studies in my review. Should I use a generic quality assessment tool for all, or should I choose three design-specific tools?

We think that the best option is to use design-specific tools. You can then be sure that you are appraising elements that are specific and important to each of the study designs of interest. The purpose of the quality assessment part of your review is to appraise the strength of the evidence you have presented. One of those strengths is inherent in the design of the study. It is not wrong to use a generic tool; however, you should be aware that using a generic tool might mask key strengths associated with study design.

Further Reading and Resources

Centre for Reviews and Dissemination (2009) Systematic Reviews: CRD's Guidance for Undertaking Reviews in Health Care. University of York: Centre for Reviews and Dissemination (www.york.ac.uk/media/crd/Systematic_Reviews.pdf). (Last accessed February 2017).

Cochrane Canada (2012) Risk of Bias Assessment of RCTs in Cochrane Reviews with Lucy Turner [Video file] (https://www.youtube.com/watch?v=0c3u_2ZoBdl).

Deeks, J.J., Dinnes, J., D'amico, R., Sowden, A.J., Sakarovitch, C., Song, F., Petticrew, M. and Altman, D.G. (2003) 'Evaluating non-randomised intervention studies', Health Technology Assessment, 7(27): 1–173. (www.journalslibrary.nihr.ac.uk/hta/volume-7/issue-27). (Last accessed February 2017).

Greenhalgh, T. (2014) How to Read a Paper: The Basics of Evidence-Based Medicine. 5th edn. Chichester: Wiley-Blackwell/BMJ Books.

Higgins, J.P.T. and Green, S. (2011) Cochrane Handbook for Systematic Reviews of Interventions (www.handbook.cochrane.org). (Last accessed February 2017).

University of Bristol, School of Social and Community Medicine (2013) Risk of Bias in Systematic Reviews (ROBIS) (www.bristol.ac.uk/social-community-medicine/projects/robis/). (Last accessed February, 2017).

WATCH...	EXPLORE...	READ...
... a video in which the editors answer your FAQ: *"Why do I need to assess the quality of the included studies?"*	... the Links Library, which gives you a host of resources to help you tackle the systematic review process.	... online resources such as example reviews, journal articles and further guidance on the review process.

Take your systematic review journey online at:
https://study.sagepub.com/doingasystematicreview2e

8

Understanding and Synthesizing Numerical Data from Intervention Studies

Michaela Brown and Marty Richardson

This chapter will help you to...

- Present and interpret the numerical results of your included studies

- Recognize whether it is appropriate to combine your studies in a meta-analysis

- Understand the basic principles of meta-analysis

- Recognize heterogeneity and learn appropriate methods to deal with it

- Present and interpret the results of a meta-analysis

Introduction

This chapter guides you through the processes of presenting and summarizing numerical data from intervention studies. We start by showing you how to present the results of individual intervention studies and the best way to interpret them. We then explore the circumstances under which it is appropriate to combine data in a meta-analysis and explain what is involved in this process. We go on to consider the importance of **heterogeneity** and how you might deal with it in your analyses. We finish by suggesting how you can present the results of your meta-analysis and interpret your findings.

Points to note

First, throughout this chapter, we use the term '**intervention study**' to refer to any study in which an intervention is evaluated. Many, but not all, intervention studies include a randomization process. Most of our examples include data from randomized controlled trials, because these are considered the gold standard of intervention studies. However, the principles discussed in this chapter apply to most types of intervention studies, unless stated otherwise.

Second, although this chapter has been written to guide you through the data synthesis process and explain the basic principles involved in a meta-analysis, it does not equip you with the skills to perform your own meta-analysis. Knowledge of the data synthesis process will allow you to interpret intervention study results correctly, and knowledge of the principles of meta-analysis will help you decide whether using this technique is appropriate for your data. However, we always recommend that you talk to a statistician at key stages during the review process if you have not performed a meta-analysis before. A statistician will be able to check that your decision as to whether or not to perform a meta-analysis is sensible. S/he can advise you on the correct methods for performing a meta-analysis using the software you have available and can also help you to understand the results. The textbook by Egger and colleagues (Egger et al., 2001) provides a useful overview of meta-analysis software. Don't forget, you can speak to your supervisor if you think you need advice from a statistician but don't know how to find one.

Third, before reading any further, it is important for you to know that a meta-analysis is not a required element of a systematic review. Meta-analysis should only be carried out as part of the review process if data from included intervention studies are sufficiently similar and it is sensible to combine them. We looked at the titles and abstracts of 288 postgraduate theses included in the Dissertation and Theses database, dating from 1990 to 2012, which reported the use of systematic review methodology across a wide range of disciplines. We identified that a minority (n = 48, 17 per cent) of these contained a meta-analysis. There are a number of conditions that must be met before deciding to meta-analyse your data; if these are not fulfilled then it is inappropriate and misleading to combine data. Don't worry though, we'll talk you through the process of making this important decision.

Finally, it is important to note that the latter half of this chapter focuses solely on meta-analysing evidence from RCTs because most of the current statistical methods use data from this type of study. However, meta-analyses of data from observational intervention studies are becoming more common. For more information on the meta-analysis of non-randomized studies please refer to Chapter 13 of the Cochrane Handbook (Higgins and Green, 2011). It is also important to note that although the examples that follow are often taken from healthcare research, the methods are also applicable to other fields, so don't be put off if your review is non-healthcare focused.

Presenting and interpreting the results of individual intervention studies

Chapter 6 focused mainly on using data tables to present key data about the included studies in your systematic review, such as study characteristics, participant characteristics and study results, and how to describe these data narratively in the text. Here, we will consider in more detail how to present and interpret the results of individual intervention studies. As numerical data can vary widely from study to study, we first look at different types of numerical data more closely. We then guide you through some of the most common types of data and the ways that these data can be presented. It is not your job to manipulate the data, as the authors of the published studies should have done this for you – use this chapter simply as a guide to help you to understand the information that is reported in the studies.

Binary data

Binary data are outcomes that can only be expressed as one of two possible responses, for example dead or alive, success or failure. These data may be presented by reporting:

- the number of individuals who experience the outcome of interest in each group and the number of patients randomized to each group (e.g. in group A, 44 of the 60 people experienced an event, in group B, 32 of the 61 people experienced an event);

- the percentage of people experiencing an event in each group and the number randomized to that group (e.g. of the 60 people in group A, 73 per cent experienced an event; of the 61 people in group B, 52 per cent experienced an event);
- **summary statistics (relative risk, odds ratio** or **risk difference).**

A summary statistic is a point estimate that is the 'best guess' of the direction and size of the treatment effect. The direction of the treatment effect tells us which treatment is better and the size tells us by how much. An associated confidence interval is usually reported alongside the point estimate and is used to describe the uncertainty around the estimate by giving the range of values within which the true effect is strongly believed to lie. Confidence intervals can be reported for a number of significance levels; the most common is the 95 per cent confidence interval, which can be interpreted as meaning that we are 95 per cent certain that the true effect lies within the range of the confidence interval. A standard 95 per cent confidence interval can be calculated using the following equation:

$$95\% \text{ confidence interval} = \text{summary statistic} \pm 1.96 \times \sqrt{\text{standard error of the summary statistic}}$$

Narrow confidence intervals indicate that the treatment estimate is relatively precise, whereas wide confidence intervals suggest that there is a high degree of uncertainty. A confidence interval that includes the value of no difference between the groups indicates that the treatments are not significantly different (we have provided the value of no difference in the information provided for each summary statistic below). However, non-significance does not always mean that there is 'no effect'. Often, small studies will report non-significant results even when there are important, real effects, which could only be detected by a much larger study.

Relative risk is the risk of an event in one group divided by the risk in the other group, where the risk is defined as the probability of the event occurring. If the risks are equal in the two groups being compared, the relative risk is 1. Therefore, the value of no difference for the relative risk is 1. If risk in group A is lower than the risk in group B, the relative risk of A compared with B is less than 1 and the relative risk of B compared with A is greater than 1. For example, if the relative risk of group A compared with group B is 0.67, this can be interpreted as meaning that the risk of an event in group A is 67 per cent of the risk of an event in group B. Put another way, there is a 33 per cent reduction in risk for people in group A relative to people in group B.

Odds ratio is the odds of an event in one group divided by the odds of an event in another group, where odds are defined as the ratio of the probability of the event occurring relative to the probability of the event not occurring. This sounds a bit complicated but these odds are the same as those used in gambling to work out your financial gain if you win. For example, odds of 3:1 mean that for every £1 you bet, you win £3. Similarly, odds are often used in medicine, where a chance of survival of 50:50 means that for every 50 patients who survive, 50 die. In the same way as relative risk, if the odds in two groups being compared are equal, the odds ratio is 1. Therefore, the value of no difference for the odds ratio is 1. If the odds in group A are lower than the odds in group B, then the odds ratio of A relative to B is less than 1 and the odds ratio of B relative to A is greater than 1. Odds ratios are much less intuitive to interpret than relative risks. For example, an odds ratio of 0.54 indicates that there is a 46 per cent reduction in odds but this does not really tell us very much. To interpret what an odds ratio means in terms of the change in the number of events across groups, it is necessary to transform the odds ratio into a relative risk. People often incorrectly assume that relative risks and odds ratios are the same. When events are rare, the value of these two measures will be approximately equal, but as risks and odds increase, large differences may exist between the two statistics. Odds ratios are sometimes chosen over relative risks due to the fact that odds ratios have strong mathematical properties, such as being able to take any value between zero and infinity.

The risk difference is the risk of an event in one group minus the risk in another group, where risk is defined as the probability of the event occurring (the same definition of risk as used to calculate a relative risk). This describes the absolute change so that if two groups are equal, the risk difference is zero. Therefore, the value of no difference for the risk difference is zero. If the risk in group A is lower than the risk in group B, the risk difference of A relative to B is less than zero and the risk difference of B relative to A is greater than zero. For example, if the risk difference of group A relative to group B is –0.39, this indicates that the risk of an event is 39 per cent lower in group A than it is in group B.

How to calculate summary statistics for binary data if they are not presented in a published paper

Let's assume that Table 8.1 shows the outcomes reported in one of your included intervention studies. The number of people who experience the event (treated here as a failure) are denoted as F_A and F_B depending on whether the people are in group A or group B, and similarly, patients who do not experience the event (treated here as a success) are denoted as S_A and S_B.

TABLE 8.1 Possible outcomes from an included study

Group	Event (failure)	No event (success)	Total
A	F_A	S_A	N_A
B	F_B	S_B	N_B

Relative risk

The relative risk is calculated by dividing the risk of an event in group A by the risk of an event in group B:

$$\text{relative risk} = \frac{F_A / N_A}{F_B / N_B}$$

An alternative way of presenting this information is the relative risk reduction, which is calculated as follows: relative risk reduction = $100 \times (1 - \text{relative risk})$.

Odds ratio

The odds ratio is calculated by dividing the odds of an event in group A by the odds of an event in group B:

$$\text{odds ratio} = \frac{F_A / S_A}{F_B / S_B}$$

Risk difference

The risk difference is calculated by subtracting the risk of an event in group B from the risk of an event in group A:

$$\text{risk difference} = \frac{F_A}{N_A} - \frac{F_B}{N_B}$$

Table 8.2 shows outcome data from an RCT. The outcome is presented as the number (n) of patients experiencing an infection, the number of patients for whom there are data that can be analysed (N), and the percentage of those patients who have data that can be analysed and who experience an infection (%). These numbers can be used to calculate relative risks, odds ratios and risk differences.

TABLE 8.2 Example of events reported in an included study

	Treatment arm			Control arm		
Trial	n	N	%	N	N	%
Smith, 2012	2	32	6	3	40	8

First, we need to rearrange the data in Table 8.2 into a 2 × 2 table, as shown in Table 8.3.

TABLE 8.3 Example of trial outcomes reported in an included study

	Infection (failure)	No infection (success)	Total
Treatment arm	2	30	32
Control arm	3	37	40

$$\text{Relative risk} = \frac{2/32}{3/40} = 0.83$$

This can be interpreted as meaning that the risk of experiencing an infection in the treatment group is 83 per cent of the risk in the control group. Put another way, there is a 17 per cent (100 × [1 – 0.83]) reduction in risk for patients in the treatment group relative to those patients in the control group.

$$\text{Odds ratio} = \frac{2/30}{3/37} = 0.82$$

This measure is much less intuitive to interpret than relative risk. An odds ratio of 0.82 means that there is an 18 per cent reduction in odds for patients in the treatment group relative to those patients in the control group, but this doesn't tell us anything about the change in the number of events for patients in the treatment group compared with patients in the control group.

$$\text{Risk difference} = \frac{2}{32} - \frac{3}{40} = -0.0125$$

This can be interpreted as meaning that the risk of an infection is 1.25 per cent lower in the treatment group than it is in the control group.

Continuous data

Continuous data are outcomes measured on a continuous scale, for example, age or height. These data may be presented separately for each treatment (e.g. with a mean and standard deviation) or as a summary statistic that measures the difference between two treatments (e.g. **mean difference** or **standardized mean difference**). If a summary statistic is not presented, we suggest you calculate this yourself as it is more meaningful than presenting the results separately for each treatment group.

The two summary statistics described below assume that the outcomes you have extracted from your included studies have a normal distribution in each arm of each study (Figure 8.1 shows how the data look graphically if they are normally distributed).

This means that the data tend to be distributed around a central point with no bias to the left or right. This assumption is not always met as data may be skewed (Figure 8.2 shows how the data look graphically if they are skewed); **skewed data** are not evenly distributed around a central point, rather they are clustered to either the left or right. Under such circumstances the mean is no longer the measure of choice. If you have concerns that your data may be skewed, speak to a statistician about the best approach to take.

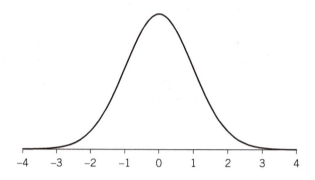

FIGURE 8.1   Example of normally distributed data

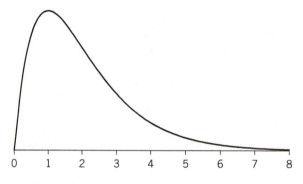

FIGURE 8.2   Example of skewed data

Mean difference

Mean difference is the absolute difference between the mean values of the outcomes in the two treatment groups. The mean difference is simple to interpret: a mean difference of 4.5 signifies that the outcome is 4.5 units bigger in one group than in the other.

Standardized mean difference

When studies assess the same outcome but measure it using different scales, the standardized mean difference is used instead of the mean difference, as it is necessary to standardize the results of the studies to a uniform scale. The standardized mean difference is a measure of the treatment effect that takes into account the variability observed across the participants. While standardized mean differences correct for different lengths of scales, they do not correct for differences in the direction of the scale (i.e. if one study uses a scale from 0–10 where 10 is good and another uses a scale from 0–10 where 10 is bad).

The standardized mean difference is more difficult to interpret than the mean difference as it is reported in units of standard deviations rather than in the units originally used to measure the outcome. The Cochrane Handbook (Higgins and Green, 2011) discusses a 'rule of thumb' for interpreting this summary statistic as proposed by Cohen (1988): 0.2 represents a small effect, 0.5 a moderate effect and 0.8 a large effect.

How to calculate summary statistics for continuous data if they are not presented in a published paper

The mean difference is calculated simply by subtracting one mean value from the other:

$$\text{Mean difference} = \text{mean in group A} - \text{mean in group B}$$

The standardized mean difference is calculated using the following equation:

$$\text{Standardized mean difference} = \frac{\text{mean in group A} - \text{mean in group B}}{\text{pooled standard deviation}}$$

For information on calculating a **pooled standard deviation** please refer to Practical Statistics for Medical Research (Altman, 1991).

Example 1: Age

If you want to know the difference between two groups in terms of their mean age you would calculate the mean difference because the outcome is measured on the same scale in both groups (Table 8.4).

TABLE 8.4 Age of participants reported in a published paper

Group	Age of participants (years)										Mean age
A	56	62	57	55	59	57	58	55	54	58	57.1
B	58	61	64	62	63	61	59	63	60	62	61.3

Mean difference = 61.3 – 57.1 = 4.2 years

The mean difference indicates that on average, patients in group B are 4.2 years older than those in group A.

Example 2: Scores on tests

If you want to know the difference between two groups in terms of their test scores and the group A test was marked out of 60 and the group B test was marked out of 80 (as shown in Table 8.5), you couldn't use the mean difference as this wouldn't take into account the fact that the two tests were marked on different scales; instead, you would need to calculate the standardized mean difference as this adjusts for the difference between the two scales.

TABLE 8.5   Calculating mean differences in two groups' scores

Group	Score										Mean	SD*	Pooled SD*
A	46	52	59	55	49	43	54	57	60	56	53.1	5.59	
B	73	77	64	59	78	66	75	74	67	69	70.2	6.20	8.34

*SD = standard deviation

$$\text{Standardized mean difference} = \frac{70.2 - 53.1}{8.34} = 2.05$$

According to Cohen's (1988) rule of thumb, discussed earlier, there is a large effect (as the standardized mean difference is greater than 0.8). This means that there is evidence of a difference between the two groups after allowing for the fact that the two tests had different maximum scores.

Ordinal data

Ordinal data fall into ordered categories, for example, mild, moderate and severe. It is common to analyse ordinal data with numerous categories as if the data were a continuous outcome, and ordinal data with few categories by grouping categories together and treating them as a binary outcome. Methods for meta-analysing ordinal outcome data are complicated and often unnecessary.

Count data

Count data are expressed as the total number of events that each participant experiences, for example, the number of infections patients experience during a clinical trial. Count data can be split into two types: counts of rare events and counts of common events.

For rare events, analyses of counts are based on rates that quantify the number of events occurring over a given time period. The summary statistic used for rare events is known as the rate ratio, which is calculated by dividing the rate of the event occurring in one group by the rate of the event occurring in the other group. For example, if in group A there are 14 events in a 24-hour period and in group B there are 3 events in a 24-hour period, the rate ratio is calculated by dividing 14 by 3, giving an answer of 4.7. This can be interpreted as meaning that the event of interest occurs 4.7 times more frequently in group A than in group B over a 24-hour time period.

For common events, the outcome can be thought of as the number of events in a group and analysed as if it were continuous data.

Time-to-event data

Time-to-event (survival) data are outcomes that measure the time taken for each participant to experience an event from a specified starting point, for example, months of survival. For those who do not experience the event of interest during the time they are observed, the length of time that they are in the trial is still recorded and they are classed as 'censored'.

It is possible to analyse time-to-event data in the same way as binary data by splitting patients into those who have experienced an event and those who have not experienced an event at a specific time period, but this requires knowledge of whether all patients have experienced the event or not at a given time point. The most common approach is to use **survival analysis**. This quantifies the data in terms of hazards, which are similar to risks (as mentioned in the binary data section) but are more unstable as they may change dramatically over time. Hazard ratios are interpreted in the same way as relative risks: a hazard ratio of 0.43 means that the risk of experiencing an event in one group is 43 per cent of the risk of experiencing an event in another group in a given time period.

Results tables

It is considered best practice to present the results of the included studies in a combined study results table. As discussed in Chapter 6, complementary text should describe any similarities and differences that you have identified across the studies rather than be focused on the results of individual trials. It is important that what you write in the text *exactly* matches what is shown in the table. Table 8.6 is a hypothetical results table showing the results of four studies in educational research.

TABLE 8.6 Example results table (educational research study data)

	Achieved 5 A*–C grades at GCSE following educational interventions		
Trial	Group A n (%)	Group B n (%)	Odds ratio (95% confidence interval)
Jones (2012)	72 (29.9)	105 (43.2)	0.56 (–1.59, 2.72)
Price (2010)	152 (29.7)	244 (48.0)	0.46 (0.22, 2.55)
Smith (2012)	98 (32.6)	136 (45.9)	0.58 (–1.55, 2.71)
Quraishy (2017)	62 (27.4)	94 (40.9)	0.55 (–1.62, 2.72)

The following is an example of the text that might go alongside Table 8.6.

> Four publications reported data on students' GCSE results following two different educational interventions designed to improve examination performance (Jones (2012), Price (2010), Smith (2012) and Quraishy (2017)). The proportion of students achieving 5 A*–C grades at GCSE ranged from 27.4 per cent to 32.6 per cent in group A and from 40.9 per cent to 48.0 per cent in group B.

Meta-analysis of data from RCTs

First things first: what is a meta-analysis and why might you want to carry one out? A meta-analysis is a statistical method that allows results from individual intervention studies to be combined to give an overall measure of the effect of one intervention compared with another (Glass, 1976). Meta-analysis allows the results from several RCTs to be combined; such analyses (usually) include a large number of patients, and therefore may be more likely to detect smaller (but still clinically significant) differences than an analysis of results from a single RCT. This means that the results of meta-analyses can be particularly useful when analysing subgroups, for example, when there are too few patients in the subgroups of individual RCTs to allow any differences to be detected. In addition to being able to detect smaller differences, any estimates detected by a meta-analysis will be more precise (i.e. have narrower confidence intervals) because the variability between patients is reduced as the number of patients increases.

The main assumption underlying a meta-analysis is that the RCTs are sufficiently similar for the results to be combined, that is, they are homogeneous. However, it is inevitable that RCTs will differ in some way or another. So, before using this method, you need to be confident that the studies you are interested in are not too different and can be grouped together, and that it is sensible to combine the results of these studies to get an overall measure of effect. The following sections outline the key steps involved in understanding if and how you might perform a meta-analysis (see Box 8.1).

Box 8.1

Key steps to consider when synthesizing data using meta-analysis

Step 1: Assess whether it is appropriate to combine your studies in a meta-analysis (i.e. check that the assumption of homogeneity is satisfied)

Step 2: Justify your decision to conduct (or not conduct) a meta-analysis in your text

Step 3: Choose an appropriate meta-analysis method

Step 4: Identify and discuss any heterogeneity in the meta-analysis results

Step 5: Present and interpret the results of your meta-analysis

Step 1: Assess whether it is appropriate to combine your studies in a meta-analysis (i.e. check that the assumption of homogeneity is satisfied)

Once you have presented the results of your included RCTs, the next task is to decide whether it is appropriate to combine the results of the studies in a meta-analysis. It is appropriate to combine study data in a meta-analysis only if the assumption of **homogeneity** is satisfied. Before being able to satisfy the assumption of homogeneity, four aspects need to be assessed. The first is that RCTs should be similar in terms of the patients they recruit; this can be checked by examining inclusion criteria and baseline characteristics across RCTs. This is a subjective approach as there is no quantitative measure of similarity.

The second aspect for consideration is that the RCTs should compare the same interventions (or exposures) and comparators; trial publications should provide detailed descriptions of each. It is important to check that these are consistent across the RCTs as, if they differ substantially, you will not be comparing like with like. For example, if you are looking at drug RCTs, it is important to check for details of treatment doses, duration of treatment and any supplementary care given alongside the investigational treatments.

The third aspect is that RCTs should report the same outcomes. It is okay if one RCT has the outcome of interest as a primary outcome, while another RCT has it as a secondary outcome – data from these RCTs can still be combined. Not only should the outcomes reported be the same, but the time frame over which they are measured should also be comparable. If the outcome of interest happens gradually over time and some RCTs are only measuring the outcome at 24 hours while others are looking at the outcome at 7 days, the event rate in the shorter RCTs will be different from the event rate in the longer trials.

The fourth aspect is that the results of the RCTs should describe similar effects (i.e. all trials conclude that one intervention is better than another, or all RCTs indicate that there is no difference between interventions), and that the corresponding confidence intervals overlap. A good way to check this is by producing a **forest plot** using a statistical package; an example forest plot is shown in Figure 8.3.

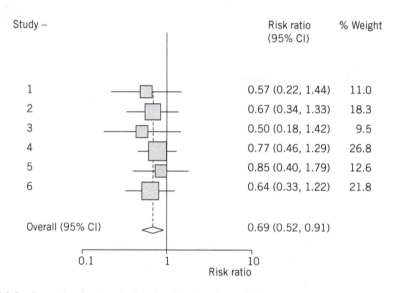

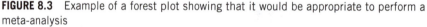

FIGURE 8.3   Example of a forest plot showing that it would be appropriate to perform a meta-analysis

The square in the centre of each line shows the point estimate of the effect recorded in each study, and the short horizontal line shows the corresponding confidence interval. The size of the square is proportional to the size of the study, so larger studies have a larger square. The length of the line is proportional to the width of the confidence interval, so longer lines indicate wider confidence intervals and therefore less accurate treatment effect estimates.

It is important to ensure that you enter the RCT results into the statistical software program in a consistent manner; results are presented comparing one group with another, so it is important to make sure that in each case the same group is used as the reference group (i.e. ensure that all RCT results are always presented as group A relative to group B). If RCT data are entered inconsistently, it might look like the RCTs' results differ greatly, when in actual fact they are similar.

When the individual study estimates of effect are relatively consistent and have confidence intervals that overlap (Figure 8.3), it is appropriate to pool results in a meta-analysis. The diamond at the bottom of the plot shows the overall estimate of the treatment effect and corresponding confidence interval obtained by performing meta-analysis. The centre of the diamond indicates the point estimate of the effect and the width of the diamond represents the width of the confidence interval. When estimates vary widely and confidence intervals do not overlap (Figure 8.4), this suggests that the RCTs are too dissimilar and that it may be inappropriate to pool the results in a meta-analysis.

If your data satisfy all of the four criteria related to homogeneity, then you are ready to obtain an overall measure of effect by performing a meta-analysis. However, before we move on to discussing how to obtain the **pooled measure of effect**, let's think about what to do if your data don't satisfy all of the criteria.

If only some of your included RCTs meet all of the criteria, then it may be sensible to perform a meta-analysis using data from only those RCTs that do meet these criteria. If this is the case, then you should also carry out a sensitivity analysis by adding the remaining studies to test the robustness of the results. Similarly, if all of your included trials meet the majority of the criteria, then it may still be sensible to combine them in a meta-analysis. In both cases you must make it clear in your report that all criteria were not met by all of the included RCTs, and you must fully explain the implications that this may have on your results. If all of your RCTs do not fulfil any of the criteria (and this is highly probable), then performing a meta-analysis would be inappropriate. In this case, combining your data would not be sensible as the overall measure of the effect would be misleading. Under these circumstances the data should be synthesized narratively.

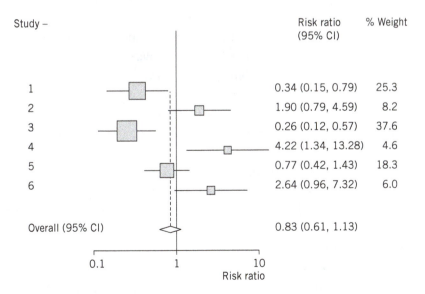

Study –	Risk ratio (95% CI)	% Weight
1	0.34 (0.15, 0.79)	25.3
2	1.90 (0.79, 4.59)	8.2
3	0.26 (0.12, 0.57)	37.6
4	4.22 (1.34, 13.28)	4.6
5	0.77 (0.42, 1.43)	18.3
6	2.64 (0.96, 7.32)	6.0
Overall (95% CI)	0.83 (0.61, 1.13)	

FIGURE 8.4 Example of a forest plot showing that it would not be appropriate to perform a meta-analysis

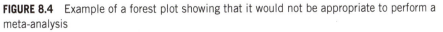

Step 2: Justify your decision to conduct (or not conduct) a meta-analysis in your text

Whether you decide to perform a meta-analysis or not, it is important that you can justify your decision in the text of your thesis. As previously mentioned, if your data satisfy all four criteria, then you are ready to perform a meta-analysis and obtain an overall measure of effect. However, a meta-analysis is not a required element of a systematic review, and if you choose not to perform one it is advisable to clearly set out the reasons for this decision. So, what might you write to explain why you have not performed a meta-analysis and how might you describe what you have done instead? The following text provides an example.

> A meta-analysis was not performed. Only a narrative summary of the data is presented. The differences across the RCTs, including poor quality of the RCT reports, diversity of protocols, and the inconsistency in reporting of outcomes, precluded a statistical synthesis of the included trial results.

Step 3: Choose an appropriate meta-analysis method

The first mistake people make when carrying out a meta-analysis is to simply pool all of the data from the individual studies as if they were all from one study. If you do this, you fail to preserve the randomization employed in each of the individual studies and you introduce bias and confounding (these concepts are addressed in Chapter 7). When randomized intervention studies are being designed, investigators put considerable effort into ensuring that the two (or more) treatment groups are similar in terms of the participants who will be enrolled. By 'lumping' participants from different RCTs together, you may no longer be comparing like with like; it is therefore important to maintain randomization when combining data from your included studies.

Another common mistake is to simply calculate an arithmetic mean of the treatment effects of the different studies. This approach is inappropriate as it gives all studies equal influence over the size of the overall effect. The results of small studies are generally deemed to be less accurate than results from larger ones, the confidence intervals around the results are usually wider so results are less precise and smaller studies are also more likely to detect a difference when it does not actually exist. For these reasons, smaller studies are given less weight in a meta-analysis. A meta-analysis needs to include a **weighted average** of the treatment effects whereby the results from larger RCTs take precedence over the results from smaller ones.

A meta-analysis can be performed in two steps. The first is to identify or calculate a summary statistic (relative risk, odds ratio or risk difference for binary data; differences in means for continuous data) for each study. The second step is to calculate the weighted average for this statistic. There are various techniques for calculating the weighted average depending on the summary statistic that is being analysed and the choice of weighting method. The techniques available all take a similar approach and are all derived from the following formula:

$$\text{Weighted average} = \frac{\text{Sum of (estimate} \times \text{weight of individual study)}}{\text{Sum of weights}}$$

There are a number of different methods available for performing a meta-analysis (see Table 8.7 for some of these) and they can be classified into two main models – 'fixed effects' and 'random effects'. The fixed effects model assumes that there is one true effect observed across all studies and that any variability between the studies is due simply to chance. In comparison, the random effects model assumes that the true effect varies from study to study but that it is centred on some overall average effect; this should not be used when there is assumed to be one true effect observed across all studies, but when there are believed to be additional differences as well as any differences due to chance alone.

TABLE 8.7   Different approaches to meta-analysis

Outcome measure	Fixed effects analysis	Random effects analysis
Binary		
Relative risk	Mantel–Haenszel, Inverse variance	DerSimonian Laird
Risk difference	Mantel–Haenszel, Inverse variance	DerSimonian Laird
Odds ratio	Mantel–Haenszel, Inverse variance, Peto	DerSimonian Laird
Continuous		
Mean difference	Inverse variance	Inverse variance
Standardized mean difference	Inverse variance	Inverse variance
Count		
Rate ratio	Inverse variance	Inverse variance
Survival		
Hazard ratio	Inverse variance	Inverse variance

Meta-analysis can be performed using one of a number of computer software packages; a systematic comparison of these is discussed in an article by Bax et al. (2007). One of the most popular software packages for this is RevMan (Review Manager, 2014), the Cochrane Collaboration's software for preparing and maintaining Cochrane reviews, which is freely available (www.community.cochrane.org/tools/review-production-tools/revman-5). Another widely used statistical software package is STATA, which is not free to download, but may be available through your academic institution. You will be able to perform a meta-analysis using STATA but, unlike RevMan, you will not be able to complete all aspects of your systematic review within it.

Step 4: Identify and discuss any heterogeneity in the meta-analysis results

Meta-analyses rely on the fact that the trials included in them are sufficiently similar to allow outcome data to be combined. However, we know that it is inevitable that trials differ in some way or another. In meta-analysis, heterogeneity is a measure of the variability between studies. It can be split into three types: **clinical heterogeneity**, which is the variability in participants, interventions and outcomes; **methodological heterogeneity**, which is the variability in trial design and quality; and **statistical heterogeneity**, which is the variability between the study results that is more than would be expected due to chance alone.

First of all, you need to examine the forest plot to identify whether there is substantial heterogeneity between studies. If the studies are estimating the same thing, you would expect their confidence intervals to overlap; if there is poor overlap, this indicates that heterogeneity is present. This 'eyeballing' approach is very subjective and is simply used to give you an initial overview of the level of heterogeneity present. Next, you would use the chi-squared test for heterogeneity to carry out a more formal assessment of heterogeneity. If you are using RevMan software (Review Manager, 2014) to undertake your meta-analysis, it will perform this chi-squared test for you. This test allows you to assess whether the observed differences in treatment effects are due to chance alone; a low p-value indicates that heterogeneity is present. This test should be used with caution when there are only a few studies being assessed, or when the number of patients recruited to each study is small, as in such cases the test is unlikely to detect heterogeneity even if a moderate amount is present. For this reason, a p-value of 0.1 is often used for determining significance, rather than the typical level of 0.05. It should also be noted that a non-significant result cannot be taken as evidence of homogeneity. The use of the chi-squared test is also problematic when there are a large number of trials; under these circumstances the test may detect clinically unimportant levels of heterogeneity.

After establishing that heterogeneity is present, you may want to calculate the degree of heterogeneity. This can be measured using the I^2 **statistic** (this can also be calculated in RevMan (Review Manager, 2014)). The I^2 statistic describes the percentage of the total variation across studies that is due to heterogeneity rather than chance, and results lie between 0 and 100 per cent. A value of 0 per cent would indicate that no heterogeneity was observed and, as the value increases, the level of heterogeneity increases. As a rough guide, 25 per cent represents low heterogeneity, 50 per cent represents moderate heterogeneity and 75 per cent represents high heterogeneity.

If you identify a large amount of heterogeneity, one way to deal with it is simply to acknowledge the problem and *not* report the results of the meta-analysis. Alternatively, you could present the forest plot but without the pooled effect (i.e.

remove the diamond from the plot) to illustrate the different treatment effects across the included intervention studies. However, it is important to ensure that you make it clear to the reader that you think it is inappropriate to combine the results as they vary considerably and that you consider that combining them would invalidate the overall estimate of the effect.

A third approach may be to report your pooled results, but include a caveat to let the reader know that you have concerns about the reliability of your results. If you decide to do this, then please note that we do not recommend using a fixed effects meta-analysis when there is a large amount of heterogeneity, as this invalidates the main assumption of the **fixed effects analysis**, that is, that there is one underlying true effect measured across all trials. A **random effects analysis** takes account of any unexplained heterogeneity between your studies but it does not explain the reasons for heterogeneity. For this reason, a full investigation of heterogeneity is still required.

Subgroups and sensitivity analysis

Heterogeneity is commonly investigated using **subgroup analysis**. Subgroup analyses determine whether different effects are observed in different subgroups of participants. For example, a larger effect may be observed in younger participants compared with the effect observed in older participants. If this is true, and there are wide differences in the ages of participants in different trials, then this could be one reason for heterogeneity. If trials present data on subgroups, you may want to meta-analyse the data for each of the subgroups to see how the overall effect compares across the different subgroups.

Another, more advanced, way to investigate heterogeneity is to use a statistical technique known as **meta-regression**. This technique adjusts the meta-analysis to take into account factors that are thought to influence the effect (such as age) (Cooper, 2010). Alternatively, you may wish to perform sensitivity analyses, including and excluding certain trials from the analysis to test the robustness of the results.

You should think in advance about specific factors that are to be considered when exploring heterogeneity and discuss these in your review protocol. If factors are identified after heterogeneity has been detected your results may be criticized because you are looking for reasons without an a priori rationale.

Step 5: Present and interpret the results of your meta-analysis

The best way to present the results of a meta-analysis is by using a forest plot and you can produce these easily using RevMan software (Review Manager, 2014). A forest plot presents the separate results of individual studies as well as the overall combined estimate of the effect. It is important to label each of the separate studies. It is also useful to present the percentage weights that have been assigned to each study.

As well as presenting the results visually in a forest plot, you need to provide complementary text, which summarizes and discusses the results. The results of the overall effect can be interpreted in much the same way as if they were from an individual study. That is, if the meta-analysis combined binary data, then the overall treatment effect would be presented as an odds ratio, risk difference or relative risk; if continuous data were combined, then the effect would be presented as a mean difference or standardized mean difference; if survival data were combined, then a hazard ratio would be presented. The case study in Box 8.2 includes further details on presenting and interpreting the results of a forest plot.

Box 8.2

Case Study

How to present and interpret a forest plot

The plot in Figure 8.5 shows an advantage for group A over group B; the point estimates are all to the left of the vertical axis indicating that all studies favoured group A over group B, and the diamond representing the pooled effect is also to the left of the axis. This advantage can also be seen in the risk ratios reported on the right, which are all less than 1. The pooled result reinforces this (risk ratio = 0.69), and

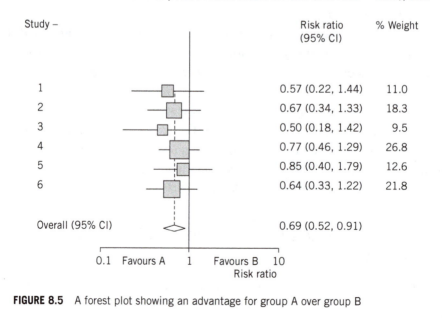

Study –		Risk ratio (95% CI)	% Weight
1		0.57 (0.22, 1.44)	11.0
2		0.67 (0.34, 1.33)	18.3
3		0.50 (0.18, 1.42)	9.5
4		0.77 (0.46, 1.29)	26.8
5		0.85 (0.40, 1.79)	12.6
6		0.64 (0.33, 1.22)	21.8
Overall (95% CI)		0.69 (0.52, 0.91)	

0.1   Favours A   1   Favours B   10
Risk ratio

FIGURE 8.5   A forest plot showing an advantage for group A over group B

the 95 per cent confidence interval suggests a statistically significant advantage for group A over group B as it doesn't contain 1 (95 per cent confidence interval = 0.52 to 0.91). The relative risk of 0.69 means that participants' risk of experiencing an event is reduced by 31 per cent (from 1 to 0.69) if they are in group A compared with if they are in group B. The 95 per cent confidence intervals all overlap, suggesting that the degree of heterogeneity is small, but this should be assessed more formally by using a chi-squared test.

Final thoughts

This chapter has focused on presenting and combining the numerical results of RCTs in a meta-analysis. Remember, this step isn't a prerequisite for a systematic review of quantitative data. If your review includes non-randomized data and you are thinking about performing a meta-analysis, then you really should speak to a statistician and/or your supervisor, as there is currently no gold standard approach for synthesizing the results of this type of research.

Key points to think about when writing your protocol

- Whether you intend to perform a meta-analysis and how you will decide if it is appropriate to do so
- What kind of outcome data you are likely to find
- What type of summary statistic you will use in your meta-analysis (if appropriate)
- How you will identify and deal with heterogeneity in your meta-analysis (if appropriate)
- Whether you will perform any subgroup analyses or meta-regression and what factors you might adjust for in these analyses (if appropriate)

What an examiner is looking for in your thesis

- Clear interpretation of the results from your included trials
- Full description of whether your included studies meet the criteria for conducting a meta-analysis
- Rationale for undertaking or not undertaking a meta-analysis
- Valid approach used to perform a meta-analysis (if meta-analysis was undertaken)
- Appropriate assessment of heterogeneity (if meta-analysis was undertaken)

Frequently Asked Questions

Question 1: What if my included studies measure the same outcome but not at the same time point?

If your studies measure the same outcome but at different time points, you might want to contact the authors of the studies to ask for more information on a common time point and then use these data in a meta-analysis. If it is not possible to get data on one time point for all studies, then it would not be appropriate to combine the data in a meta-analysis; you should only combine the data that are measured at the same time point.

Question 2: What if the outcomes are defined differently across the studies (e.g. different definitions of a common primary study outcome)?

If outcomes are defined differently across studies, it is advisable to perform sensitivity analyses whereby studies that define outcomes differently are removed and/or replaced to test the robustness of the overall results.

Question 3: What if the studies I have included in my meta-analysis are of varying quality?

If the studies vary greatly in quality, it is sensible to perform a sensitivity analysis. A sensitivity analysis may involve, for example, excluding lower-quality results and rerunning the meta-analysis. This will test the robustness of the overall results of your original meta-analysis.

Question 4: What if I only found one trial?

If you have only identified one suitable trial for inclusion in the review, then it will not be possible to synthesize your data in a meta-analysis; instead you should simply present a narrative description of the results of the single trial.

Question 5: If I have only two included trials, is it worth carrying out a meta-analysis?

Two trials is the minimum number of trials required before you can perform a meta-analysis. However, the accuracy of the meta-analysis results increases with the number of included studies. So, if you only identify two trials that are appropriate for inclusion, you can still perform a meta-analysis but you will need to explain the limitations of including only two trials when you write up your thesis.

Question 6: What if the studies report the same outcome but use different effect measures?

If some studies present the outcome using a relative risk and others present the same outcome but using an odds ratio, check the data that are reported and, if possible, calculate the appropriate effect measure yourself. If the paper does not provide sufficient data for you to do this, contact the authors of the paper and ask for them. Once you have the same effect measure for each study, you can include all of them in a single meta-analysis.

Question 7: What if my included studies are not intervention studies?

If your systematic review does not include intervention studies, and instead includes studies that evelute the association(s) between two or more phenomena or variables, then the data presented in your included studies may appear to be quite different from the data that are presented in the examples in this chapter. For example, you may find that your included studies present summary statistics that are different from the summary statistics described in this chapter (i.e. relative risk, odds ratio, risk difference, mean difference and standardized mean difference). A comprehensive guide to summary statistics, or 'effect sizes' from a range of different types of study, is provided in *The Essential Guide to Effect Sizes* (Ellis, 2010). The guide also discusses meta-analyses of different effect sizes, although we would highly recommend seeking advice from a statistician if you want to perform meta-analysis to synthesize data from non-intervention studies.

Further Reading and Resources

Crombie, I.K. and Davies, H.T. (2009) *What is Meta-analysis?* Newmarket: Hayward Medical Communications (www.bandolier.org.uk/painres/download/whatis/Meta-An.pdf). (Last accessed February 2017).

Ellis, P.D. (2010). *The Essential Guide to Effect Sizes: Statistical Power, Meta-analysis, and the Interpretation of Research Results*. Cambridge: Cambridge University Press.

Higgins, J.P.T. and Green, S. (2011) Cochrane Handbook for Systematic Reviews of Interventions (www.handbook.cochrane.org). (Last accessed February 2017).

Moore, R.A. and McQuay, H.J. (2006). *Bandolier's Little Book of Making Sense of the Medical Evidence*. Oxford: Oxford University Press.

Review Manager (RevMan) Version 5.3 (2014) [Computer program]. Copenhagen: The Nordic Cochrane Centre, The Cochrane Collaboration.

Whitehead, A. (2002) *Meta-analysis of Controlled Clinical Trials (Vol. 7)*. Chichester: John Wiley and Sons.

WATCH...   EXPLORE...   READ...

WATCH...	EXPLORE...	READ...
... a video in which the editors answer your FAQ: *"Do I have to do a meta-analysis as part of my systematic review?"*	... the Links Library, which gives you a host of resources to help you tackle the systematic review process.	... online resources such as example reviews, journal articles and further guidance on the review process.

Take your systematic review journey online at:

https://study.sagepub.com/doingasystematicreview2e

systematic review to find the review's 'take home messages'. As a student, academic and systematic reviewer, you have a responsibility to the readers to ensure that your discussion of findings and your conclusions are accurate, evidence-based, appropriate and applicable to your review question.

How do I write my 'Discussion' and 'Conclusions' sections?

Your 'Discussion' and 'Conclusions' sections need to be clearly structured and make logical sense to the examiner. When writing your 'Discussion' and 'Conclusions' sections, remember that systematic reviews are designed to combine available data from a range of sources, so *there should be very limited discussion of individual studies*. Instead, the majority of the discussion needs to focus on what the research tells you when you consider the data overall. We recommend including the points set out in Box 9.1, although the exact order in which you discuss each point may vary depending on your review question.

Box 9.1

Main components of the discussion and conclusions

- First, start with a brief overview of review question and methodology. Then, answer the following questions:

  - What were the main findings of my review?
  - How do my findings fit with previously published research?
  - What are the strengths and limitations of the included studies?
  - What are the strengths and limitations of the review process?
  - Can the findings be generalized?
  - What are the implications of the review?
  - What conclusions can be drawn from the review?

Brief overview of review question and methodology

By the time the reader arrives at your discussion section, they will have already taken in a lot of information. As such, it's a good idea to first remind the reader of your review question and methodology so as to refresh their memory. This should be a clear and concise sentence or paragraph, which summarizes the aims of the review and the methodology that you used.

Example:

This manuscript used systematic review methodology to investigate the association between expressed emotion and shame in family carers of adults with long-term mental health difficulties. (Cherry et al., 2017)

What were the main findings of my review?

Next should come a simple statement summarizing the main finding of your review. If there isn't sufficient evidence from which to draw a conclusion then you need to make this clear in your text. There is no need to repeat the 'Results' section here – the purpose is to remind the reader of the overall key findings so that they have a reference point when reading the rest of your discussion.

Example:

All studies assessing the efficacy of oral flecainide and propafenone reported favourable results in comparison to other treatment strategies. Oral sotalol was not found to be as efficacious as intravenous digoxin-quinidine. (Saborido et al., 2010)

How do my findings fit with previously published research?

At this stage, you may wish to consider outlining how your findings fit with the research that you outlined in the 'Introduction' section of your thesis, and wider empirical and theoretical literature, where relevant. Do your findings contradict common practice or national policy? Do the data you have support existing theory? Are you surprised by your findings, or do they make sense when interpreted in light of the wider literature base? To answer these questions, you will likely have to do some additional reading, but it will be well worth it, in our opinion.

Example:

Collectively, these data are consistent with the notion that carers who experience shame within the context of their own, or service users', perceived characterological deficits, may engage in emotionally over-involved behaviours in an attempt to promote a positive self-image. (Cherry et al., 2017)

Students can find this process challenging, particularly if they have struggled to interpret the main findings of their review. If this is the case for you, then we recommend that you discuss with your supervisor how best to link your findings to the wider literature base, while reflecting on *why* you think that this may be the case (i.e. could it be a reflection of the strengths and limitations of the included studies, or of the review process itself?).

What are the strengths and limitations of the included studies?

Consider the strengths and limitations of your included studies. If the quality of your included studies is good, then you will have more confidence in the results of your studies and the conclusions of your review. Re-familiarize yourself with the results of your quality assessment exercise (Chapter 7). How consistent are the findings across different studies? How similar are the participants or outcome measures used? This is your chance to summarize your view on the extent to which data from the included studies allowed you to answer your review question.

Example:

Overall, the methodological quality of the included trials was poor. All stated that patients were randomly allocated to treatment groups; however only four studies described the method of randomization and only two of these noted how allocation was concealed. The majority of trials included either no post-treatment follow-up or less than 6 months' follow-up. There were 15 studies with post-treatment periods of 6 months up to a maximum of 12 months. (Greenhalgh et al., 2009)

What are the strengths and limitations of the review process?

It is important to discuss the strengths and limitations of the review process itself. This allows you to explain why you made the methodological decisions that you did, and to reflect on how these decisions may have influenced your review findings and the quality of your review. If you can correctly identify the strengths and limitations of your systematic review, then this will help you to interpret your findings in the appropriate context, thus demonstrating insight and reflection on your part.

When doing so, you may wish to reflect upon whether your inclusion and exclusion criteria were appropriate (Chapter 3). It may be that because of your broad inclusion criteria you ended up with a number of studies that actually did not address the question you were asking, or that the participants were so different across studies that you ended up 'comparing apples with oranges'. If you invested time in the development of your research question (Chapter 3), then this should not happen, but sometimes it does.

You may also choose to discuss whether your search strategy was comprehensive and appropriate (Chapter 4). For example, did you include non-English papers, or theses? Did you find an abundance of literature or was there very little? Was this because of what was available, or because the search strategy was inappropriate? If you found a great deal of literature you may have decided to limit your research question – this is where you can discuss that decision and the implications that you consider it had on the review.

This section can also be used as a platform to highlight the strengths of your research and to make it clear to the examiner that you understand the review process and your findings. As such, don't forget to reflect upon the steps taken to increase the robustness of your review. For example, did anyone (a peer, or your supervisor) help you with screening and selection (Chapter 5) or cross-check your extracted data (Chapter 6)? Did you assess the quality of your included studies (the answer to this should be yes and this is a strength of your review) and if so, did anyone help you with this (Chapter 7)? Did you perform appropriate analyses (Chapter 8) and, if so, did you seek the advice of others when conducting these? Make sure that you demonstrate that your review is clear, thorough, reproducible and transparent.

You should finish this part of the discussion with a statement about whether you believe you have all, or at least a representative sample, of the available evidence relating to your question. This gives the reader your view on whether the appropriate literature has been identified for consideration.

Example:

Application of the inclusion criteria to the results of the searches identified 15 papers for inclusion in this review, a surprisingly small number given the recent growth in editorials and review pieces advocating the application of attachment theory to the study of patient–doctor communication. Nonetheless, piloting of the search strategy and supplementation of the results of the electronic search with hand searching and searching of reference lists of included papers allows confidence in the conclusion that all relevant research was included in this systematic review and that conclusions arising from this review can be based on synthesis of all available evidence. (Cherry, 2013)

Can the findings be generalized?

This question can be answered by drawing together what has been explored in the previous sections. You need to focus this part of your discussion on the implications of the review and its generalizability to your research question and professional practice. When doing so, it's important to consider to whom the results apply, and whether caution should be used when translating the results to certain populations.

Example:

> Studies also reported variations in the number of participants studied (...) Method of selection also varied, from self-selecting students to randomised groups. Self-selecting students may have different characteristics than students chosen randomly to participate. Given the nature of emotional intelligence, it is possible that self-selecting students may be more motivated to respond, more assertive, and generally may score higher on the intrapersonal dimension of emotional intelligence than those who may not respond to requests for participants. This may lead to a polarisation of responses, thus jeopardising the generalisability of findings. (Cherry et al., 2012)

What are the implications of the review?

Every systematic review has implications, be they clinical, educational, research or policy-related. First, the implications of your review should be discussed in terms of the relevant client groups or stakeholders. For example, in healthcare reviews of effectiveness, implications are generally considered in terms of patient care or public health, and for educational reviews, the implications for students or teachers are generally discussed.

Second, this section should also include a discussion of the need (if any) for future research. Avoid saying, 'More research is needed' and try to focus on the study (or studies) that you would like to see take place. Give clear direction about study design, choice of outcome measure, participant groups and so on. It often helps to base these implications on the findings of your quality assessment exercise by identifying where included studies were found to be lacking.

There is currently a vibrant debate regarding the role of systematic reviews in making recommendations for policy. The emerging consensus is that the findings of one systematic review are not sufficient to allow policymakers to draw firm conclusions; the results of several systematic reviews may need to be considered by experts, who may also take into account risk, cost and patient preference before making policy decisions.

Example:

Future research should consider and address the methodological and conceptual limitations of currently published findings. It should aim to assess the relationship between attachment style and objective, behavioural outcomes, transferable to the clinical setting, with the goal of establishing a theoretical, observable link between attachment style and communication. Such research should be adequately powered and should consider incorporating a longitudinal study design to ensure the most rigorous and conclusive findings. (Cherry, 2013)

What conclusions can be drawn from the review?

The end of the 'Discussion' section should summarize the conclusions that can be drawn from your review. There is no consensus on how much detail should be in the 'Conclusions' section. Reviews of effectiveness papers tend to have very short 'Conclusions' sections; the conclusions tend to be, 'Yes, the treatment works and we should be using it,' 'No, it does not work and we should not be using it' or 'We don't know if it works because there isn't sufficient (high-quality) research available.' Social science researchers often use the 'Conclusions' section to explore the options relating to future action that is required as a result of the findings of the review. In contrast, the conclusions of qualitative reviews often explore the richness and context of the data that have been reviewed. There is no right or wrong way, and we suggest that you take the lead from your supervisor in following departmental or institutional preference.

Example:

Uncertainty in the available clinical data means there is insufficient evidence to support a recommendation for the use of the pill in the pocket strategy in patients with paroxysmal atrial fibrillation. (Saborido et al., 2010)

Common pitfalls and how to avoid them

From our collective experience of supervising students, we can tell you that one of the most frustrating things for a supervisor is to read an excellent thesis that falls apart towards the end because the student didn't take sufficient time to fully consider their findings and write their discussion and conclusions. Box 9.2 summarizes some of the most common reasons that students write poor discussion and poor conclusions.

Box 9.2

Common reasons why students write poor discussion and conclusions

- Didn't answer or address the review question
- Didn't leave sufficient time at the end of the project to adequately examine and reflect upon their data
- Didn't have enough confidence in themselves and their experience to draw firm conclusions from the data – too scared of 'getting it wrong'
- Had too much confidence in themselves and made grand, sweeping, over-generalized statements
- Had data that did not match the results they were hoping to get
- Didn't understand their data or their analysis and so couldn't adequately conclude anything from their review
- Didn't critically appraise their work or its implications

Not answering the review question

The most important aspect of the 'Discussion' and 'Conclusions' sections is that you actually address your review question (see Chapter 3). This may sound obvious, but it is surprising how many students fail to answer their review question. This most frequently happens when students don't clearly define their review question, or don't have a clear protocol to follow. The students who have made these mistakes often end up wandering their way through the evidence and are still wandering while writing their discussion because they didn't have a clear idea of their final destination, or they found something else that they thought was more interesting or important and ignored their original question.

Too little time

It is important to work back from your submission date and set a research timetable to ensure that you meet your target deadlines (see Chapter 2). Unlike other research projects where you're encouraged to meet timelines because of external commitments to others, when you're undertaking a systematic review as a student, you're working primarily independently and therefore self-discipline is required. Sometimes the best-laid plans go awry due to unforeseen circumstances – you had to wait longer than you had planned for papers from the library, or your dog ate your hard drive midway through your write-up! What's important is that you don't take that lost time from the time you've allocated to the write-up, especially the write-up of the discussion and conclusions. You'd be surprised how frequently this happens, particularly when the student isn't sure of their data or how to discuss them. Results need to be mulled over or considered during a walk in the park. This will not happen if you are writing up your discussion at midnight the night before your thesis is due to be submitted. It is easy to spot these kinds of reports – we have frequently seen well-conducted systematic reviews that have been carried out meticulously with almost nothing written in the discussion and conclusions because the student spent all of their time and energy on the description of what they did and far too little time writing up what it all meant.

Unsure of yourself and your opinions

If you chose a topic of genuine interest to you, then this is less likely to be an issue than if your topic area was unfamiliar to you, or worse, bored you from the very beginning. You've probably spent months reading around and summarizing the research in a topic area that you already care about, and are likely to already hold, or at least want to develop, an opinion about this specific issue or topic. So be confident enough to say what you think. Others can disagree with your opinion, but a well-formulated interpretation and discussion of your data is what is expected of you at this level (see Chapters 6 and 7). What your examiner wants to see is evidence of the thought processes and critical thinking that brought you to your conclusions about the data. Your examiner wants you to show that you have explored the implications of your data and wants to see how you think current practice, or your approach to your professional work, will benefit from the review that you have carried out. The examiner of your thesis might not always agree with your conclusions, but if you have presented a clear case as to why you came to those conclusions, then you have succeeded in your work.

Too much confidence

Be careful not to be too confident, or sweeping, in your discussion or conclusions; both need to be firmly grounded in the context and limitations of the included data and also the review process. If you didn't include grey literature then say so – but don't then conclude that you've summarized all of the available evidence and go on to draw conclusions with 100 per cent certainty. Every review and study has its limitations; it's important to recognize them and not to include broad statements without references or supporting data to back them up.

The data do not say what you want them to say

This happens far more frequently than most people would like to admit. If you are carrying out a review in a topic area that interests you, then you probably already have an opinion about it. All too often, these opinions are not upheld by the research findings that you summarize. This can be a good finding and can provide you with a starting point for your discussion; it's often very interesting to read discussions that say that 'Current practice in the area is X but the research says Y' and to read the reviewer's take on the reason(s) for this finding. What you must not do, however, is try to adapt your data to match your views. It can be frustrating to have mentally written your discussion before properly interpreting the data only to find that you have to reformulate your arguments. It is far better to take the time to rethink your ideas during the review process, rather than be challenged by an examiner or peer reviewer at a later date.

You do not understand your data

This is a real problem and usually happens when you don't leave sufficient time to explore your findings (see Chapters 6 and 7). It also often occurs when statistical analysis has been carried out and you're unfamiliar with the analysis and/or what the results really mean (see Chapter 8). Equally, this can be a problem when all of your included studies use different outcome measures, or research participants come from very diverse settings. It's important to understand what your data mean before you attempt to discuss them or draw conclusions. This might mean spending a bit more time considering your data, chatting to a statistician or your supervisor, doing some wider reading or simply taking a break from your review for a few days. Whatever you do, it's important to fully understand the implications of your findings. If the study outcome measures or participants are too diverse to statistically synthesize, then say so. If you can't draw conclusions from the data due to the presence of heterogeneity, then that's okay. You can recommend that future research focuses on a more homogeneous set of participants or outcomes.

Lack of critical appraisal

The examiner marking your thesis will be checking whether you have demonstrated your ability to critically examine the evidence and that you understand what the data mean. This is something that the majority of students struggle with – they can describe the data that they have extracted but the majority fail to provide their reflection on what the data actually mean. Critical appraisal is important because it shows that you understand the data and the limitations of the research. It's not sufficient to assess the quality of studies and report the findings in a table in the 'Results' section but not refer to the table again. Good and well-thought-out critical appraisal is what separates exceptional students from average students, and it demonstrates a reviewer's ability to not only discuss findings but to understand their meaning in terms of their clinical, educational or policy implications.

It can be frustrating for an examiner to read a thesis where the student follows all of the steps but doesn't think about what the findings mean; if one study reports a strong treatment effect for drug A but only tests it on two people, then you need to develop the skills to interpret these findings in relation to the study that found no effect on 1000 people. A discussion should never be a list of 'Smith said, Jones said and Walley said'. It needs to examine and discuss the included studies as a group, highlighting where there are similarities and differences. Then you need to discuss what you think are the possible reasons for these similarities and differences. This is what critical appraisal means and it is a vital part of every systematic review. Critical appraisal skills can be difficult to develop but there are a number of excellent books and online educational materials to help you. Further information can be found on our website (https://study.sagepub.com/doingasystematicreview2e).

Final thoughts

You're now coming to the end of the eight specific chapters focusing on the practical elements involved in conducting and reporting a systematic review within the format of a postgraduate thesis. Throughout this book, the systematic review process has been likened to a journey. As with any journey, unless you know the route well, you would expect to consult your map numerous times along the way, particularly if you get lost. Treat this book, in particular Chapters 3 to 9, like your map. Turn down page corners, highlight text and scribble notes to yourself in margins. Revisit chapters that discuss concepts or methods that you are unsure about and skip through chapters discussing those aspects that you are most confident about. Most importantly, make sure that you keep this book with you throughout the review process as it can act as a handy guide, particularly when you feel lost. Don't close this book just yet, though. The next chapter is essential reading for any student who is undertaking a systematic review as their Master's thesis, because it is dedicated solely to dissemination – after all, it would be a shame not to tell the world about your excellent systematic review after all this hard work, wouldn't it?

Key points to think about when writing your protocol

- Most protocols don't require sections on discussion and conclusions because when you write your protocol you usually have no idea what you will find

What an examiner is looking for in your thesis

- Sensible discussion of study results based on intelligent interpretation of the data
- Orderly discussion of important points – keep discussion of similar points together
- Reflection on your methodological and analytical choices and explanation of how these choices may have influenced your conclusions
- Conclusions that come from critical consideration and are supported by evidence from included studies

Frequently Asked Questions

Question 1: What if I don't have any studies to discuss?

It would be unusual to carry out a systematic review as part of a Master's degree with no included studies, particularly given that a large proportion of the marks for your review will come from your ability to quality assess the included studies, and to extract and synthesize relevant data from them. If, however, you choose to progress with no studies, then your 'Discussion' section is likely to be the most important part of your review, as it should contain a lengthy explanation of the reasons why you didn't find any studies and the research implications arising from your review. It would be important, in such a case, to explain that you carried out the review because you felt that there should be studies conducted in the topic area. The fact that you didn't find any studies implies either that the topic area should be highlighted as a research priority or that it isn't generally considered to be important. We recommend that you explore both interpretations. Be sure to include a discussion of the strengths and limitations of your review process too; even though you didn't find any studies, there will be adequate room to discuss your methodological approach and its pros and cons.

Question 2: What if I disagree with the findings?

It can be frustrating when you have a mental picture of what you think you will find, but then the data suggest something entirely different. In this case it is important to have an open mind and to try to interpret your findings with respect to the data. If you expected to find an effect or relationship but didn't, you might want to think about why you expected to find that result. Are there methodological considerations in the included papers that may have influenced the findings? For example, did the papers consider only participants aged over 65, whereas you based your hypothesis on participants aged 18–65? In cases such as this, it is often valuable to discuss your findings with your supervisor or a peer; often students can't see the forest for the trees, and find that getting other perspectives really helps them to reframe and reinterpret unexpected data.

Question 3: What if I discover that the way I have been doing things is wrong?

At this point, it is probably too late to redo your review. The best that you can do is make sure that you reflect on what went wrong, why it went wrong and how this may have influenced your findings. It might be something out of your control, such as you couldn't access any papers from a certain journal. It might be that you missed out a key search term, or your review question was far too broad. As long as you reflect on the potential implications of your (perceived) errors on the conclusions and the implications arising from your review, you are demonstrating awareness and reflection. It happens to the best of us, so don't beat yourself up too much. Discuss your concerns with your supervisor and try to account for what has happened when writing your 'Discussion' and 'Conclusions' sections.

Question 4: What if there's no clear answer to my review question because my results are conflicting?

This often happens, so don't panic! We recommend that you discuss this with your supervisor, and think about potential reasons for any divergence. For example, did your included studies differ widely in their use of outcome measures, or their participant groups? Was there heterogeneity in study design? If so, then these points can all be reflected upon in your discussion, and may form a solid basis for recommendations for future research or practice (e.g. it may be beneficial for researchers to focus upon standardizing their methodological approaches or reporting styles in future research).

However, don't assume that the fault lies solely with the available research; it's also important to pay careful attention to your research question and inclusion and exclusion criteria – were they too broad or narrow? What might you have done differently, in hindsight, and how can you best reflect upon this in the discussion so as to demonstrate your learning? It's far better to demonstrate to the examiner that you have noticed and reflected upon these limitations than to hope the examiner won't notice – they probably will!

Further Reading and Resources

Booth, A., Papaioannou, D. and Sutton, A. (2016) *Systematic Approaches to a Successful Literature Review*. 2nd edn. London: SAGE.

Bui, Y. (2014). *How to Write a Master's Thesis*. 2nd edn. London: SAGE.

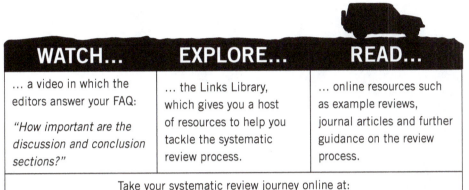

WATCH...	EXPLORE...	READ...
... a video in which the editors answer your FAQ: *"How important are the discussion and conclusion sections?"*	... the Links Library, which gives you a host of resources to help you tackle the systematic review process.	... online resources such as example reviews, journal articles and further guidance on the review process.

Take your systematic review journey online at:
https://study.sagepub.com/doingasystematicreview2e

10

Disseminating My Review

M. Gemma Cherry and Gerlinde Pilkington

This chapter will help you to...

- Understand the importance of disseminating your systematic review

- Think about identifying and delivering to 'target audiences'

- Gain an awareness of the different ways in which your review can be disseminated

- Gain the confidence to disseminate your review widely and successfully

Introduction

In this chapter, we first discuss why we think it is important to disseminate your systematic review. We then present tips for successful dissemination, before outlining some common avenues for dissemination. Finally, we conclude the chapter with frequently asked questions regarding dissemination. By doing so, we hope to give you enough confidence to take your thesis beyond an academic exercise.

Why should I disseminate my research?

For some of you, submission and approval of your thesis may feel like the final destination. It is a significant achievement and you should be proud of attaining your new academic standing. However, we don't think that your journey should end here. We tell students that if we were in charge, all postgraduate students undertaking a systematic review for their thesis would be required to at least think about disseminating their review to an audience wider than that of their supervisor and examiner(s). We would also ask them to include a **dissemination strategy** in an appendix of their thesis, and perhaps a draft manuscript for submission to a peer-reviewed academic journal. Of course, students are very pleased that we do not have the power to enforce this.

However, we do think you should consider how the results of your review could be disseminated. We find that some students are hesitant to take this next logical and, it might be said, ethical step. We do not think there is any need for hesitancy. We have read many systematic reviews with the potential to make a valuable contribution to research and practice, the results of which were not seen by anyone beyond the student and their supervisor and examiners. This makes us understandably frustrated, because a systematic review is much more than a learning exercise in fundamental research skills – it's an important piece of research in its own right, and one that deserves to be disseminated. Why? The answer is simple – your work can only advance your field of study and make a difference to others if people are aware of it! Sharing the results of your work can have an impact – on other students, the wider academic community, policymakers, practitioners and the public. Dissemination is also likely to have personal benefits. For example, it's likely to boost your CV (and self-esteem!) while helping you to gain further experience of the research process. Dissemination can also be a powerful vehicle for networking, which can help you to make valuable contacts in your field.

But surely no one would be interested in *my* work!

From our experiences, we have found that the majority of students tend to underestimate the value of their research. In fact, the most common reasons given by students for not disseminating the results of their systematic reviews are that they do not consider their reviews to be of a sufficiently high standard, or that they do not feel 'qualified' to disseminate the results. However, students are frequently pleasantly surprised by the feedback when they do decide to share their research results.

Where do I start?

If you're now thinking, 'Okay, I'm interested … but where do I start?', Box 10.1 contains some key tips and points that may help you when thinking about disseminating your work, regardless of your subject area, discipline or field.

Box 10.1

Tips for successful dissemination

Tip 1: Act promptly

Tip 2: Decide on your target audience(s)

Tip 3: Think creatively about the best way to reach your target audience(s)

Tip 4: Devise a dissemination strategy

Tip 5: Keep your audience in mind

Tip 6: Be mindful of copyright issues

Tip 1: Act promptly

The best time to disseminate your systematic review is probably just after you submit your thesis, as all of your hard work is still fresh and clear in your mind. However, students often say that dissemination is the last thing on their mind at this time! It's important to get the ball rolling as soon as possible with your chosen dissemination method(s), particularly given that your systematic review is a summary of the available relevant evidence pertaining to a specific and, importantly, a current review question. If you delay disseminating the results, then you risk the results becoming out of date, thus reducing your systematic review's relevance. Inevitably, some methods of dissemination will take more time than others, and we discuss these in more detail later on in the chapter. However, to ensure relevance and timeliness, our first tip for successful dissemination is to start as soon as possible.

Tip 2: Decide on your target audience(s)

The next step is to ask yourself, 'Who would benefit from knowing the results of my systematic review?' There are likely to be a number of different audiences that will benefit from, or be affected by, the results of your research. These are summarized in Table 10.1, together with the benefits of disseminating to each group.

TABLE 10.1   Potential target audiences for your review

Potential audience	Benefits of dissemination
Other students	• Encourages their journey and instils hope • Provides reference points for own research • Encourages a culture of publication and dissemination
Researchers	• Informs future research by adding new perspectives or strengthening existing research findings • Helps ensure that research is not duplicated
Academics	• Helps to promote and facilitate evidence-based teaching • Ensures academics draw from the most up-to-date knowledge base • May help when supervising future research projects
Policymakers and local government	• May help to contribute to policy development • Generates interest and debate
Practitioners at different levels	• Informs decision-making, even if findings are inconclusive • Helps when planning for change in practice or innovation • Encourages evaluative culture
Service users/individuals with lived experiences of the phenomena that was studied	• Promotes empowerment • Informs decision-making, even if findings are inconclusive • Facilitates meaning-making or understanding
The general public	• Raises or promotes awareness of the subject area and topic being studied

Tip 3: Think creatively about the best way to reach your target audience(s)

Once you have decided on your target audience(s), it's important to think about how best to reach them. Insomuch as there is a range of target audiences who may benefit from your findings, there are also a variety of dissemination strategies available to you. We use the term 'traditional' methods of dissemination to refer to methods such as publication in peer-reviewed journals or academic books, presentation at local, national and international conferences, and **thesis archiving/indexing**. Traditional methods of dissemination are an excellent idea if your primary target audience includes researchers, clinicians and/or academics, as these are the ways in which these people are made aware of research findings.

There are also numerous 'alternative' methods of dissemination. These methods may help to widen both the audience, and the impact, of your work. There are too many alternative methods of dissemination to list exhaustively here, but examples include academic social media, informal presentations to local services or groups, short reports in newsletters, summaries posted on online forums or websites, blog entries, podcasts or audio files, media sound bites ... the list goes on! Don't forget the importance of word of mouth too! A quick search of the Internet may reveal groups with a vested interest in your results, such as third sector organizations and stakeholder groups, who may value your research contributions and want to use them or share them with others. We summarize a few common methods of dissemination, together with their pros and cons, in Table 10.2.

TABLE 10.2 Common methods of dissemination, and their pros and cons

Dissemination method	Potential audience	Pros	Cons
Peer-reviewed journal article	Academic peers and researchers Practitioners	Good addition to your CV Academic 'currency' Prestige – raises your profile	Can be a lengthy and time-consuming process Some journals may not publish systematic reviews There may be a fee to publish It is hard on your ego when they reject your submission – so be thick-skinned
Conference proceedings	Academic peers and researchers Practitioners	Abstracts are often published and searchable Good for networking with academic peers Can choose method of dissemination (e.g. poster presentations are more informal than oral presentations)	May not feel comfortable presenting Costs of travel/accommodation Cost of printing, including mistakes (poster) May require time off work/study
Thesis archiving/ indexing	Academic peers and researchers	Institutional archiving requires little effort Online repository upload is a free way of disseminating your review Can be found by search engines	Be careful to check copyright issues Might be important to choose indexed keywords carefully Not all Master's theses are archived, and not all institutions have electronic repositories
Blogging	Academic peers and researchers Service users General public	Free way to share ideas Adds to academic discourse Gives you good practice in writing for a variety of audiences	Takes effort and time to build a readership and provide content Could there be issues with appropriate content? May have to pay for domain name/upkeep

(Continued)

TABLE 10.2   (Continued)

Dissemination method	Potential audience	Pros	Cons
Microblogging	Academic peers and researchers Policymakers Practitioners Service users General public	Easily accessible Can share other researchers' content Good for networking and keeping up to date with current research	Takes effort and time to build a readership and provide content Not specifically for academic use – don't mix your social and academic profiles if you want to appear professional
Academic social networking site(s)	Academic peers and researchers	Can upload documents and share research content Can network and make contact with academic peers Keeps you up to date with other research	Requires some effort to build a network and appropriate profile Regular upkeep may be required

When thinking about dissemination, remember that each thesis is different, which means that each student's dissemination strategy is different. It's important to be creative and to remember that your supervisor is well placed to recognize the contribution that the results of your research might make to the professional practice of others. S/he may be in a position to offer you advice in the first instance on how to disseminate the findings of your systematic review.

Tip 4: Devise a dissemination strategy

We recommend that you devise a clear dissemination strategy and discuss and agree this strategy with your supervisor. When thinking about a dissemination strategy, it's helpful to think about:

- the most appropriate ways to reach your target audience(s);
- the audiences that you may *cut off* by selecting or prioritizing certain methods of dissemination over others;
- the time that you (and your supervisor) have available for dissemination;
- your motivation and enthusiasm for dissemination;
- your skill set(s);
- the findings of your systematic review.

A clear dissemination strategy will act as a guide or map for your dissemination journey, prevent you from losing focus and, hopefully, keep you motivated and on track! As mentioned previously, a dissemination strategy also makes an excellent addition to the appendix of your thesis, and demonstrates a commitment to good practice right from the start.

Tip 5: Keep your audience in mind

Successful dissemination requires you to shift the focus of the article to suit the needs of your target audience. For example, it would be unrealistic to expect your thesis, in its entirety, to be published in a newspaper, or narrated as a podcast – people would switch off almost immediately, irrespective of how well written it may be! Adapting your thesis to suit different target audiences may seem like an onerous task, yet students tell us that they are often surprised by its similarity to the process of dissertation writing. Prompts for writing for dissemination are shown in Box 10.2.

Box 10.2

Prompts for writing for dissemination

- DO keep the reader in mind; avoid assuming expert knowledge, but don't 'dumb it down' either
- DO write concisely; avoid tangents and digressions
- DO tell a story to your reader
- DO emphasize the strengths and novelty of your work
- DO seek feedback from others
- DO look at examples, and stick to guidelines and word counts, where appropriate
- DO structure your work carefully
- DON'T feel as though you have to include everything – key points are often enough
- DON'T overuse jargon, unless appropriate for the audience
- DON'T self-plagiarize, and think carefully about copyright
- DON'T lose your work's fidelity or key messages along the way

Tip 6: Be mindful of copyright issues

Our final tip is to always check copyright law, particularly if you want to disseminate your thesis in several ways. So long as you have the copyright to your work, then you are free to disseminate it however you see fit! But you *must* be sure of this so as to avoid difficulties further down the line!

Copyright applies to all manner of creative works, but especially intellectual property. Your thesis is your intellectual property, of which you are automatically the copyright owner. However, there may be issues with archiving/indexing your thesis if it contains third-party materials such as photos or figures, or if you have borrowed extensive extracts from published or unpublished works (even when cited or attributed appropriately) and permission has not been sought from the copyright holder – in these instances please check with your institution for clarification and assistance. Be aware that if you have signed agreements with government or funding bodies who have a stake in the intellectual property rights to your thesis, you may also need to check on your rights to publish or deposit your thesis electronically.

In addition, be mindful that most publishers require you to assign them the copyright to your work when your article is accepted for publication in one of their journals – in effect many academics do not have the copyright to their articles. This may have a bearing on whether you can deposit your thesis in a repository, as some publishers consider theses to be 'prior publications'. In these circumstances, it may be necessary to place restrictions on the deposited thesis, so that only an abridged or shortened version is available for a period of time, or only the record title is visible for a set period of time (i.e. the full text can't be accessed until an 'embargo' period has passed). Your institution should be able to provide you with further information and guidance. Also, be aware that some peer-reviewed academic journals may allow authors to distribute or make available different versions of their articles. For example, an academic may be permitted to distribute an earlier version of the published article on a social networking site without contravening any copyright laws. If you have any doubts or queries about copyright, you must contact the publisher for guidance.

Serious about dissemination? Read on...

By now, we hope that you are starting to think seriously about disseminating your thesis. We now briefly discuss some key methods of dissemination in more depth: dissemination through publication in a peer-reviewed academic journal, dissemination in the form of conference proceedings, dissemination through thesis archiving/indexing and dissemination through academic social media.

Dissemination through publication in a peer-reviewed academic journal

By now, you will be familiar with peer-reviewed academic journals, as you will likely have sifted through hundreds, if not thousands, of journal articles while carrying out your review. There's a good reason for this – peer-reviewed academic journal articles are often seen as currency in the research community, and, as such, publication in a peer-reviewed journal is an excellent option if you want to reach academic, clinical or research audiences. It is important to keep in mind that most journals publish only a small proportion of the submissions that they receive, and therefore the process of publication can often be frustrating, time-consuming and difficult for would-be authors. We outline eight key steps involved in disseminating your review through publication in a peer-reviewed journal (see Box 10.3).

Box 10.3

Steps involved in disseminating through publication in a peer-reviewed academic journal

Step 1: Think very carefully about the suitability of your review for publication in a peer-reviewed academic journal

Step 2: Pick an appropriate journal

Step 3: Decide on authorship (and author order)

Step 4: Turn your thesis into a paper

Step 5: Write your covering letter

Step 6: Submit your paper

Step 7: Receive/respond to reviewers'/editors' comments

Step 8: Receive final outcome

Step 1: Think very carefully about the suitability of your review for publication in a peer-reviewed academic journal

Before you start, it's important to think very carefully about the suitability of your thesis for publication in a peer-reviewed academic journal. Most academic journals apply stringent standards and checks to the papers that they publish, and therefore it's important to make sure that your work doesn't fall at the first hurdle. We recommend that you reflect upon the scientific rigour of your work, the importance of your findings and the conclusions that you were able to draw. How can the quality assurance of your work be communicated? You should apply a quality assessment tool to your review, as discussed in Chapter 7, to see whether it meets quality standards – you can be sure that the journal's peer reviewers will do this, so beat them to it and address any issues. These issues do not preclude publication in a peer-reviewed academic journal, but may require some careful phrasing or reframing in your submission (e.g. pointing out the limitations of the review and the potential implications of these for the review's conclusions). Alternatively, you may wish to consider 'repackaging' the results of your systematic review by writing a discussion paper, in which you reflect upon the lack of evidence. This may be of particular value in fields where evidence is lacking, and direction and guidance for further research is needed.

At this stage, it's also essential to consider the timeliness of your review. How much time has passed since you did your searches or completed your thesis? Do your searches need updating to ensure that your review findings are not out of date? If there's a time lag between searching and submission, then this is likely to be picked up at the peer-review stage. Have you checked for any similar systematic reviews that may have been published *after* you completed your thesis? It might sound obvious, but it's an important step as there's no point trying to publish your work if someone has already beaten you to it! These considerations may take some time, but in our opinion it's time well spent, as it may potentially help you avoid disappointment later on. Gauge others' opinions as to the suitability of your review for publication at this stage, including your supervisors. This may help you to view your work more objectively and spot potential limitations that may otherwise have passed you by.

Step 2: Pick an appropriate journal

Once you are satisfied that the work contained within your thesis is eligible and suitable for publication in a peer-reviewed academic journal, it's important to carefully select the most appropriate one. When doing so, it's helpful to consider several factors.

The first is the subject area and readership of the journal. Which journals publish work in a similar topic area to yours? Do these journals accept systematic review articles or do they prioritize primary research? Have there been any calls for review articles lately from these journals? It may be helpful at this stage to consider where the included papers in your review were published, as this normally gives a good indication of the key journals in your field. A brief email or letter of enquiry to the journal's editor may help to answer some of your questions, and to clarify the relevance and appropriateness (or otherwise!) of your proposed submission.

The second is the prestige and quality of the journal. Prestige and quality are traditionally measured in terms of '**impact factor**' – a term used to refer to the average number of times an article in that journal has been cited (i.e. referenced) over the past year. Put more plainly, an impact factor of 1.0 indicates that you may expect your article to be cited once in the year post-publication, whereas an impact factor of 4.0 would indicate four citations over that same 1-year period. Generally speaking, many academics would argue that the higher the journal's impact factor, the better. However, impact factor isn't everything – you should also consider the context of the topic area and target audience of your work. For example, some fields of study are relatively small; although your review may have a significant impact and be cited widely within that field, articles published in journals in niche areas will probably be cited less than articles published in more mainstream journals, thereby leading to a lower impact factor for niche journals. Furthermore, if one of the goals of publication is to inform practice, reaching your audience through a journal with an appropriate readership has more impact than publishing in a more prestigious journal. It is also important to note that a journal needs to have been indexed in Web of Science for at least 3 years before an impact factor can be calculated, which means that newer journals do not have an assigned impact factor. A journal's ranking within the field often gives a more balanced view of its prestige than impact factor alone. There are several websites dedicated to this, which can be easily found via online search engines.

Third, consider cost. We are in the middle of a transition from print to online publishing, which is an exciting time for the research community. In light of this, some peer-reviewed academic journals have begun to offer 'open-access publication', which means that anyone can view their publications as long as they have Internet access. This is in contrast to journals that require a subscription before articles can be viewed. There are obvious advantages to open-access publication, not least that it widens the readership beyond those who subscribe to a particular journal. However, there are also costs – literally! The fees for publication in an open-access journal can be substantial, so it's imperative to check at this stage whether your institution is willing to cover the cost. If not, cross open-access journals off your list and start again.

Finally, think about structure and length. Often the length of your article determines your choice of journal; if you have a lot to say, then consider journals with more generous word limits, and remember that different types of articles are often allocated different word limits. If you wish to submit a concise summary, then this may not be as much of a concern.

At this stage, students often find that they've narrowed their choice down to three or four potentially suitable journals. Remember, it is worth aiming high (i.e. choosing good-quality journals) to start with, even if you don't think you've got a shot at acceptance. You might be very pleasantly surprised, or, at the very least, you may receive useful reviewers' comments, which may help you to address any issues with your review prior to submitting to another journal!

Step 3: Decide on authorship (and author order)

The next step is to discuss and decide on authorship. The term 'authorship' refers to who is listed as an author on your submitted paper, together with the order of authors. Position within an authorship means different things in different disciplines, but generally indicates an author's degree of involvement in, and contribution to, the paper. The first author should always be the person who has made the largest contribution to the final manuscript, and would normally be either the principal investigator or the researcher who has conducted the research and written up the results (you!). Authors are then listed in terms of decreasing contribution to the manuscript. In some contexts, being last author is seen to be almost as prestigious as first author – this position is normally reserved for the project manager or lead supervisor. However, this doesn't always carry across different disciplines, so it's important to check the degree of responsibility, contribution and prestige attached to each position in an authorship list. Ask your supervisor if you aren't sure.

Determining authorship sounds simple but in practice can be challenging. It may be that your academic institution has an existing policy on the publication of research findings from thesis projects. This policy may outline the inclusion of supervisors as authors on all publications. If your institution does not have a publication policy, and you have not had this discussion with your supervisor, then now is the time. You may automatically want to include your supervisors as authors, which may indeed be appropriate, but it's important to consider their contribution to the final manuscript. The majority of peer-reviewed journals have guidelines on what constitutes inclusion as an author; the International Committee of Medical Journal Editors (ICMJE, www. icjme.org) suggests that, in order to be eligible for authorship, you must have made a 'substantial contribution' to the work and the drafting or revising of the manuscript, in addition to approving the version for submission and agreeing to be accountable for the work published. These guidelines apply to any author, and so, in addition to considering your supervisors' contributions, you should also reflect upon your fellow students' contributions: did a friend help you with your screening or selection stages, and if so, does this constitute a substantive scientific contribution? Probably not, but this needs to be clear and transparent from the start of their involvement so as to avoid any difficulties or conflict later on.

Step 4: Turn your thesis into a paper

This is another step that sounds deceptively easy – you've already done the hard work, right? However, transforming your thesis into a draft paper for submission to a journal requires skill, time and patience. You may have to update elements of your review, as previously discussed, which can feel like a lot of additional work (which is why we suggest you write the paper as you are finishing writing your thesis). You'll also likely need to compress your work into a concise and readable article that tells a story to the reader. It can be heartbreaking to delete paragraphs that you've spent hours getting just right, but the key to writing a journal article is succinctness. You may wish to request the input of your co-authors at this stage, particularly if you're not able to view your work objectively.

When writing your manuscript, it's essential to conform to the journal's guidelines for authors, otherwise your paper will be immediately returned to you. This means adhering to the journal's preferred referencing style, formatting style (including font, spacing and language requirements) and word limit. Journals often also request that tables and figures be submitted separately to the final manuscript, so expect to put something like *INSERT TABLE 1 HERE* in the final submission in place of the original table. Journals often send out anonymized manuscripts for peer review, and so they may ask you to anonymize your final submission or include a separate title page. They may also ask for additional requirements, such as keywords or bullet points that summarize the key findings of your review. These requirements should all be clearly stated in the author guidelines, but can take up valuable time and often differ between journals, making formatting frustrating.

Step 5: Write your covering letter

When you submit your manuscript, you'll normally be expected to include a brief covering letter to the editor (see Box 10.4 for a real-life example of a successful covering letter). This is a valuable opportunity to promote your work, and one that should not be underestimated. We recommend that you address your letter to the editor personally (their name can usually be found on the journal's home page) so as to show your interest in that particular journal. It's often helpful to keep letters short by:

- outlining the title of your review and its main findings;
- explicitly stating the novelty of your review and what it adds to the existing literature base;
- explaining why it is likely to be of interest to the journal's readership;
- politely requesting that it be considered for publication in the journal.

Box 10.4

Example covering letter to an editor of a peer-reviewed academic journal

Dear [insert editor's name here]

As you may recall, we were in correspondence last year regarding a systematic review that myself and my colleagues from the UK were conducting. We have

(Continued)

(Continued)

now finished the review, which is entitled 'Guilt, Shame and Expressed Emotion in Carers of People with Long-Term Mental Health Difficulties: A Systematic Review', and wish to submit it for consideration by *Psychiatry Research*. The systematic review narratively synthesizes the findings of 10 studies, reported in eight papers, which investigate the relationship between guilt or shame and expressed emotion in carers of people with long-term mental health difficulties. This is an area which, to the best of our knowledge, has not been systematically explored to date, yet which we feel can add a valuable contribution to the literature base. In particular, we hope that the findings of the review may facilitate a greater understanding of the psychological processes underpinning expressed emotion. We feel that the submission is timely in light of recent work outlining the importance of understanding family interventions at a process level, including an increased awareness of the psychological factors associated with the development and maintenance of high expressed emotion. We also feel that the paper would be of relevance and interest to your readers, and would fit well with the scope and remit of the journal. As such, we hope that it will be considered for publication.

Thank you very much.

Sincerely,
[Student]

Step 6: Submit your paper

Again, this step sounds like a simple process but it can take some time. Normally, manuscripts are submitted to journals electronically. This usually requires researchers to first create an account with their journal of choice by following the instructions on the journal's home page. Once this has been created, you'll be asked to add in your co-authors, and you'll usually have to select areas of interest and keywords for the paper too. Finally, you'll be asked to submit each of your files electronically and in the correct file type (i.e. manuscript, figures, tables etc.) and then approve a PDF proof of the final submission. Ensure that you allow a good few hours to make sure that you get this right, otherwise you may fall at the first hurdle (i.e. the paper never even gets considered!). It's also important to check that you provide the correct contact details – this sounds self-explanatory, but you'd be surprised at the number of students that provide their university email address, even though they are about to graduate!

Step 7: Receive/respond to reviewers'/ editors' comments

In the majority of instances, members of the journal's editorial team evaluate submissions. The purpose of this is to ensure that submissions are of a suitable quality, relevance and format to be sent out for peer review. Sometimes you'll hear back from the editor immediately. S/he may request additional materials or edits, or merely reply with a thank you, but no. The latter can be disheartening, but we prefer to look at the positives – we would rather be told quickly than wait months to find out the same outcome, and it may not be a reflection of our work but rather of the level of interest that the journal has received.

The majority of the time, articles are sent to a jury of peers (usually three or four academics, researchers or clinicians in the field) to be evaluated, normally against a standardized checklist or set of criteria. As you can imagine, this may take some time, as the submission first has to be sent out to other people, and then their comments have to be received, collated and sent back to you. Furthermore, most reviewers are not paid for their time but rather offer their services in a voluntary capacity. As you can imagine, their paid work can often take precedence over reviewing papers, therefore leading to delays. Most journals' home pages contain information about how long you can expect to wait before you receive a response, so we recommend that you be patient and try your hardest not to contact the journal unless you've been waiting longer than what would reasonably be expected.

Occasionally, the editor may reply to say that they wish to accept the submission in its current form. If this happens to you, then well done! It's a very rare occurrence, so you should be very proud of yourself. The most common outcomes, however, are either an outright 'no' or 'revise and resubmit'. If it's a 'no', then please try not to get disheartened. In 1937, Krebs' and Johnson's seminal paper, about (you guessed it!) the Krebs cycle, was rejected by *Nature* before later being accepted by *Enzymologia* (Holmes, 1993), so you're in good company. Hopefully you will receive some constructive feedback alongside the 'no', which may be helpful when you submit to your second-choice journal. We suggest that you return to Step 4 and begin the process again. However, although it might be tempting to address all comments before submitting to your second-choice journal, only address comments if you're certain that, by doing so, you will improve the quality of the paper – it's often not worth the effort to tailor the paper to a single reviewer as you are likely to receive feedback from people with different opinions in your next peer review.

If the response is a 'revise and resubmit', then, well done. This is a good outcome, although it may feel disheartening to have to do even *more* work on your paper. There are often no guarantees that your work will be accepted pending changes, but it gives you an opportunity to demonstrate why your work is worthy of publication.

It's important to note that you might be asked to revise and resubmit a paper several times to the same journal, so keep your spirits high each time. Box 10.5 contains some tips for revising and resubmitting; additional pointers can be found in the excellent article by Paltridge (2013).

Box 10.5

Tips for revising and resubmitting your manuscript

- Carefully consider the reviewers'/editors' comments.
- Try to take emotion out of your interpretation; it's not a personal attack (this is where the thick skin comes in).
- Make amendments in line with suggestions, where appropriate.
- Don't feel as though you have to address *all* comments; if you disagree, or the comments are contradictory, then clearly and politely outline your decision to disregard comments.
- Track changes or note the location of your changes or edits in the text.
- Outline your responses to the reviewers'/editors' comments in a point-by-point letter, addressed to the editor.

  o Begin by thanking the reviewers for their good suggestions and their help in improving the manuscript; they generally aren't paid for the role, so it's important to express your appreciation.
  o Respond to each point in turn, and don't forget to acknowledge positive comments. This is often a strategic move, as it reminds the editor of the novelty and worth of your paper, which they'll likely have forgotten by the time they receive your response!
  o Indicate location of change in paper (using line and page numbers).
  o Clearly outline the changes you've made to your paper, using direct quotations from the paper where appropriate – you could do this in a table or in prose form.

- Take the opportunity to check for errors in your original submission when responding to comments (and fix them!).

Step 8: Receive final outcome

Congratulations, you're nearing the end. Hopefully, you will receive a 'yes' from the journal, in which case we say a big 'well done' to you! Expect to receive proofs of your article some time after the acceptance; these are often accompanied by queries from the copyediting team. Reply promptly and take the opportunity to check for additional errors in the manuscript – this is your last chance! Once published, celebrate by giving signed copies of your manuscript to everyone you know! If it's a no, then don't worry. It's common to receive a negative response even after several cycles of revising and resubmitting. It can feel really disheartening, but consider their reasons for rejection – might you need to revise your style before submitting to another journal? When you're ready, revisit Step 4 and begin again. Don't lose heart; plenty of papers are rejected from numerous journals before being accepted for publication.

Dissemination in the form of conference proceedings

Local, national and international conferences are also great places to disseminate your research, particularly to clinical and academic audiences, as they often represent a snapshot of the most cutting-edge research around. As a student, there are many benefits to disseminating your work in the form of conference proceedings (i.e. oral or written communication). For example, you don't have to wait until you have finished your review; in fact, you can apply to present your work at almost all stages of the review process, from protocol to completion. Not only does this give you the opportunity to hone your skills in succinctly communicating your work to others in the field, but you are also likely to receive valuable feedback from others, and may also be able to spot studies of relevance to your review before they are published. Conference attendance also enables you to meet like-minded others, make valuable connections and contribute to advancing your own research profile and your field of study.

There are numerous ways in which you can find out about conferences in your topic area. For example, you could try searching the Internet, signing up to relevant mailing lists, looking for calls for applicants to conferences, speaking to your supervisor or connections in your field, keeping an eye out for advertisements in relevant peer-reviewed academic journals … the possibilities are almost endless. Our advice to you is to think small as well as big; local university-based or clinical conferences are as good a place to start as any, and may help you to build your confidence before applying to a national or international conference. Institutions often organize conferences for postgraduate students to discuss their work – if you are offered this opportunity, then do participate, you're likely to learn a lot!

When applying to present at conferences, there are a few things that we recommend you consider. First, think about funding. Often, local conferences charge a nominal fee, yet national or international conferences can be costly. As well as the conference attendance fee, which can vary between conferences, you also need to factor in travel and accommodation costs. It's worth having a funding strategy in place before agreeing to attend a specific conference, but don't worry if you can't afford to self-fund. Often, conferences offer reduced rates for students, but have a look to see whether your university has a conference budget that may cover you, and you can also check for wider institutional or national grants that would cover your costs.

Next, it's important to think about the type of contribution that you would like to make, and the time frame available to you. Would you like to do an oral presentation, which is typically a short (10–30 minutes) presentation with slides in front of a group of conference delegates, or would you feel more comfortable preparing a poster, which you then talk about? Usually, posters are displayed throughout the conference, and there are dedicated sessions in between oral presentation sessions when delegates have the chance to look at posters and ask questions about the research. In both cases, consider what the application process is like. Do you have time to prepare a poster (it will have to conform to certain size and format requirements, and will take time and money to print)? What is the deadline for applications? Who will be your co-authors? Usually, conferences require that you submit a short abstract of your work, which may take some time to prepare. These are then peer reviewed and the outcome fed back to you in due course, so it's also important to think about the deadline for abstract submissions and so on in your planning process. Sometimes, you may apply for an oral presentation and instead be asked to give a poster presentation, so think carefully about whether you would accept this option if it was offered to you.

Finally, once you've been accepted as a delegate, it's important to be well prepared. There are lots of excellent resources available to help guide you through the conference process, from the design of a presentation or poster through to the day itself. We have included some on our website (https://study.sagepub.com/doingasystematicreview2e) that may be helpful to you. Don't forget to include your conference proceedings on your CV too; they are something to be very proud of!

Dissemination through thesis archiving/indexing

We use the term 'archiving/indexing' to refer to the electronic or physical storage of a thesis within a repository or library. Thesis archiving/indexing is a relatively straightforward method of dissemination, and one that may be mandatory for postgraduate students upon award of their degree. Most universities have their own repositories whereby students can archive/index their work electronically (i.e. upload a final version of their thesis as a PDF or Word document). There are also online repositories that span institutions and countries, such as ProQuest (www.proquest.com), OpenThesis (www.openthesis.org) and the British Library's e-theses online service (www.ethos.bl.uk). To give you an example of how wide-reaching these repositories can be, ProQuest is accessed by over 3000 institutions worldwide, and disseminates and archives over 90,000 graduate theses per year. Access and costs for other reposi-tories vary (e.g. indexing is free in ProQuest but a subscription is required to access full-text copies of theses by other people).

Not all institutions offer Master's students the opportunity to archive/index their thesis, but we would strongly recommend that you archive your work if this option is available to you, as it's an excellent way to expand the audience of your system-atic review. Many indexes also allow students to place a restriction on access rights, for example, for a 2-year period, so that they have time to publish or disseminate their findings. However, it's worth checking whether this option is available to you, together with the copyright agreements for online indexers, *before* you deposit your work, so as to avoid any nasty surprises later on.

Dissemination through academic social media

Although peer-reviewed journal articles still hold a great deal of value in the world of academia (and probably always will), researchers are increasingly using more creative ways to share their ideas and findings to a much wider audience (including academ-ics, peers, practitioners, politicians, stakeholders and the public), thus increasing both the potential impact of their work and their academic/professional profile. In particu-lar, using social media for academic purposes (or using specific academic social media) is increasing in popularity. We use the term 'social media' to refer to platforms used for blogging, **microblogging**, networking and sharing content. Used appropriately, social media is an instant way to publicly share your views or links to interesting arti-cles, comment or share the work of peers, and establish connections and engage with others in your field. Different platforms can allow you to:

- create a public profile with academic interests, specialisms;
- upload your own published/unpublished papers as PDFs or share links to your work;
- establish a network of contacts who can send messages and engage with content;
- instantly receive feedback, encouragement and dissemination from others;
- engage with current discourses and debates in your field, and discover new work;
- stay up to date with current research and practice – for example, conferences often use searchable hashtags to help users identify specific content for events;
- gain experience of academic writing.

Don't forget, social media isn't foolproof: you'll need to get used to conventions and norms, set up and manage accounts, and take time to explore how different social media sites operate and how to get the best from your chosen platform(s). More infor-mation about social media can be found on our website (https://study.sagepub.com/doingasystematicreview2e); Mark Carrigan's book, *Social Media for Academics* (2016), also provides an excellent introduction to the world of academic social media, and is worth a read if you choose this method of dissemination. A word of caution though: as with any method of online dissemination, always be sure to read the terms of service before posting anything online, and pay special attention to copyright issues. Furthermore, make sure that you are aware of institutional rules – for example, are you required to include a disclaimer that your posts reflect your views rather than those of your institution? You can normally find out more about specific policies from your institution, but this is well worth checking before starting out.

Final thoughts

We hope that this chapter has encouraged you to consider how the results of your review could be disseminated to a range of audiences. We wish you well in your dissemination journey, and would love it if you could help us to make this chapter even more comprehensive by feeding back to us your dissemination strategies via our website (https://study.sagepub.com/doingasystematicreview2e).

Before you rush off, there's one more point that we'd like to make. The final two chapters of this book are for students who have specific journeys in mind: reviews of qualitative evidence (Chapter 11) and reviews of **cost-effectiveness** evidence (Chapter 12). We still encourage you to read them, even if you don't plan to carry out these types of reviews, but be aware that, while they touch on points already discussed in previous chapters, they are designed to be very topic specific.

Frequently Asked Questions

Question 1: When should I disseminate my systematic review?

Obviously, it wouldn't be appropriate to focus all your efforts on disseminating your review before you've written your thesis, as this must take priority! However, this doesn't mean that you can't take small steps towards disseminating your work early on. For example, as discussed earlier, it's an excellent idea to register your review on the PROSPERO database as soon as you can, provided that your review relates to health and social care, welfare, public health, education, crime, justice, and/or international development. The PROSPERO database includes basic protocol details for each registered review, so even if you don't take any further dissemination steps, at least your protocol is out there for all to see.

Many conferences have a closing date for submission of abstracts for consideration for oral or poster presentations, so it's also worth making sure that you don't miss these while writing your thesis. You don't need to have finished your review to submit an abstract (although it often helps if your abstract includes your results and conclusions); instead, you can say that your oral or poster presentation will include a discussion of the main findings of your review.

With respect to your completed review, if you don't want to be drafting an academic journal article while finalizing your thesis for submission, then why not consider taking the time between submission and graduation to prepare your manuscript for publication in a peer-reviewed academic journal, taking time to scope out the journals and begin the submission process?

Question 2: Do I need to list my supervisors as co-authors even if they haven't helped me to prepare my review for submission to a peer-reviewed journal?

This is a common worry faced by students. If your institution does not have a policy for publication, then we would advise you to refer back to the journal's guide for authors and/or the ICMJE guidelines, and agree potential authors' contributions as early as possible. Having said that, the contributions made by a supervisor to a systematic review, and those made by a co-author, may differ. For example, a supervisor may not substantially re-write a section of a discussion, whereas a co-author may. Transparency is the key: discuss how to manage this early on, and keep returning to published guidance if it becomes blurry.

Question 3: My supervisors haven't mentioned publication – what should I do?

If your supervisors haven't mentioned publication, please don't dismiss it out of hand. This does not mean that your work is unpublishable: they may not think you want to publish, or may be too busy to have given it any thought. Having said that, if they raise concerns about whether your work is of a publishable standard, then listen to these concerns carefully and consider how best to proceed.

Question 4: I received permission from the author of a quality assessment tool to include it in the appendix of my thesis for examination purposes. What does this mean for dissemination?

This is a tricky one. If the measure is freely available in the public domain without copyright restrictions, then you are free to disseminate it how you wish (e.g. by including it in the appendix of a journal article, or by posting it on academic social media). However, if it is not (e.g. if it has been published in a subscription-only peer-reviewed academic journal) then you *must* check copyright before disseminating it in any way other than that permitted by its author (e.g. even by archiving/indexing your thesis with it in the appendix). You can't be too careful!

Further Reading and Resources

Beller, E., Glasziou, P., Altman, D., Hopewell, S., Bastian, H., Chalmers, I., Gøtzsche, P.C., Lasserson, T., Tovey, D. and the PRISMA for Abstracts Group. (2013) 'PRISMA for abstracts: Reporting systematic reviews in journal and conference abstracts', *PLoS Med*, 10(4): e1001419.

Carrigan, M. (2016) *Social Media for Academics*. London: SAGE.

Kamler, B. (2008) 'Rethinking doctoral publication practices: Writing from and beyond the thesis', *Studies in Higher Education*, 33(3): 283–94.

Paltridge, B. (2013) 'Referees' comments on submissions to peer-reviewed journals: When is a suggestion not a suggestion?', *Studies in Higher Education*, 40(1): 106–22.

Piper, P. (2014) 'Writing your journal or conference abstract', *Journal of Pediatric Surgical Nursing*, 3(2): 47–50.

Thompson, B. and Kamler, P. (2013) *Writing for Peer Reviewed Journals: A Strategy for Getting Published*. London and New York: Routledge.

WATCH...	EXPLORE...	READ...
... a video in which the editors answer your FAQs: *"Should I publish the results of my review? How do I decide on authorship?"*	... the Links Library, which gives you a host of resources to help you tackle the systematic review process.	... online resources such as example reviews, journal articles and further guidance on the review process.

Take your systematic review journey online at:
https://study.sagepub.com/doingasystematicreview2e

Reviewing Qualitative Evidence

M. Gemma Cherry, Helen Smith, Elizabeth Perkins
and Angela Boland

This chapter will help you to...

- Understand both the principles of qualitative evidence synthesis and how these differ from the principles of quantitative evidence synthesis

- Define a review question for a qualitative evidence synthesis

- Understand different approaches to synthesizing qualitative research

- Recognize challenges specific to qualitative evidence synthesis

Introduction

We are assuming that, since you are reading this chapter, you are thinking about conducting a systematic review of qualitative evidence. In this chapter, we revisit the principles outlined in previous chapters but place emphasis on systematically reviewing qualitative evidence. As such, it's important that you've at least scanned the other chapters so that you have an understanding of the principles involved in conducting a systematic review. In this chapter, we outline why we think **qualitative evidence synthesis** is important and discuss how the steps you take can differ from those involved in **quantitative evidence synthesis**. We discuss different methods of qualitative evidence synthesis before outlining some of the challenges, rewards and pitfalls associated with qualitative evidence synthesis. We conclude with frequently asked questions.

Why should I carry out a systematic review of qualitative evidence?

Historically, systematic reviews of the effectiveness of healthcare interventions have dominated (see, for example, reviews produced by the Cochrane Collaboration), on the assumption that decision makers want to know 'what works' so that they can allocate scarce resources effectively. However, as interventions become more complex, and evidence-based policymaking becomes the 'norm', so the demand for systematic reviews of other types of evidence has grown. While systematic reviews of quantitative evidence generally allow determination of whether something works (or not), systematic reviews of qualitative evidence allow *how* something works to be explored in more depth. Qualitative evidence syntheses typically ask questions that go beyond 'Does this intervention work?' by, for example, asking 'Why and how does this intervention or policy work?', 'How acceptable is this intervention to end users?' or 'What are the barriers and facilitators to implementation of an intervention?' (Lavis, 2009). Bringing together the findings from qualitative research can lead to a greater understanding of the sensitive issues that research frequently addresses, and can provide rich data relating to the impact of a condition, intervention or policy on the lived experiences and feelings of those involved. Qualitative evidence synthesis can also allow for gaps in the literature base to be identified, and meta-level themes, theories, explanations, insights and/or conclusions to be developed.

There are a number of reasons why we advocate that students carry out a systematic review of qualitative evidence as part of their postgraduate studies, not least because qualitative evidence synthesis provides an excellent opportunity for students to learn, and then apply, the principles of systematic reviewing. If your topic area of interest lends itself to qualitative evidence synthesis, then we encourage you to go ahead. It will be an excellent learning experience for you, both as a student and as a researcher.

Differences between qualitative and quantitative evidence synthesis

As described in previous chapters, a systematic review, unlike a traditional literature review, uses explicit and rigorous methods to identify, select, appraise and synthesize all relevant information pertaining to a specific question, in order to generate new cumulative knowledge. Systematic reviews of quantitative evidence generally follow a series of distinct steps, which are outlined in Chapters 2 to 10. These steps are clear and well tested, and are recognized as the gold standard for systematic reviews of quantitative evidence. However, these steps leave little room for interpretation, and are particularly used in reviews of clinical effectiveness where the conclusions often take the form of 'A is better at treating X than B, but isn't as good as C'.

Researchers carrying out systematic reviews of qualitative evidence also follow a series of defined steps, but these steps are less prescriptive than those involved in systematic reviews of quantitative evidence, particularly with respect to quality assessment, analysis and synthesis of data. This is, in part, reflective of the breadth of qualitative philosophies, methodologies and methods currently available, which we have briefly summarized in Table 11.1.

There has been a lot of debate about whether it is feasible and acceptable to synthesize qualitative evidence derived from different theoretical perspectives and analytical approaches (Dixon-Woods et al., 2005). Some authors argue that, when synthesizing data, the original studies should share similar methodologies, while others take the more pragmatic view that even data from diverse studies can be combined (Dixon-Woods et al., 2005). The main point to take from this debate is that there is no standard approach for synthesizing qualitative research. As such, the good news is that in systematic reviews of qualitative evidence, you have the freedom to decide on how best to analyse your data. On the flip side, this means you have to defend your chosen analysis technique and make it very clear in your write-up why you've chosen one method over another. While five researchers performing the same quantitative meta-analysis should come up with exactly the same conclusions, five researchers answering the same qualitative review question may end up with five completely different sets of conclusions, depending on each researcher's choice of analysis, synthesis method and theoretical standpoint. Reviews of qualitative evidence may provide richer conclusions than reviews of quantitative data due to the potentially greater depth of analysis. There are fewer right and wrong answers with qualitative evidence synthesis, but be warned, this type of synthesis requires the researcher to be reflective and flexible in their approach.

TABLE 11.1 Common qualitative philosophies, methodologies and methods of analysis

Term	Definition
Phenomenological studies	Phenomenology is sometimes considered a philosophical perspective as well as a research approach. It focuses on people's subjective experiences and interpretations of the world. These experiences are called lived experiences. The goal of phenomenological studies is to describe the meaning that these experiences hold for each person. In phenomenological research, people are asked to describe their experiences as they perceive them, most commonly either through an interview or through written accounts. To understand someone's lived experience, the researcher is required to identify what she or he expects to discover and then deliberately put aside these ideas; this process is called bracketing. Only when the researcher puts aside her or his own ideas about the phenomenon is it possible to see the experience from the eyes of the person who lived the experience.
Ethnographic studies	Ethnography has been the most common research approach used by anthropologists to study people all over the world. Ethnographic studies involve the collection and analysis of data about different groups or cultures. Ethnography can be defined as the systematic process of observing, detailing, describing, documenting and analysing particular patterns of a culture (or subculture). In ethnographic research, the researcher frequently lives with the people or groups being studied and becomes a part of their culture. This is called participant observation. Data are also collected through formal and informal interviews. Data collection and analysis occur simultaneously. As understanding of the data occurs, new questions emerge. The end purpose of ethnography is the development of cultural theories.
Grounded theory studies	Grounded theory is a qualitative research approach developed by two sociologists, Glaser and Strauss (1967). Grounded theory involves the generation of theory through the collection and analysis of data. Data are gathered in naturalistic settings and primarily involve observation and interviews. Data collection and data analysis occur simultaneously using a process called constant comparison. This means that as data are gathered they are compared with the data previously gathered. Grounded theory involves the coding of data using concepts. These codes and concepts are reviewed and refined as data collection progresses. As data are gathered, adjustments are made to the theory to allow for the interpretation of new data that are obtained. There are a number of key theorists who are associated with grounded theory but they adopt different approaches to actually doing grounded theory.
Action research studies	Action research became popular in the 1940s as a result of the work of Kurt Lewin (1946). Action research aims to improve practice and involves studying the effects of the action that was taken. Solutions are sought to practice problems. Action research does not aim to generalize the findings of the study. In action research, the implementation of solutions occurs as an integral part of the research process.
Discourse analysis	Discourse analysis is a research approach used across a range of disciplines in the humanities and social sciences, including linguistics, education, sociology, psychology, social policy and geography. Discourse analysis encompasses a number of approaches to analysing different forms of communication, including written, spoken, visual or sign language. All approaches to discourse analysis look beyond the sentence and are primarily, although not exclusively, concerned with naturally occurring language use. Within discourse analysis, the different approaches reflect different theoretical perspectives on the nature of language. In some approaches, language plays a key role in creating and shaping identities and social relations; it is not seen as neutral. In order to understand the work language does, discourse analysis can draw on perspectives such as applied linguistics, conversation analysis, pragmatics, rhetoric, stylistics and text linguistics.

Do I follow the same steps as in a quantitative review?

If you're thinking, 'Hang on, I've just trawled through the whole book and now you're telling me the principles differ between reviews of qualitative and quantitative evidence!,' then don't worry, you haven't wasted your time. There are a number of common key steps involved in conducting a systematic review, be it of quantitative or qualitative evidence, which we have outlined in great detail in Chapters 2 to 10. The key differences lie in data extraction, quality assessment and data synthesis. However, if you have just picked up this book and flipped to this chapter without reading the previous chapters, then *stop*! Make yourself a drink, get comfy on the sofa and read the book from the beginning. You'll understand a lot more about what's covered in this chapter if you already have an idea of the general principles of systematic reviewing.

The main principles of systematically reviewing qualitative evidence map onto those of reviewing quantitative evidence, and are outlined in Box 11.1.

Box 11.1

Main principles of qualitative and quantitative evidence synthesis

Step	Review of qualitative evidence	Review of quantitative evidence
1	Plan review	
2	Perform scoping searches, define review question and inclusion and exclusion criteria, and write protocol	
3	Literature searching	
4	Screening titles and abstracts	
5	Obtaining papers	
6	Selecting full-text papers	
7	Theoretical standpoint and synthesis plan	Data extraction
8	Data extraction and quality assessment	Quality assessment
9	Analysis and synthesis (qualitative)	Analysis and synthesis (quantitative)
10	Writing up, editing and disseminating	

As you can see from Box 11.1, like a systematic review of quantitative evidence, there are 10 key stages to a systematic review of qualitative evidence. Most of these steps will be exactly the same regardless of whether you're reviewing qualitative or quantitative data. However, some will require additional considerations, and so we'll discuss each step from a qualitative evidence synthesis perspective, highlighting where the steps differ from those involved in a systematic review of quantitative evidence.

Ten key steps in a systematic review of qualitative evidence

Step 1: Planning your review

The first step is to plan your review by considering the time, resources and tools available to you. Chapter 2 provides a comprehensive guide to this step – we recommend that you (re)read this chapter before going any further. It's worth bearing in mind that certain steps of a qualitative evidence synthesis may take longer than if you were conducting a systematic review of quantitative evidence, so don't forget to factor this into your timelines.

Step 2: Performing scoping searches, defining your review question and inclusion and exclusion criteria, and writing your protocol

Chapter 3 discusses the importance of establishing a clear research question, and lays out a number of steps for you to follow. The main additional points that you need to consider when conducting a systematic review of qualitative evidence are:

- Is my review question clear and applicable to the available qualitative data?
- Have I developed a set of inclusion and exclusion criteria applicable to qualitative evidence synthesis?

It may well be that you begin your research with what you believe is a clear question. For instance, you may want to know mothers' views on treating fever in their infant children. Or you may want to understand the experience of mothers who have to return to work and need to place their infants in nurseries. These may seem like quite straightforward questions, but very few qualitative research studies will have asked exactly these questions. Indeed, it is more likely that studies have addressed these questions within broader studies, such as those relating to basic care issues or the role of day-care nurseries. This is where scoping searches relating to childcare would prove useful. They allow you to take a look at the current state of the literature and evaluate the suitability of your question. Alternatively, as you carry out your scoping searches you may identify that there are other, more important, issues within each of these topics, and you may decide that you want to modify your question and follow where the research leads. This is a very acceptable qualitative approach but, be aware, it can often take up a great deal of time.

The second task that differs somewhat from the steps involved in quantitative evidence synthesis is the development of your inclusion and exclusion criteria. While systematic reviews of quantitative evidence clearly define inclusion and exclusion criteria, often by using mnemonics such as PICOSS (Participants, Intervention, Comparison, Outcomes, Setting and Study Design), these inclusion criteria are not all relevant to systematic reviews of qualitative evidence. Rather than trying to devise a PICOSS table, we recommend that you think of your inclusion criteria in terms of **PICo**: **P**opulation, phenomena of **I**nterest (which may be either a condition or an intervention) and the **Co**ntext (Joanna Briggs Institute, 2014).

Conceptualizing the components of a review idea, or topic area, in terms of PICo helps you to plan what kind of studies you intend to include in your review without being so specific that you risk excluding a potentially relevant paper. This approach also provides your supervisor, the examiner and/or other readers with a significant amount of information about the focus, scope and applicability of your review in relation to their needs. Table 11.2 provides two examples of PICo tables for qualitative evidence synthesis.

TABLE 11.2 Example PICo tables

Review question	What are the views of mothers regarding treatment of fever in their infant children?	What experiences do mothers returning to work and placing their infants in nurseries report?
P	Mothers with infant children	Mothers with new infants
I	Views around treatment of fever in infants	Coping with emotional distress
Co	Home	Day-care nurseries and home

Other alternatives to PICOSS include: **ECLIPS(E)**, developed to address questions relating to health policy and management; **SPICE**, developed specifically for questions in the field of library and information services (Wildrige and Bell, 2002); and **SPIDER**, developed specifically for qualitative evidence synthesis (Cooke et al., 2012). These are summarized in Table 11.3.

TABLE 11.3   Alternatives to PICOSS

ECLIPS(E)		SPICE		SPIDER	
E	Expectation: What do you want to find out?	S	Setting	S	Sample
C	Client group: Who are you interested in?	P	Perspective: Whose views are you interested in?	P	Phenomenon of Interest
L	Location	I	Intervention: What is the phenomenon of interest?	I	
I	Impact: What's changed as a result of the policy/management change?	C	Comparison: What are you comparing the intervention with?	D	Design
P	Professionals	E	Evaluation: What was the result?	E	Evaluation
S	Service			R	Research type

When developing and refining your review question, we recommend that you follow the principles laid out in Chapter 3, modifying your inclusion and exclusion criteria accordingly. However, be aware that the time it takes to develop a review question for systematic reviews of qualitative evidence is often longer than the time it takes to develop one for systematic reviews of quantitative evidence. Amend your timelines accordingly, and begin this process with patience and curiosity. A final word of advice – setting out your plans in a protocol is a great way to organize your thoughts (and your time!). We discuss how to write and structure a protocol in Chapter 3, so we recommend that you revisit that chapter and follow the steps outlined in Table 3.3 when writing your protocol.

Step 3: Literature searching

Chapter 4 talks you through the steps required to search for evidence. The general principles are the same when searching specifically for qualitative studies. However, you need to think carefully about how you are going to find studies that have addressed your specific research question within broader qualitative studies. A specific, detailed and complex search strategy may not be as helpful here as in a review of quantitative evidence, particularly given that some papers may have relevant data that may be hidden in the depths of a larger study. Rather than try to put together a complicated search, it might be better to consider combining a number of free-text words relating to your PICo/SPICE/SPIDER/ECLIPS(E) table, using AND, OR and NOT. Using a broader and less precise search strategy will yield more titles and abstracts to examine during screening. This, in turn, means that you will have to look at more full-text papers than if you were conducting a review of quantitative evidence with very narrow and tightly defined parameters. However, this broader approach allows you to identify 'fuzzy' papers that you might not otherwise have found. It's also worth searching a variety of databases. For reviews conducted in the field of health and healthcare, MEDLINE is not necessarily the preferred choice when searching for qualitative research. We recommend that you start by searching CINAHL, as this database has indexed qualitative studies more completely and for longer than other databases (Flemming and Briggs, 2007). Other databases to consider, depending on your topic area, are PsycINFO (psychology-related disciplines), ERIC (education-related disciplines), Social Sciences Abstracts, Sociological Abstracts and Web of Science (which includes the Social Sciences Citation Index). Have a look at Table 4.2 in Chapter 4 for more ideas. Be aware that sometimes qualitative researchers can be quite creative with the keywords they use in article titles, and so you might wish to spend some time, before you start searching, familiarizing yourself with key index terms and subject headings that are relevant to your review question.

When formulating your search strategies, we recommend that, in addition to terms reflecting your topic, you add generic terms (such as 'qualitative' or 'findings'); reviewers from the School of Health and Related Research (ScHARR) organize these under the abbreviation ESCAPADE (see Table 11.4). Also, don't forget to supplement your enquiries with searches of reference lists of retrieved papers, hand searching of specific journals and also searches using Internet search engines. This stage, as with all searches, will be trial and error, but it is worth investing time to ensure that your searches have the appropriate balance of sensitivity and specificity (as mentioned in Chapter 4).

TABLE 11.4 ESCAPADE

E	Exploratory methods – Include search terms related to the methodology of interest, such as 'focus group', 'grounded theory' or 'action research'
S	Software – Include search terms related to the software researchers may have used to analyse their data, such as 'NVivo' or 'Nudist' or 'MaxQDA'
C	Citations – Include key references, both in your specific research area and more globally in the qualitative research arena
A	Application – Consider searching terms related to the wider application of potentially relevant studies, such as 'ethnography' or 'psychology'
P	Phenomenon – Include search terms related to the phenomenon of interest, such as 'perceptions', 'attitudes', 'viewpoints', 'standpoints'
A	Approaches – Consider searching for different methodological approaches, such as ethnography
D	Data: Think how researchers may have 'labelled' their data in their paper, and include terms such as 'stories', 'narratives', 'themes'
E	Experiences – Similarly, consider how researchers may have conceptualized participants' experiences, using search terms such as 'encounters'

Note: Reproduced with permission from Andrew Booth, ScHARR, University of Sheffield, UK

This is a good time to raise the question of how many studies you need to include in a systematic review of qualitative evidence. It is an important question and one frequently posed by students conducting systematic reviews. One approach is to draw upon methods from primary qualitative research – that is, you will search only until you have retrieved sufficient studies to demonstrate that any additional studies do not provide any new information. In other words, you have, in qualitative terms, reached saturation. Another approach would be to take the standard systematic review approach – that is, to carry out a comprehensive and exhaustive search of the literature to identify all relevant evidence pertaining to your review question. Neither approach can be considered the 'right way', although purposive or **theoretical sampling** are increasingly recognized as being appropriate and feasible approaches when undertaking qualitative evidence synthesis, provided that the included studies portray all likely insights on the topic (Hannes and Macaitis, 2012). What is important, however, is that you decide on your approach, describe it clearly and, in the 'Discussion' section of your thesis where you discuss the limitations of your review, point out how your decision might have impacted on the conduct of the research and, very importantly, on your findings and your conclusions. It is worth thinking about how you might deal with this issue before you start your review. Discuss your plans with your supervisor and consider including a section in your protocol on how many studies you will search for and/or include in your final review.

Step 4: Screening titles and abstracts

As we said earlier, if you use a broad and inclusive search strategy, then you will have lots of studies to sift through at this stage. Remember, as discussed in Chapter 5, creating and piloting your screening and selection tool, and screening studies against your inclusion and exclusion criteria, can take up a lot of your time so factor this into your plans. Also, be aware that, compared with a review of quantitative evidence, it is likely to be more difficult to spot potentially relevant papers at this stage, because some of the titles of qualitative papers are conceptual. It's therefore important to pay close attention to the abstracts as well as the titles of citations, and to be inclusive rather than exclusive to maximize your chances of obtaining relevant full-text papers.

Step 5: Obtaining papers

If you're going to be inclusive when screening titles and abstracts, then it is likely that you will be obtaining more papers than your peers who are carrying out reviews of quantitative evidence. Don't worry. There isn't a limit on the number of full-text papers that you can obtain. Just make sure that your institution has sufficient budget to pay for your inter-library loans and that you have allowed sufficient time to carry out this stage of your review.

Step 6: Selecting full-text papers

It follows that if you are being inclusive during screening, then you will have more studies to select from than your peers who are carrying out reviews of quantitative evidence. Take your time. Read each study carefully to identify all relevant data and, using your inclusion criteria, make a decision about its applicability to your review. Again, factor in an appropriate amount of time for this stage. Usually, this step in the review process is carried out by two people independently, to bring an element of rigour to the process. If your institution permits co-working (see Chapters 1 and 2), you may find that it's possible to work together with another student on your course who is also conducting qualitative evidence synthesis. Ideally, the two of you should sift through the full text of papers that have made it through the title/abstract screening process. You should each decide which papers meet your inclusion criteria, noting the reasons for excluding any studies on your screening and selection tool as you go along (more on this in Chapter 5). You should then meet to compare your decisions and discuss any disagreements, seeking arbitration from your supervisor if you are unable to reach a consensus on a paper.

Step 7: Determining your theoretical standpoint and synthesis plan

Now you've got a final list of your included studies, it's important to consider your theoretical standpoint and your synthesis plan. This needs to be done before you start quality assessing studies, extracting data or producing tables, because it is argued that the synthesis of qualitative data needs to be based on a defined philosophical stance (Estabrooks et al., 1994). Ring and colleagues provide a detailed discussion of the relevant literature (Ring et al., 2011), but essentially, in qualitative evidence synthesis, you have to choose how you want to analyse your data before you start, because it will influence the data you extract, how you look at your data and how you draw conclusions from them.

Insomuch as there are many ways to analyse primary data (see Table 11.1), there are also many methods of qualitative evidence synthesis. If you quickly search the Internet using the term 'qualitative evidence synthesis', you'll likely find the terms '**qualitative meta-narrative**', '**qualitative meta-aggregation**' and '**qualitative meta-summary**', among others. There are, in fact, about 20 different approaches to qualitative evidence synthesis (for overviews of the methods, see Dixon-Woods et al., 2005; Barnett-Page and Thomas, 2009). Each of the terms above refers to a slightly different approach. The plethora of terms also masks the fact that there are some basic similarities across the different approaches. In fact, many synthesis methods draw on established approaches used in primary qualitative data analysis, such as **constant comparison**, **thematic analysis** and descriptive and explanatory accounts.

We appreciate that, in contrast to quantitative data synthesis, the world of qualitative synthesis can appear to be very complex and confusing. In fact, one of the most common questions that students ask us is how they should synthesize their qualitative data. Broadly speaking, methods of qualitative evidence synthesis can be very roughly categorized into **integrative approaches** or **interpretative approaches**. In integrative syntheses, data from primary studies are considered comparable and therefore suitable for aggregation. Integrative syntheses summarize data where the concepts or themes are already quite well defined or specified. For example, in our review of health system barriers and facilitators to the uptake of interventions to prevent malaria among pregnant women (Hill et al., 2013), the key concepts (health system barriers facilitators, interventions to prevent malaria and pregnant women) had already been clearly defined up front. As such, we weren't concerned with developing these concepts and categories, but rather used these existing concepts and categories to extract, describe and summarize data from multiple studies. As you can see from this example, integrative syntheses are therefore 'deductive' in their approach.

On the other hand, interpretative syntheses are concerned with generating concepts, and then developing theories that link together concepts and which are grounded in the findings of the included qualitative studies. In an interpretative synthesis, concepts and categories are not fixed in advance; instead, it is the purpose of the review to identify these. In this way, interpretative synthesis takes an **inductive approach**.

Table 11.5 displays some of the most common types of integrative and interpretative qualitative synthesis methods, many of which are adaptations of methods used to analyse primary qualitative data. There is considerable overlap in the methods, and they are not completely distinct. For example, most integrative syntheses will include some interpretation, and most interpretative syntheses will include an element of integration. Along this spectrum from integrative to interpretative, methods that are more interpretative include **critical interpretative synthesis** (CIS), grounded theory, **meta-ethnography** and **meta-study**, while those that are more integrative include **framework synthesis, thematic synthesis**, meta-aggregation and meta-summary.

When deciding on a method for synthesizing qualitative evidence, it is important to keep in mind that there is no single correct approach. In many published syntheses, reviewers appear to choose the method based solely on familiarity and fit with their theoretical standpoint (Lockwood et al., 2015). This is not ideal, as the method is driving the question rather than the other way around. Rather than choosing your method of synthesis on the basis of your, or your supervisor's, familiarity with the method, it is better to make an informed decision based on: a) your research question; b) the time, resources and expertise available to you; c) the type and availability of data that you will be reviewing; and d) the anticipated output or synthesis product and what it will be used for.

TABLE 11.5 Methods of qualitative evidence synthesis

Method	Outline	Type of synthesis	Seminal references
Framework synthesis	Applies 'framework analysis' – a structured and transparent method of analysing primary qualitative data. Begins with an a priori framework of concepts and themes against which data are extracted and synthesized. Charts that map the features of each theme or topic area identified allow further interrogation of the data.	Integrative	Oliver et al. (2008)
Grounded theory for synthesis	Based on the well-established primary research method of grounded theory, where theory is inductively derived through the concurrent collection and analysis of data. Constant comparison is the most widely used element of grounded theory, and in a synthesis it is used to compare new categories with existing ones and relate them to the emerging theory. Grounded theory synthesis takes primary research to a higher order and more abstract level.	Interpretive	Eaves (2001); Kearney (1988)
Meta-ethnography	A method for combining participant findings and author interpretations from primary ethnographic studies, to produce new meaning or theoretical understanding. A meta-ethnography produces a 'higher-order' interpretation and often produces explanatory theory. It is currently the most widely adopted method of qualitative data synthesis.	Interpretative	Noblit and Hare (1988); Britten et al. (2002)
Meta-study	Meta-study comprises three components – meta-data analysis (analysis of findings), meta-method (analysis of methods) and meta-theory (analysis of theory). The idea behind this approach is to scrutinize the findings and methods and explore the theoretical assumptions across the included studies. The synthesis aims to develop a new interpretation and/or new or overarching theory based on the three components.	Interpretative	Paterson et al. (2001)
Qualitative meta-aggregation	A pragmatic and process-driven approach that avoids re-interpretation and instead presents the findings of included studies accurately and as intended by the original authors. Meta-aggregation assembles the conclusions of primary studies (however reported) and pools them on the basis of similarity in meaning; it is analogous and predicated on meta-analysis. The output tends to be generalizable recommendations for policy and practice.	Integrative	Lockwood et al. (2015)

(Continued)

TABLE 11.5 (Continued)

Method	Outline	Type of synthesis	Seminal references
Qualitative meta-narrative	An interpretative approach to qualitative data synthesis, which allows for synthesis of findings from research containing many different theories arising from many different disciplines and study designs. Often used to explore a topic by highlighting the contrasting and complementary ways in which researchers have studied the same or a similar topic.	Integrative and interpretative	Greenhalgh et al. (2005)
Qualitative meta-summary	A relatively new approach to qualitative evidence synthesis, qualitative meta-summary is an aggregative method whereby findings from individual studies are accumulated and summarized rather than transformed into a higher-order theory or interpretation. The approach produces a 'map' of the content of included qualitative studies and attempts to 'quantify' the frequency of each finding, even going as far as calculating 'effect sizes'.	Integrative	Sandelowski et al. (2007)
Textual narrative synthesis	An approach to qualitative evidence synthesis that can be used to combine different types of evidence. Rather than identifying themes or concepts, textual narrative synthesis prepares narrative summaries of included studies. Typically the study characteristics, design, methods and findings are reported in a standardized way in tables so that commonalities and differences among studies can be identified.	Integrative	Lucas et al. (2007)
Thematic synthesis	An approach to qualitative evidence synthesis that borrows from methods used to analyse primary research. Developed by reviewers at the Institute of Education in London, thematic synthesis has been applied to reviews of acceptability and appropriateness of health interventions. In thematic synthesis, codes are identified inductively, and constantly compared and regrouped into themes. Descriptive themes are further developed into analytical themes, similarly to higher-order interpretation in meta-ethnography.	Integrative and interpretative	Thomas and Harden (2008)

Considering the type of question you wish to answer is a good place to start. As you can see from the information in Table 11.6, within the field of healthcare, some reviews of qualitative evidence ask questions about health-related behaviours or experiences of illness. To answer these questions, it may be important to identify concepts and metaphors relating to behaviours and experiences of ill health. As such, meta-ethnography is commonly used as the synthesis method, as this approach allows for the development of theories or hypotheses of health behaviour for further testing. Other qualitative reviews ask questions relating to the appropriateness or acceptability of interventions. Such reviews generally include studies of people's views or perspectives, and tend to use thematic synthesis to identify descriptive (and sometimes analytical) themes across multiple studies. Some review questions are concerned with implementation of interventions or policies; if quite a lot is known already about the types of barriers and facilitators to implementation, a form of framework synthesis can be used, which permits reviewers to extract and synthesize data in line with existing concepts or themes.

Second, you might also wish to consider the time, resources and expertise available to you. Some interpretative methods (such as meta-ethnography) are very time-consuming as they involve moving from description to re-interpretation of data across multiple studies; these methods also generally require expertise or at least familiarity with ethnographic research methods, and/or knowledge of the topic area. Thematic synthesis, framework synthesis and meta-aggregation are more integrative and can be less time-consuming.

TABLE 11.6 Examples of different types of synthesis according to the review question

Review question or aim	Examples	Synthesis or analysis method
To understand health-related behaviours or experiences, or responses to illness	What factors are considered important by patients, caregivers and healthcare providers in contributing to antiretroviral medication adherence?	Meta-ethnography
	What factors underpin recognition and response to symptoms of meningitis in under-fives?	
To explore the need, appropriateness or acceptability of interventions or policies	What are women's views of oral contraceptives?	Thematic synthesis
	Children's perspectives of interventions to promote school attendance?	
To identify factors influencing implementation of interventions or policies	What barriers and facilitators affect implementation of educational interventions to promote hand hygiene?	Framework synthesis

Third, it is also worth considering the type of data that you will be reviewing. Rich or thick accounts of findings (often derived from anthropological or **ethnographic studies**) will generally sustain interpretative synthesis using meta-ethnography or grounded theory, whereas studies that report thin or largely descriptive data may be more suited to aggregative approaches such as thematic synthesis, framework synthesis or meta-aggregation.

Finally, a further consideration is the output you expect to produce and how you anticipate it being used. For example, the output of some integrative reviews (thematic synthesis, framework synthesis) is more relevant to policymakers or those developing and implementing interventions than more interpretative reviews, which produce more complex and conceptual outputs that require practitioners to interpret relevance to their own context (e.g. meta-ethnography, grounded theory, critical interpretative synthesis) (Thomas and Harden, 2008; Barnett-Page and Thomas, 2009). This is unlikely to be the deciding factor for you as a postgraduate student, but it's worth bearing in mind, especially if you plan to publish your systematic review in a peer-reviewed academic journal (see Chapter 10 for more information).

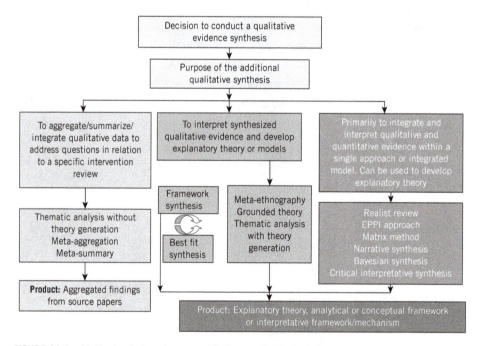

FIGURE 11.1   Methods of choosing a qualitative synthesis technique

Note: We have permission to reproduce this figure, adapted from published guidance from the Cochrane Collaboration Qualitative Methods Group (Noyes and Lewin, 2011), from Andrew Booth at ScHARR

Whatever approach you use, you need to ensure that you provide the reader with a clear overview of the method you have chosen and your reasons for choosing it. You must also take extra care not to break the first 'golden rule' of qualitative evidence synthesis: never violate the philosophical foundations (i.e. paradigm) of the primary research included in your review (Sandelowski and Barroso, 2007). We won't go into too much more detail on the different approaches available, as there are a number of excellent books and sources for each method of qualitative synthesis, which we reference in the 'Further Reading and Resources' section at the end of this chapter. We recommend that you consult Figure 11.1 and read up on your chosen approach *before* you attempt to carry out any form of data extraction or synthesis. Speak to your supervisor(s) and make sure that you don't make your analysis decision for the wrong reasons. Examples of incorrect reasons for choosing a synthesis method are displayed in Box 11.2.

Box 11.2

Incorrect reasons for choosing a particular synthesis method

- Assuming a technique is correct because it was the one used most frequently in the literature you have read
- Deciding on the technique used by a former student because they had experienced few problems and had passed their Master's degree
- Choosing a method that was widely discussed at a conference you attended
- Deciding against one method because you know someone who had a bad experience using it
- Choosing a particular technique because your supervisor or peers told you to

Step 8: Data extraction, data presentation and quality assessment

The next step is to extract and present data from, and quality assess, your included studies.

Data extraction and presentation

There are some commonalities between data extraction for qualitative and quantitative evidence syntheses; namely, you must ensure that you provide the reader with a clear overview of the studies that you have included, their similarities and differences, and your view of their findings. As such, we first recommend that you revisit Chapter 6 and re-familiarize yourself with the principles of data extraction. There are, however, some additional considerations with respect to data extraction from qualitative studies, which we summarize here. Principally, you must always ensure that your data extraction is tailored to your synthesis approach, theoretical standpoint and the aim of your review.

Irrespective of your synthesis approach, the first thing to do is identify and present key descriptive information from each study in a way that is informative and helps to summarize the key characteristics of the studies in your review. An important starting point is to extract standard descriptive information that gives the reader an overview of the characteristics of each study. Some simple headings to use in your 'Study Characteristics' table are:

- Author(s)
- Date of publication
- Country
- Study setting
- Sampling approach
- Data collection methods

If you extract this information in a standardized way across all included studies, this will allow you to write a short paragraph (usually at the beginning of the 'Results' section of your thesis) describing any important overall trends or patterns identified from the studies included in your review.

Next, you need to decide what data you need to extract to help you answer your review question. For more integrative (aggregative) reviews, it is usual to extract data (or themes) reported in the findings section of papers and which are supported by direct participant quotes. Interpretative reviews tend to take a more inclusive approach, and reviewers extract any and all data that help to address the question, including author interpretations found in the 'Discussion' section.

The ways in which you extract and collate data from the included studies will differ depending on your approach to synthesis. For aggregative reviews (e.g. framework synthesis, **textual narrative synthesis** or thematic synthesis), key concepts and themes may already be quite well defined, so it is your job to identify these within each study, and to summarize them as a whole. Specifically, in framework synthesis, you may begin with a highly structured table containing the concepts, issues and themes that are known to relate to your question. For example, in a review of barriers and facilitators to community distribution of misoprostol (Smith et al., 2016), the types of barriers were generally well known and were documented within an existing framework of possible factors affecting implementation of health system interventions. The reviewers therefore used this framework to systematically extract findings relating to knowledge, skills and attitudes of healthcare providers, acceptability among recipients of care, health service delivery factors and factors relating to the health system and political context. For other types of aggregative review you may begin with a small number of known concepts and themes, which you then add to as you become familiar with the studies and identify additional concepts or ideas or findings.

Conversely, if you are using a more interpretative approach, this will require a greater level of immersion in the findings of included studies. For example, when conducting a meta-ethnography, begin, as you would approach analysis in a primary research study, by familiarizing yourself with the findings sections of the studies, reading and rereading and making notes about possible themes and concepts as you go. Continuously and iteratively revise this initial list of inductively derived themes as you read through your included studies. This is analogous to constant comparison in primary data analysis – where themes and concepts in one paper are compared to those in other papers. Ideally, you want to reach a point where all of the studies are accounted for and no new themes arise. This list of themes can then be used as a framework against which to extract data and findings from each study. In meta-ethnography, sometimes a distinction is made between 'first-order' themes (findings derived from the findings section) and 'second-order' themes (derived from authors' interpretations). However, increasingly, this approach is seen to be less important as all reported findings are a product of an author's interpretations.

Irrespective of synthesis approach, there are some key data extraction challenges which you would be wise to consider.

- Transparency. However you decide to extract and collate data it must be systematic and transparent, and you should be able to describe the process in detail in your final write-up. You need to maintain an 'audit trail' between the included studies, data extraction and synthesis of the findings.
- Contextual information. You need to extract and preserve information about contextual factors from the included studies to help explain differences across studies. This information is most useful when comparing studies against each other to detect patterns within themes. You can look for explicit differences between studies in relation to, for example, geographical location, socio-economic conditions, participant groups or type of intervention (if relevant).
- Sufficient data. There is an assumption that you will be able to find sufficient data to extract from within the studies included in your review. However, poor-quality reporting (e.g. lack of supporting quotes, thin description of themes and data) may limit the contribution of data from individual studies.
- Internal consistency. You need to pay attention, just as you would in primary analysis, to whether the extracted data actually relate to your review question, and make sure that the data you extract clearly illustrate the theme and contribute to some aspect of your review question. It is quite easy to become distracted

by interesting but less-relevant findings in the included studies. For this reason, you might consider having another reviewer independently extract or cross-check some or all of your extracted data.

- Authenticity. It is really important, especially for more interpretative reviews where concepts and themes are arrived at inductively, that you check that the themes you identify and decide to report on in your synthesis are actually developed from data in the included studies and not from your own 'armchair theorizing'.

- Iteration. Data extraction is a necessary part of the synthesis process, but extracted data do not constitute the final product of the synthesis. Rather, data provide the basis for summarizing, interpreting, reshaping and theorizing (i.e. the creative part of making meaning out of the data). In interpretative reviews, this process is likely to be iterative, as you move from initial themes and extracted data into a more distilled version that considers how the themes are interrelated. It is likely you will move back and forth between the individual studies, extracted data and the emerging model or theory. We recommend that you do not do this in isolation; perhaps discuss this with your supervisor and/or peers before you choose any final overarching model or hypothesis.

We have provided you with the basics to get going on data extraction, but you'll find more insight into the data extraction process for different types of review in the further reading section at the end of this chapter, and on our companion website (https://study.sagepub.com/doingasystematicreview2e). Similarly, how you choose to present these data is, to some extent, up to you; we recommend that you have a read around your chosen approach, take a look at other systematic reviews that have analysed qualitative data using your choice of synthesis method, and explore how other authors have presented their data.

Quality assessment

You need to assess the quality of your included studies, but whether you do this before or after data extraction is up to you. When making that decision, it's important to note that although the basic principles of quality assessment apply to reviews of both qualitative and quantitative evidence, there are some differences. Namely, you might decide to exclude 'low-quality' studies from your review, or you may choose to include all studies but report details of their quality as a narrative. Again, this depends on your synthesis approach; integrative (theory testing) and interpretative (theory generating) analyses may differ in their inclusivity. If you're planning on excluding low-quality studies, however, then you would be wise to carry out quality assessment *before* data extraction, so that you don't waste your time needlessly extracting data from some papers.

There are many ways to assess the quality of qualitative evidence. Flexibility is required when carrying out quality assessment, as the included studies will almost certainly be based on different qualitative research approaches; there isn't a hierarchy of evidence like there is with quantitative study designs. Both the Centre for Reviews and Dissemination report (2009) and the report by Ring et al. (2011) provide excellent overviews of the quality assessment options for qualitative studies. If you want to use a tried and tested approach for appraising qualitative research, many reviews of qualitative evidence employ either the critical appraisal checklist for qualitative studies developed by the **Critical Appraisal Skills Programme (CASP)**, or a variant of this (CASP, 2002).

There are some basic quality assessment considerations that you may want to apply to qualitative studies. These include:

- Was the research guided by a clear question?
- Was the research conducted in an ethical and rigorous manner?
- Was there clear information about the methods that were used to collect and analyse the data?
- Did the research provide information that indicates the perspective of the researcher(s)?
- Did the research provide information regarding whether the findings have been verified (i.e. have a resonance with the kind of people who participated)?

Additionally, when quality assessing qualitative research, it is important to consider a number of issues that are not relevant when quality assessing quantitative research. These include the congruity between the stated philosophical perspective and the research methods, whether the theoretical standpoint of the researcher was considered and/or addressed, whether participants' voices were adequately represented and whether there was a statement as to the theoretical or cultural location of the researcher. As there is no accepted gold standard quality assessment tool, then what is important is that you clearly present the assessment that you carried out, why you chose that particular approach and what impact your approach had on the findings of your review. It is usual to report on study quality, drawing out broad strengths and weaknesses across the studies, when describing the characteristics of the included studies at the beginning of the findings section.

An important challenge to be aware of is that the data extraction process, and therefore the overall synthesis, is dependent on the quality of the reporting of qualitative research in included studies. Often through your quality assessment process you will identify weaknesses in how sampling, data analysis and the methods used to enhance trustworthiness were reported. However, poor reporting does not always mean poor study quality. For this reason, many reviewers prefer to include studies assessed as poor quality because they can still make valuable contributions to the synthesis.

Step 9: Analysis and synthesis of qualitative data

This section outlines arguably the most important, but challenging, step in conducting a qualitative evidence synthesis. As we have highlighted in the preceding sections, qualitative evidence synthesis takes a more iterative approach to sampling and data extraction than the linear steps taken in a review of quantitative data. This iteration continues into the analysis or synthesis phase of a review. Here we describe the basic principles and steps to get you started on bringing together and making sense of the data from across your included studies.

Generally speaking, if your review is integrative (aggregative) and aims to assemble data across studies (e.g. meta-aggregation, framework synthesis or textual narrative synthesis), then you should focus on summarizing data according to concepts or themes found in the studies that are largely well specified already. These key concepts and themes are defined and listed prior to data extraction. Data are extracted and synthesized in line with these categories. Commonly, the process of arriving at the categories involves a degree of iteration between the individual studies, the emerging list of themes and concepts, and the final distilled list of categories. The synthesis output tends to be written descriptions of each theme, usually with illustrative quotes from included studies, an indication of which studies contributed data to the theme and some degree of contextualization of the findings (e.g. noting any distinct patterns in the findings per theme).

Interpretative reviews, which aim to integrate the themes and concepts from included studies into a higher-order interpretation, naturally take a more inductive and iterative approach to synthesis, requiring deeper immersion in the findings of individual studies. Concepts and themes are identified during the extraction and analysis of data from included studies. This may involve moving to and from the included studies to refine and regroup the concepts into the final product, usually a theory or a model that is grounded in the data from the included studies. To give an example, the synthesis process for a meta-ethnography of care-seeking for childhood illness (Colvin et al., 2013) involved the following steps: three reviewers discussed the initial core findings extracted from studies and drafted a thematic framework to organize these findings. Each reviewer re-reviewed a subset of studies to identify findings that contributed to the thematic framework. The reviewers then compared notes, revised the framework and elaborated on the meaning of the themes. At this point, the findings relevant to each theme were compiled into one table, which made it easy for the reviewers to look across all of the data per theme. From further interrogation of the contents of the table, the reviewers together identified three overarching themes that were reported in the synthesis, and these were used as the basis for a conceptual model for understanding household pathways to care and decision-making.

A final word on synthesis. Software designed for use in analysis of primary qualitative data can be used in synthesis. Some reviewers use NVivo to organize extracted data, and the **Joanna Briggs Institute** has developed a software package called **Qualitative Assessment and Review Instrument (QARI)** for meta-aggregation. **EPPI-Reviewer** is another software package developed by the **Evidence for Policy and Practice Information Coding (EPPI)** Centre at the Institute of Education in London, specifically to support qualitative data synthesis. The important thing to note here is that, just like in primary data analysis, the software helps you organize, manage and retrieve your extracted data, but it will not do the hard work and synthesize data for you. You may have to pay to use these software packages so check with your supervisor as s/he might already have access to them. Space does not allow us to provide extensive detail relating to the various ways in which you might use software in a synthesis, but take a look on the Internet and read around this topic to help you get started.

As you will note from reading this section, synthesis of qualitative data, just as analysis in primary research, is not straightforward and requires you to use different techniques and tools concurrently. It is often hard to describe exactly what has been done, but you must confidently put into words how you synthesized your data and finalized your results, whether these take the form of a summary of findings under thematic headings or a more elaborate model or theory that explains the data found within multiple studies. As previously discussed, we suggest that you take a look at the further reading section at the end of this book and visit our companion website for additional information and resources (https://study.sagepub.com/doingasystematicreview2e). Choose an appropriate text relating to your approach to synthesis, and spend some time familiarizing yourself with the requirements or recommendations associated with that approach.

Step 10: Writing up, editing and disseminating

When writing up a systematic review of quantitative evidence, reviewers generally focus on the transparency of the review process and the explicit methods that have been followed, with emphasis placed on minimization of bias. The same principles apply when writing up a review of qualitative evidence. Keep your target audience (in your case, your examiner) in mind, and be explicit about your theoretical standpoint and the limitations of your review process in your write-up. Qualitative evidence synthesis gives you great freedom in your approach to analysis and synthesis, but it also means that when you write up your research you have to be very clear about why you made your decisions, and how your decisions have impacted on your conclusions. The write-up is your chance to demonstrate that you have thought through your review from start to finish. When writing up your review, it may be useful to consult the **ENTREQ** statement to help you to report the common stages of qualitative evidence synthesis (Tong et al., 2012). This framework provides guidance on how to write up the searching, screening and selection, quality assessment, data extraction and data synthesis parts of your 'Methods' section. It may also be helpful to consult the **CERQual** website (www.cerqual.org) for guidance on how to transparently assess and report the confidence of your review's findings. Don't forget to also make a plan for disseminating your review – we consider this to be an essential part of the review process! Chapter 10 provides more information about dissemination.

Final thoughts

We hope that this chapter has provided you with a useful introduction to the (sometimes complex) world of qualitative evidence synthesis. As a student, it's worth bearing in mind that there is currently an ongoing debate relating to the appropriateness of conducting systematic reviews of qualitative research. Some researchers see the drawing of conclusions from qualitative data at a population level, rather than at the level of individual research studies, as a difficult, if not impossible, task. Each qualitative research project is different, and each researcher brings their own perspectives and theoretical standpoint to the analysis. Interpretation and reporting of data are therefore subjective; it's not as easy as saying 'Ten people died because they had drug X.' Because qualitative research starts with a view that phenomena are created and shaped within the social and historical context in which they are experienced, it becomes quite tricky to make comparisons among phenomena located in a very different time and context. In addition, a successful synthesis of findings relies on the reviewers' ability to identify the ideological, philosophical and methodological similarities between studies in order to allow the findings to be compared in a robust way. Basically, you sometimes need to make a calculated guess, on the basis of what has been said, about whether other conditions may or may not have been likely. Bear this in mind when you are carrying out your review.

Qualitative research is carried out for the purposes of illumination and interpretation. Qualitative research synthesis, therefore, allows reviewers to construct greater meaning from the results of primary studies. Such synthesis is needed to allow for the translation of findings into policy, and so we advocate qualitative evidence synthesis and applaud you for choosing this path for your Master's thesis. Methods for synthesizing data from qualitative research are evolving and make the process both challenging and rewarding. In terms of your thesis, it can provide you with an opportunity to explore a variety of research approaches and gain a new perspective on the conduct of qualitative research and its use in practice.

Key points to think about when writing your protocol

- Clarity in your review question and inclusion and exclusion criteria
- Acknowledgement that a variety of qualitative research approaches might mean that synthesis of evidence is difficult
- An explicit statement of your preferred methods for data extraction, quality assessment and data synthesis

---

What an examiner is looking for in your thesis

- Critical in-depth analysis of your findings
- Critical appraisal of the review process and data analysis approach adopted
- Reflection on your methodological and analytical choices and explanation of how they may have influenced your conclusions
- Where appropriate, provision of alternative conclusions from the available data

---

Frequently Asked Questions

Question 1: Can I combine qualitative and quantitative evidence within a single systematic review?

Yes, and these types of reviews are sometimes called integrative or mixed-method reviews. However, it's important not to underestimate how challenging these reviews can be to carry out. Few studies deal with topics in the same way, and as a result it is often difficult to provide concrete conclusions about a particular topic using this type of approach. First, you need to be clear about why you are doing the review and specify the research question that you are attempting to address. Second, you need to set out what prompted you to combine the two types of data – was it to gain as comprehensive an understanding of a particular topic as possible or was it to generate new insights into a particular phenomenon? Sandelowski et al. (2007) make a distinction between assimilation, where the findings are incorporated into each other, and configuration, where the findings are used to generate new, or modify existing, theoretical or narrative accounts. Other authors use terms such as aggregation and integration to reflect the different types of activity associated with systematically reviewing qualitative and quantitative studies. The approach most often adopted when undertaking a systematic review that combines qualitative and quantitative studies is to undertake separate systematic reviews of the 'evidence', assessing each body of research using methodologically, theoretically and disciplinarily appropriate criteria, and then to bring them together once each synthesis has been completed. However, despite the appeal of integrative reviews, particularly when answering more complex and multifaceted questions, there are some unresolved methodological issues with such reviews, including the uncertainty over which evidence should be synthesized first and how best to integrate the findings from two types of synthesis. As such, we wouldn't recommend this approach as an option for postgraduate students carrying out a systematic review as part of an academic accreditation.

Question 2: Can I undertake a systematic review of qualitative studies on any topic?

In short, yes. As long as qualitative research has been undertaken you can conduct a systematic review. Methods for conducting qualitative evidence syntheses have been developed largely within the fields of health and social care, but there is no reason why the methods cannot be applied to other domains such as, for example, education, environmental science or agriculture.

Question 3: Can I only review qualitative studies that adopt the same methodological approach?

No. Currently there are differing views among those involved in qualitative evidence synthesis. Some researchers believe that only studies drawing upon the same research tradition should be combined, while others take a more pragmatic view and suggest that any type of qualitative evidence can be summarized to answer a particular question. You should decide where you place yourself in this debate and be prepared to justify your stance.

Question 4: How many papers should I include in a qualitative evidence synthesis?

There is no set answer or agreement on this, as it largely depends on the number of studies identified in your comprehensive search of the literature. Sometimes the number of studies that meet your inclusion criteria is simply too large to work with (perhaps more than 50 individual studies). In this case, you may decide to limit the number of included studies. You can do this in several ways. One, you may revisit your review question and eligibility criteria and narrow them further. Two, you may adopt **purposive sampling**, whereby papers are selected for inclusion on the basis of particular criteria such as rich description or conceptual clarity. We encourage you to refer to Finfgeld-Connett (2008) and Dixon-Woods et al. (2006) for examples of qualitative evidence synthesis using purposive sampling. Finally, theoretical sampling can be used, whereby papers are randomly sampled and included in your review until data saturation is reached. However, there is currently little guidance on how best to use the latter two approaches in the literature.

Question 5: Do I have to use computer-assisted qualitative data analysis software to synthesize my findings?

No. Just like in primary qualitative research, computer-assisted qualitative data analysis software (CAQDAS) such as NVivo or MaxQDA can help you to manage and organize qualitative data, but its use is not mandatory. The key to producing a rigorous and comprehensive synthesis of qualitative evidence is to be organized, and to have a clear plan for data extraction and synthesis. Data can be extracted from included studies into a table using a word-processing package or into a spreadsheet just as easily as it can be compiled in an NVivo project file. Further sorting and categorization of data extracts can also be done using computer software. The choice is yours, but your decision should depend on how familiar you are with the various software packages available to you.

Question 6: Should I exclude studies that are assessed as being of poor quality?

There is a lot of debate about this and various different viewpoints exist. Some reviewers think assessment of methodological quality is not essential, as poorer-quality studies tend to contribute less to the synthesis anyway. Some reviewers, particularly those who use more 'aggregative' methods of synthesis, advocate that all studies should be quality assessed, and poor-quality studies should be excluded from analysis. Other reviewers, particularly those using meta-ethnography as a synthesis approach, do not advocate excluding studies based solely on quality, because even studies that do not describe data collection or analysis methods clearly can still make a valuable contribution to the synthesis. So, in summary, your decision to include or exclude poor-quality studies from your analysis will depend on the type of synthesis you are conducting and whether you judge that the poor-quality studies still have something to add to your synthesis.

Question 7: Do I extract data from the 'Discussion' and 'Conclusions' sections of a paper, or just the 'Results' section?

Data extraction for qualitative evidence synthesis is not as straightforward as for syntheses of quantitative data. Qualitative evidence can be presented in many formats, usually as themes, but often as diagrams, tables or other mapping of data. As such, it's crucial to decide what you plan to class as 'evidence'. For some reviewers, only data (or themes) that are illustrated with direct quotes constitute evidence. Others take a more inclusive approach, whereby all data and/or themes are extracted regardless of supporting quotes. In meta-ethnography, all relevant data, including author interpretations (found in the 'Discussion' section) are extracted, whereas when adopting a more integrative approach, only research findings substantiated with excerpts or quotes (usually found in the 'Results' section) are extracted for synthesis.

Question 8: Where can I find out more about qualitative evidence synthesis?

Many international organizations support and promote qualitative evidence synthesis. These include:

- The Cochrane Qualitative and Implementation Research Group (formerly the Cochrane Qualitative Research Methods Group), which supports the inclusion of qualitative systematic reviews in the Cochrane Database of Systematic Reviews and supports methodological work on qualitative evidence synthesis approaches. The group has produced specific guidance on how to search, appraise, extract and synthesize data from qualitative research (Noyes et al., 2015).
- The EPPI-Centre, based at the Institute of Education, University College London, which is at the forefront of methods development and training for research synthesis. The Centre produces systematic reviews in diverse disciplines including health, education, finance and economics, social care and international development.
- The Joanna Briggs Institute, which is an international not-for-profit research and development organization based at the University of Adelaide, South Australia, that promotes and supports the synthesis, transfer and utilization of qualitative evidence.

Further Reading and Resources

Bearman, M. and Dawson, P. (2013) 'Qualitative synthesis and systematic review in health professions education', *Medical Education,* 47(3): 252–60.

Booth, A., Papaioannou, D. and Sutton, A. (2016) *Systematic Approaches to a Successful Literature Review.* 2nd edn. London: SAGE.

Centre for Reviews and Dissemination (2009) Systematic Reviews: CRD's Guidance for Undertaking Reviews in Health Care. University of York: Centre for Reviews and Dissemination (www.york.ac.uk/media/crd/Systematic_Reviews.pdf). (Last accessed March 2017).

Gough, D., Oliver, S. and Thomas, J. (2013) *Learning from Research: Systematic Reviews for Informing Policy Decisions: A Quick Guide.* A paper for the Alliance for Useful Evidence. London: Nesta.

Gülmezoglu, A., Chandler, J. and Shepperd, S. (2013) 'Reviews of qualitative evidence: A new milestone for Cochrane', *Cochrane Database of Systematic Reviews,* 8(11).

Hannes, K. and Lockwood, C. (2012) *Synthesising Qualitative Research: Choosing the Right Approach.* Oxford: BMJ Books/Wiley-Blackwell.

Joanna Briggs Institute (2014) Reviewers' Manual (www.joannabriggs.org). (Last accessed February 2017).

Noblit, G. and Hare, R. (1988) *Meta-Ethnography: Synthesizing Qualitative Studies.* Thousand Oaks, CA: SAGE.

Noyes, J., Hannes, K., Booth, A., Harris, J., Harden, A., Popay, J., Pearson, A., Cargo, M. and Pantoja, T. on behalf of the Cochrane Qualitative and Implementation Methods Group (2015) 'Chapter 20: Qualitative research and Cochrane reviews', in J.P.T. Higgins, S. Green (eds), *Cochrane Handbook for Systematic Reviews of Interventions* Version 5.3.0 (updated October 2015). The Cochrane Collaboration. (http://qim.cochrane.org/supplemental-handbook-guidance). (Last accessed March 2017).

Paterson, B., Thorne, S., Canam, C. and Jillings, C. (2001) *Meta-Study of Qualitative Health Research: A Practical Guide to Meta-Analysis and Meta-Synthesis (Vol. 3).* Thousand Oaks, CA: SAGE.

Petticrew, M. and Roberts, H. (2008) *Systematic Reviews in the Social Sciences.* 2nd edn. Oxford: Blackwell.

Ring, N., Ritchie, K., Mandava, L. and Jepson, R. (2011) A Guide to Synthesising Qualitative Research for Researchers Undertaking Health Technology Assessments and Systematic Reviews (www.healthcareimprovementscotland.org/programmes/clinical__cost_effectiveness/programme_resources/synth_qualitative_research.aspx). (Last accessed September 2016).

Sandelowski, M. and Barroso, J. (2007) *Handbook for Synthesizing Qualitative Research.* New York: Springer Publishing Company.

Seers, K. (2012) 'What is a qualitative synthesis?', *Evidence Based Nursing*, 15(4): 101.

Toye, F., Seers, K. and Allcock, N. (2014) 'Meta-ethnography 25 years on: Challenges and insights for synthesising a large number of qualitative studies', *BMC Medical Research Methodology*, 14(1): 80.

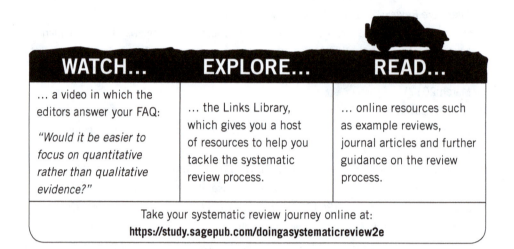

WATCH...	EXPLORE...	READ...
... a video in which the editors answer your FAQ: *"Would it be easier to focus on quantitative rather than qualitative evidence?"*	... the Links Library, which gives you a host of resources to help you tackle the systematic review process.	... online resources such as example reviews, journal articles and further guidance on the review process.

Take your systematic review journey online at:

https://study.sagepub.com/doingasystematicreview2e

12

Reviewing Economic Evaluations

Angela Boland, Sophie Beale and
M. Gemma Cherry

This chapter will help you to...

- Develop your economic systematic review question

- Search for economic evidence

- Critically appraise economic evidence

- Draw conclusions from economic data

Introduction

This final chapter is written specifically to guide you as you undertake a systematic review of economic evaluations. First, we outline the purpose of a systematic review of economic studies. Second, we describe the types of economic studies you are likely to identify when searching for economic evidence. We also guide you through the key steps you are likely to take when reviewing economic evidence, highlighting where the process differs from other systematic review processes.

Points to note

We feel that we must make several points clear about this chapter. Economic reviews are important but most students are not equipped to conduct them unless economics is their main area of study. We encourage these students to read on. This chapter focuses on economic evaluations of healthcare interventions – our area of expertise. However, we are confident that the universal principles described in this chapter will also be useful if you are reviewing economic evaluations from any other field of study.

The main purpose of this chapter is to help you to complete your systematic review of economic evaluations on time and without too many problems along the way. We've assumed that you have studied, are studying or at least understand the basic principles of economic evaluation. If you are interested in learning how to carry out an economic evaluation or how to build an economic model then, sorry, you will need to look elsewhere for information and you might find it helpful to consult the health economics textbooks and journal articles recommended on our website (https://study.sagepub.com/doingasystematicreview2e).

Reviews of economic evaluations fall into two types – reviews *of* economic evaluations and reviews *for* economic evaluations (Anderson, 2010). This chapter is written to help you complete a review *of* economic evaluations. The most frequently asked question in reviews of economic evaluations in the field of healthcare is, 'For a specific group of people, is intervention X cost-effective when compared with intervention Y?' This chapter has been written with this question in mind.

Undertaking a review of economic evaluations is similar to undertaking a quantitative review. This chapter can be read as a stand-alone chapter, but you will find it more useful if you have already read Chapters 2 to 10. Each of these chapters contains information that will improve the content and quality of your thesis. In this chapter we offer you *additional* information that is specific to a review of economic evaluations.

What is a systematic review of economic evaluations?

A systematic review of economic evaluations is similar to any kind of systematic review of quantitative or qualitative evidence, in that it aims to bring together all of the available relevant evidence to answer a specific question. As with other types of review, a systematic review of economic evaluations might be designed to answer a specific question to inform decision-making; it might be conducted to summarize methodological arguments with a view to reaching consensus; or it might be carried out to search for data to inform an economic model or an economic evaluation. Some reasons for carrying out economic reviews are shown in Table 12.1.

TABLE 12.1 Reasons for carrying out a review of economic evaluations in healthcare

Why might you carry out a review of economic evaluations in healthcare?	Example
To find out which of two drugs offers value for money for a specific group of patients.	Is pemetrexed cost-effective compared with gemcitabine for patients with non-squamous non-small cell lung cancer?
To identify the different types of economic models used in economic evaluations within a specific topic area.	What is the best way to model the costs of cardiac care in patients with multi-vessel disease?
To identify the available quality-of-life evidence for a specific group of patients so that you can then use this information in your own economic evaluation.	What is the best source of quality-adjusted life year values for patients with breast cancer in the UK?

What type of studies might I find in a review of economic evaluations?

There are many types of economic evidence and these include economic evaluations, economic reviews, cost analyses, commentaries, editorials and letters. You can find economic evidence explicitly stated in the title or abstract of economic studies or lurking in the depths of a wide range of publication types. For the purposes of this chapter, we focus primarily on economic evaluations and there are four main types: **cost-minimization analysis** (CMA), **cost-effectiveness analysis** (CEA), **cost–utility analysis** (CUA) and **cost–benefit analysis** (CBA). These four types are usually grouped together and called **full economic evaluations** as they consider both the costs and benefits of healthcare interventions or programmes. **Partial economic evaluations** either do not involve a comparison between alternatives or do not relate costs to benefits; this type of study includes **burden-of-illness/cost-of-illness studies** (BOI/COI), **cost–consequence analyses** (CCA) or simply **cost analyses**.

In general, economic evaluations describe the costs *and* benefits of alternative courses of action, usually comparing innovative interventions with interventions that are gold standard or best practice. As shown in Table 12.2, the four types of full economic evaluation identify, measure and value the costs of interventions and comparators in the same way; they only differ in the way they identify, measure and value the benefits arising from the interventions and comparators. In healthcare, the most commonly used methods of economic evaluation are CEA and CUA. Both of these approaches use **incremental cost-effectiveness ratios** (ICERs) to summarize their results. For example, CEAs often report results in terms of **incremental cost per life year gained** (cost per LYG) and CUAs often report results in terms of **incremental cost per quality-adjusted life year** gained (cost per QALY).

TABLE 12.2   Types of economic evaluation studies

Full economic evaluations	Characteristics
Cost-minimization analysis (CMA)	Benefits are proven to be equivalent. Focus is on costs. Costs are measured in currency (e.g. £ or $).
Cost-effectiveness analysis (CEA)	Benefits are unidimensional and measured in natural units (e.g. cost per LYG). Costs are measured in currency (e.g. £ or $).
Cost–utility analysis (CUA)	Benefits are multidimensional (e.g. quality and quantity of life) and typically measured in QALYs. Costs are measured in currency (e.g. £ or $).
Cost–benefit analysis (CBA)	Both benefits and costs are measured in currency (e.g. £ or $).
Partial economic evaluations	**Characteristics**
Burden-of-illness (BOI)/ cost-of-illness studies (COI)	Economic burden of a disease is measured and the maximum amount of money that could potentially be saved, or gained, if a disease or condition no longer existed is estimated.
Cost-consequence analysis (CCA)	Different costs and benefits of the interventions being compared are not aggregated. Benefits are measured in natural units (e.g. number of people cured) and costs are measured in currency (e.g. £ or $).
Cost analysis	No mention of outcomes; focus is solely on costs.

QALY = quality-adjusted life year; LYG = life year gained

What are the key terms used in economic evaluations of healthcare interventions?

Some of the key terms used in economic evaluations of healthcare interventions and programmes are listed in Table 12.3. If you are planning to undertake a systematic review of economic evaluations then you need to be, at the very least, familiar with these terms as you won't be able to carry out your review successfully if you don't understand the terminology being used.

TABLE 12.3   Key terms used in economic evaluations of healthcare interventions and programmes

Key term	Definition
Cost-effectiveness	Extent to which costs and health effects of an intervention or programme can be regarded as providing value for money
Discounting	Technique used to enable comparison of costs and/or benefits occurring in different years
Incremental cost-effectiveness ratio	Summary of all changes in costs and benefits between the different interventions or programmes
Perspective	Viewpoint adopted in the economic evaluation. Examples include patient, health service and society
Quality-adjusted life year	Outcome measure that captures both length of life and quality of life
Sensitivity analysis	Technique used to test the robustness of economic results to uncertainty in parameters or methodologies
Utility	Measure of well-being or benefit gained from a healthcare intervention or programme

Box 12.1

Key steps to consider in the systematic review process

Step 1: Planning and managing your review

Step 2: Performing scoping searches, identifying the review question and writing your protocol

Step 3: Literature searching

Step 4: Screening titles and abstracts

Step 5: Obtaining papers

Step 6: Selecting full-text papers

Step 7: Data extraction

Step 8: Quality assessment

Step 9: Analysis and synthesis

Step 10: Writing up and editing

Ten key steps in the systematic review process

Box 12.1 outlines 10 key steps in the systematic review process that we recommend you follow when doing a review as a Master's thesis. Most of these steps are exactly the same regardless of whether you are reviewing economic, clinical, educational or environmental papers. However, some steps do require additional considerations and we'll discuss each step from the perspective of an economist carrying out a review of economic evaluations. We also highlight where the steps differ from those commonly used in other types of evidence synthesis.

Step 1: Planning and managing your review

Before you rush off to work on your review, you need to take time to think about how you are going to plan your review activities from now until the day that you submit your thesis. A successful systematic reviewer learns to multitask and works to deadlines. During the review process, you will ask yourself a number of questions: Do I have the full-text papers of all of my included studies? What quality assessment checklist am I going to use? What software package shall I use to store my data? What is the submission date for my thesis? Do I have sufficient time to really think about the data I've extracted before I write my 'Discussion' and 'Conclusions' sections? Has my systematic review answered the research question? There are many different elements to manage during the review process, and these are discussed in Chapter 2. You will also find useful information that will help you to make sure that your review progresses smoothly – so don't forget to read, and then reread, this chapter!

Step 2: Performing scoping searches, identifying the review question and writing your protocol

Scoping searches

One of the first tasks we recommend that you carry out is your scoping searches. Scoping searches are the searches that you undertake when you are still pondering the precise wording of your review question – you use simple search terms and search only a selection of relevant sources of information. The results give you an idea of the quantity of economic evidence available to you before you carry out your main search. Chapters 3 and 4 provide detailed advice on how to carry out scoping searches.

The results of your scoping searches may be disappointing in that either you identify too many, or too few, relevant studies. If this is the case, we suggest that you meet with your supervisor and agree a plan of action so that you know exactly what to do if your 'main' search identifies too many or too few relevant studies. Unfortunately, it is not unusual to identify only one or two (or even zero) relevant economic studies when looking for healthcare-related economic evidence, especially if the focus of your search is a drug or device that has only recently been introduced to market. Your supervisor might think that not finding any studies is a valid result in itself, or might suggest that you broaden the scope of your review question so that additional economic studies can be included. Just remember, however, that to get good marks for your thesis you need to demonstrate that you have critical appraisal skills – this is difficult to do if you don't have any studies to critique. On the other hand, identifying too many studies means that your review question is too broad and, if this is the case, you need to think about the best way to narrow the focus of your review question (e.g. by limiting your definition of population or choice of economic evaluation method).

Identifying the review question

Whatever the reason for carrying out a review of economic evaluations, you need to be certain that you are asking a question that can be answered. For example, you may be interested in whether the cancer drug pemetrexed offers value for money to the health service. Unfortunately, the question 'Is pemetrexed cost-effective?' is too broad and, therefore, not easy to answer. Working through the PICO and PICOSS headings described in Chapter 3 will help you to formulate a review question that you can answer (see Box 12.2).

Box 12.2

Developing an answerable review question

What is the cost-effectiveness of pemetrexed (INTERVENTION) versus gemcitabine (COMPARATOR) in the first-line treatment of patients with non-squamous disease in non-small cell lung cancer (POPULATION) in the UK NHS (SETTING) using data from cost–utility studies (OUTCOMES/STUDY DESIGN) published between 2000 and 2016 (TIME FRAME)?

Developing your review question can be a lengthy process and one that always benefits from discussions with others. As the review question that you want to answer becomes clear, your inclusion criteria will also become clear. As discussed in Chapter 3, your inclusion criteria describe the key characteristics that a study must have if it is to be included in your review – think carefully about population, intervention, comparator and outcomes. In addition, you might want to address issues of study design (e.g. by choosing only full economic evaluations), language (e.g. only searching for studies published in English) and time frame (e.g. including only papers published after 2000). In systematic reviews of economic evaluations, reviewers often specify the method of the economic studies to be included in the review (e.g. only include CEAs, or only include full economic evaluations). However, this is not always the case. Where the quantity of economic evidence available is limited, reviewers are less likely to restrict inclusion by economic evaluation method. Whether you do, or don't, apply any restrictions, you need to fully justify this decision in the 'Methods' section of your thesis.

It is good practice to state each of your inclusion criteria explicitly in your report; you could list them in a table alongside any exclusion criteria. Table 12.4 shows two very different sets of inclusion and exclusion criteria for use in two different reviews of economic evaluations.

TABLE 12.4   Examples of inclusion and exclusion criteria

	Inclusion criteria	Exclusion criteria
Review question: Is pemetrexed cost-effective compared with gemcitabine in the treatment of patients with non-squamous, non-small cell lung cancer in the first-line setting using data from cost–utility analyses from 2000 to 2016?		
Population	Chemotherapy naïve, first-line, non-small cell lung cancer, non-squamous disease	
Intervention	Pemetrexed or gemcitabine	
Comparator	Any chemotherapy	
Outcomes	Cost per QALY gained	
Study design	Cost–utility analysis	Cost-minimization analysis, cost–benefit analysis, cost-effectiveness analysis, editorial, letter, poster, abstract, methodological paper, partial economic evaluations
Setting	UK National Health Service	Non-UK
Language	English language	
Time frame	2000–2016	

	Inclusion criteria	Exclusion criteria
Review question: Are public health interventions aimed at low socio-economic groups a cost-effective use of resources?		
Population	Focus on people with low socio-economic status and/or health inequalities	
Intervention	Public health interventions	Pharmacological interventions
Comparator	Any	
Outcomes	Cost per LYG, cost per natural unit of effectiveness	
Study design	Full economic evaluations	Editorial, letter, poster, abstract, methodological paper, partial economic evaluations
Setting	Any	
Language	English language	
Time frame	1990–present day	

QALY = quality-adjusted life year; LYG = life year gained

If you are finding it difficult to define your review question, then read Chapter 3 again and make sure that you follow the key steps that are discussed in the chapter; namely, identify a topic that interests you, carry out scoping searches, focus your ideas to define the scope of your review and finalize your review question. There's no real rush, time spent developing your review question is always time well spent.

Protocol

We always encourage students to write a review protocol, no matter what the topic area under review. A protocol doesn't have to be complicated or lengthy, but it should outline how you intend to search for evidence, screen and select studies, and report and critically appraise findings. It must also describe any planned data analyses. The time that you spend thinking about and writing your protocol will not be wasted. At times during the review process you may feel as though you are not making much progress, or you may feel uncertain about which task to do next. Having a protocol that is clear and well thought out means that, on such occasions, you can simply refer to it and take your own advice.

Step 3: Literature searching

Let's assume that you have carried out your scoping searches, refined your review question and written your protocol. You now need to think about your search strategy, that is, how you are going to search for economic evidence.

There are two key questions to consider:

- What bibliographic databases do you want to search for economic evidence?
- What key search terms do you want to use?

Databases

Most of the commonly searched health and social sciences bibliographic databases also index economics studies. Useful bibliographic databases for the identification of economic evaluation papers relating to health and social sciences include: MEDLINE, EMBASE, NHS Economic Evaluation Database (NHS EED), Health Economics Evaluation Database (HEED), Health Management Information Consortium (HMIC) and PsycINFO. Other useful databases that include economic studies are: Economics and Social Data Service, EconLit, Social Care Online, Educational Resources Information Centre (ERIC), Education-line, Current Education and Children's Services Research (CERUK), and Association of Public Health Observatories (APHO). See Table 4.2 in Chapter 4 and our website for a list of useful web addresses (https:// study.sagepub.com/doingasystematicreview2e).

Large numbers of papers containing economic evidence are published each year and are indexed in different databases and on Internet websites. Depending on the focus of your review, you will need to choose your databases and websites carefully. For example, economic evaluations of healthcare interventions are found primarily in established medicine-related databases (e.g. MEDLINE and EMBASE), whereas economic evaluations of public health interventions are more likely to be found on governmental and public sector websites (e.g. National Institute for Health and Care Excellence (NICE) and APHO). If you have doubts about this part of your review, we recommend that you turn to a librarian or information specialist for assistance.

Search terms

To make sure that you identify all relevant economic evidence, you should think about using a broad search strategy. The economic data that you are interested in may be hidden in the depths of the text rather than being easy to spot in the title or abstract. Your objective is to identify all relevant economic evidence so that you can be sure that you are capturing the cost and benefit information that you need to answer your review question. Don't be too specific. We believe that it pays to be inclusive rather than exclusive when it comes to choosing economic search terms to identify studies. Performing a broad search means you'll find more papers than you would if you were to carry out a narrow search. So, for example, use the terms 'cost' or 'economic' rather than 'economic evaluation' and you will find more studies (as shown in Table 12.5). The extra time it takes you to look through the titles and abstracts of your retrieved papers is worthwhile, even if you find only one additional relevant economic study.

TABLE 12.5 Table of costing studies identified using different search terms

Bibliographic databases searched: 2000–2016	Number of hits (Jan. 2017) – using 'cost' as a keyword	Number of hits (Jan. 2017) – using 'economic evaluation' as a keyword
MEDLINE (health)	355,936	46,988
NHS EED (economics)	41,357	4,138
PsycINFO (psychology)	70,859	8,112
ERIC (education)	17,695	3,029

You need to think carefully about the search terms that you use. For example, if you are only searching for economic evaluations based on the results of randomized controlled trials (RCTs), you probably won't pick up any economic papers that fail to mention RCTs in the title or abstract (see Table 12.6) – even though the authors mention RCTs in the main body of the text. Also, don't be tempted to use the abbreviation 'RCT' in your searches – on MEDLINE you will find approximately 12,000 hits using the keyword 'RCT' but nearer 459,000 when using the keywords 'randomized controlled trial'.

If you can, it is a good idea to ask a librarian or information specialist to check that the search terms you are planning to use will pick up all relevant studies. If you can't do this, then just check that your search terms are picking up the key economic studies that you have already identified from your scoping search results and through discussions with your supervisor. If your main search strategy is not picking up all of these studies it is time to rethink your search terms and rerun your searches. See Chapter 4 for further explanation regarding how to develop your search strategy and improve the accuracy of your searching.

TABLE 12.6 Impact of using search terms that are 'too' specific

Search terms used in MEDLINE (1948–)	Number of hits (search date: 15/02/17)
(gemcitabine and lung cancer and RCT and cost).mp.	2
(gemcitabine and lung cancer and randomized controlled trial and cost).mp.	18
(gemcitabine and lung cancer and cost).mp.	89

Step 4: Screening titles and abstracts

The fourth step in the review process is to use your inclusion and exclusion criteria to screen the titles and abstracts of the papers identified from your main searches. You need to refer to your criteria as you read through the titles and abstracts in order to identify the papers that are potentially eligible for inclusion in your review based on your specific criteria. Remember, you don't need to have the full-text papers in front of you at this stage, as you are only reading through titles and abstracts.

Step 5: Obtaining papers

For some students, obtaining full-text papers can be a welcome distraction but for others it is the most boring task in the world. You must try to obtain the full-text papers of all of the economic papers that you included in Step 4. If you are unable to obtain a paper, you need to let your supervisor know and acknowledge this problem when writing up the limitations of your review.

Step 6: Selecting full-text papers

When selecting full-text papers for inclusion in your review, you follow the same process as you do when screening titles and abstracts. However, this time you have the full-text papers in front of you (in paper or in electronic format). The full text gives you the information you need to decide whether or not a study should be included in your review. You must check through the full-text paper of each study carefully so as to ensure that you don't miss any relevant information using your explicitly stated inclusion and exclusion criteria. Only after having done this will you be able to confidently include or exclude a paper from your review.

Step 7: Data extraction

The next step in your systematic review is to carry out data extraction. However, before you can begin to extract data from your economic evaluations you need to design a data extraction form. We suggest that you turn to Chapter 6 and read the sections on designing and piloting data extraction forms. Chapter 6 also includes useful advice on how to efficiently extract data from studies, and provides examples of data extraction tables that have been well thought out.

The type of data that you extract from economic evaluations differs substantially from the data that you extract from other types of studies. However, the structure of most published reviews of health economic evaluations is straightforward and we suggest that you consider including the following data in your data extraction tables:

- Table 1: Study characteristics: study reference, identify whether full-text paper or abstract, type of study, intervention, study population, country, time period, industry affiliation
- Table 2: Economic costs and outcomes: study reference, type of model (if used), perspective, assumptions relating to costs, assumptions relating to outcomes
- Table 3: Cost items and data sources: study reference, cost items and cost data sources, price year, currency, discount rate
- Table 4: Efficacy and outcomes sources: study reference, efficacy data, efficacy data sources, outcomes, outcome data sources, discount rate
- Table 5: Cost-effectiveness results and conclusions: study reference, total costs, total outcomes, ICERs, authors' conclusions
- Table 6: Sensitivity analysis: study reference, summary of sensitivity analyses and results

As a student, you will probably be working independently. However, it is worth trying to find someone (suitably able) to check your extracted data for inaccuracies and/or transcription errors. This is particularly important if your included studies contain large, complex data tables. In terms of responsibility, this systematic review is your project and you must be accountable for all decisions made and tasks undertaken. One benefit of working alone is that you can be sure you have adopted the same approach to data extraction across all studies. As mentioned in Chapter 2, check with your supervisor regarding your institution's policy on working independently.

Step 8: Quality assessment

Let's assume that you have just completed your data extraction exercise. You are now getting to know your included studies and probably feel in control of your economic review. The next stage in the systematic review process is the critical appraisal (or quality assessment) of your included studies. Not all reviewers of economic evidence quality assess their included studies. However, if you are aiming to produce the best review that you are capable of writing, then this is a step that you cannot afford to skip.

The quality of economic evaluations varies. Most economic evaluations are carried out by individuals with expertise in economics but some are conducted by clinicians or social scientists who are interested in exploring cost-effectiveness questions but do not have the necessary skill base to do this well. It is, therefore, really important that you are able to identify research that has been conducted and reported to a high standard so that you do not give equal weight to studies of variable quality.

Whether you carry out quality assessment before, after or during data extraction is a personal choice. Everyone has a preference – go ahead with the method that suits your style of working. Remember, you need to quality assess each included study and it is up to you whether you do this on paper or electronically.

There are many different quality assessment tools available for the critical appraisal of health economic evaluations and some are easier to use than others. Examples of quality assessment tools can be found on our website (https://study.sagepub.com/doingasystematicreview2e). The majority of available tools ask the same pertinent and probing questions. We suggest that you use a short version of a checklist by Drummond and colleagues (Drummond et al., 1997). The short version of the checklist is shown in Table 12.7. As a student writing a thesis, we consider this 10-point checklist to be the most appropriate tool for you to use. If you are feeling very enthusiastic, you could use the full 35-point version of this checklist (Drummond and Jefferson, 1996; Drummond et al., 1997). The questions posed in the Drummond checklist are generic and so can be used in the quality assessment of any economic evaluation, no matter what the field of study. The questions will lead you to consider the elements of the economic study that are most important. Remember to allow yourself sufficient time to think through your answers.

TABLE 12.7   Short checklist for assessing economic evaluations

Drummond et al. (1997) checklist questions
1   Was a well-defined question posed in answerable form?
2   Was a comprehensive description of the competing alternatives given (i.e. can you tell who did what to whom, where and how often)?
3   Was the effectiveness of the programmes or services established?
4   Were all of the important and relevant costs and consequences for each alternative identified?
5   Were costs and consequences measured accurately in appropriate physical units?
6   Were costs and consequences valued credibly?
7   Were costs and consequences adjusted for differential timing?
8   Was an incremental analysis of costs and consequences performed?
9   Was allowance made for uncertainty in the estimates of costs and consequences?
10   Did the presentation and discussion of study results include issues of concern to users?

Source: Box 3.1, *Methods for the Economic Evaluation of Health Care Programmes by* Drummond et al., (1997). By permission of Oxford University Press

There are also tools for assessing the quality of health economics models. The report by Philips et al. (2004) presents a useful review of guidelines for good practice in decision-analytic modelling in health technology assessment.

In an ideal world, you would be able to ask someone with sufficient time and suitable qualifications to read through the results of your quality assessment exercise to check the consistency of your judgements across your included studies. However, if you don't live in an ideal world (and who does?), then make sure you mention this issue when writing up the limitations of your review.

Finally, don't forget that there are also tools for assessing the quality of systematic reviews and it is always a good idea to review the quality of your own systematic review (see Chapter 7 for more details).

Step 9: Analysis and synthesis

When it comes to the systematic review of economic evaluations there are no established methods for data synthesis, other than narrative synthesis (see Chapter 6 for a discussion of narrative synthesis). So don't worry, it is probably not appropriate for you to perform a meta-analysis or a meta-ethnography. How you write up your narrative synthesis will depend on the information you have reported in your data tables. Your data tables often reveal that the results of your included studies are different: some studies may demonstrate that 'Intervention X is cost-effective compared with intervention Y', while others may conclude that 'Intervention Y is cost-effective compared with intervention X'. If this is a feature of your review then all that you can do in your narrative synthesis is report what you have found. You also need to acknowledge patterns (similarities and differences) in the data and in the magnitude of the reported ICERs.

There is no need to describe and then scrutinize each included study on its own merits; you need to spend your time thinking carefully about what the data are saying as a collective. Anderson (2010) argues that even trying to do this is a wasted effort as the individual papers included in systematic reviews of economic evaluations are often inherently different from each other, and attempting to compare studies with different perspectives, time frames and local settings is futile. Our alternative perspective is that economic reviews, if carried out using systematic and rigorous methods, can be just as informative and useful for decision-making and student learning as any other type of systematic review. We agree that reviews of economic evaluations usually comprise very different studies; however, we believe that this is an important observation in itself. The information described and critiqued within a review of economic evaluations may serve many purposes, including summarizing what is currently known about a topic, helping to inform a policy decision, or identifying parameter values to use in an economic model or economic evaluation. Even if your review concludes that the results of the economic studies are too diverse to enable comparison, this can be a useful finding in itself.

Step 10: Writing up and editing

A successful review of economic evaluations (and any other type of review) is one that adds information to the existing knowledge base and answers the review question posed. This may sound obvious to you, but believe us, not all reviewers manage to write 'Discussion' and 'Conclusions' sections that succinctly summarize the available data or meaningfully interpret the results of all of the hard work that has been undertaken. See Chapter 9 for more information about writing your 'Discussion' and 'Conclusions' sections.

Reviewing the literature is mainly a technical exercise until this stage in the review process, and it is widely agreed that 'Discussion' and 'Conclusions' sections are the most difficult sections of any review to write. As a reviewer you need to think carefully about the information you have collected and decide whether there are enough data of sufficient quality to answer your review question. You really must take the time to match the extracted economic data with the results of your quality assessment exercise and then meaningfully interpret what you have found. There is no right or wrong way to do this. Planning your discussion and thinking through the key issues before putting pen to paper is always a good way to start. The questions raised in Table 12.8 might help you to clarify and organize your ideas.

TABLE 12.8 Writing the 'Discussion' section of an economic review

	Key questions/issues to think about when writing the discussion
Number of studies	Are there sufficient studies to answer your review question? If there are very few published economic evaluations included in your review, then you need to discuss the possible reasons for this. Perhaps your inclusion criteria were too strict or you didn't search enough databases, or maybe your topic was out of date or too new?
Quality	Economic evaluations are often inherently flawed. It is important that you acknowledge the link between study results and study quality in your 'Discussion' section. It is misleading to report that all included studies demonstrated that intervention A was cost-effective compared with intervention B if you don't mention that some of the studies didn't include all relevant costs, some overestimated benefits and others used limited perspectives.
Intervention and comparator	Do you have sufficient information about the intervention and comparator in each study to confidently compare them and draw conclusions? Do most of the studies in the review describe the same interventions and comparators with the same level of detail? Do any of the studies compare interventions with comparators that are no longer in use?
Perspective	Do all of the studies in the review adopt the same perspective? If not, is there a reason for this? Does the choice of perspective influence the results of the study? Narrow perspective/viewpoint: for example, patient. Wider perspective/viewpoint: for example, society.
Rate of discounting	No matter what the discount rate used in a study, it is helpful if the authors explore the impact of using different discount rates as part of their sensitivity analyses, including using a rate of 0 per cent. Watch out for studies that only discount costs *on* benefits, and studies that apply different rates to costs and benefits. What is the approach taken in most of the studies and why?

	Key questions/issues to think about when writing the discussion
Price year and currency	Are all of the resource items used in the economic evaluations from the same price year and estimated in the same currency? Probably not. You need to be aware of how different price years and currencies might affect the size of the calculated ICERs and how this might influence decision-making.
QALYs	Where do the QALY estimates come from? From the general public or from a patient survey? What tools are used to derive utilities? Are the values used comparable across studies? Do you think there are better sources of utility values for this population?
ICERs	Are the estimated ICERs of a similar size? Are the results of the studies in agreement? If not, why not? What are the key drivers of the analyses? Are the drivers common to all studies? Can you make an overall judgement about whether or not the intervention is cost-effective compared with the comparator(s)?
Sensitivity analysis	Do the authors address uncertainty in their analyses? What are the main sources of uncertainty in the economic evaluations? How is this uncertainty handled?
Generalizability	Discussion of generalizability is paramount. Even if all of the evaluations in your review are expertly undertaken and assessed to be of excellent quality, if they are all inherently different in their approach to estimating cost-effectiveness, then you need to think about whether the results of the studies can be used to answer the review question. When conducting an economic review it is always possible that even studies that meet strict inclusion/exclusion criteria will fail on the test of generalizability. For example, some authors might include the costs of interventions that are not routinely used in all settings, others might employ a slightly wider definition of the patient population, while others might use published cost data from non-routine sources. Often this list is endless and it is crucial to describe overall results in light of issues of generalizability so that the reader is clear about the circumstances under which the results of the review are valid.

QALY = quality-adjusted life year; ICER = incremental cost-effectiveness ratio

Final thoughts

Congratulations! You've made it – you have completed your review of economic evaluations. Is there a little voice in your head daring you to think about publishing your review? We hope so! Increasingly, reviews of economic evidence are being published in a wide variety of journals, not only specialist health economics journals. For example, you may come across a review of economic evaluations in a clinical journal or an economic review of housing alternatives in a health economics journal. You might also want to think about submitting an abstract of your review to a local, national or even international conference. We discuss these methods of dissemination further in Chapter 10, but are of the opinion that if you have followed the advice in this book then your systematic review will pass even the highest of peer-review obstacles. Go on, put yourself (and your review) out there and get your results published.

Key points to think about when writing your protocol

- Present a clearly stated economic review question with as much detail as possible
- Be comprehensive when you outline your plans for searching for economic evidence
- Quality assessment tool – explain why you think the tool you will use is appropriate

What an examiner is looking for in your thesis

- A clearly stated economic review question
- Appropriate search terms used and relevant databases searched for evidence
- Quality assessment of included studies
- Structured discussion showing how the quality of studies may influence the conclusions of the review
- Pertinent discussion of generalizability of results
- Statement relating to whether you were able to answer the review question

Frequently Asked Questions

Question 1: Can I do a review of economic evaluations that are unrelated to health?

Yes. Health economics is not the only branch of economics that employs methods of economic evaluation – environmental, housing and transport economics do too.

Question 2: What if the prices/currencies used in my included studies are all from different years?

This is often the case. You must decide whether you need to compare the cost data from your included studies at a single point in time. You should think about whether this level of comparability is critical to the interpretation of the data and how converting prices/currencies to a **base year** might affect decision-making. If you decide to convert your prices/currencies to a base year, then you can search the Internet for up-to-date and useful information on how to do this. Again, it is a good idea to discuss your planned approach with your supervisor.

Question 3: What do I do if the economic evaluations that I am interested in all adopt different viewpoints/perspectives?

You need to make sure that the issue of viewpoint/perspective is intelligently discussed in your thesis. It is misleading to conclude that most of the results discussed in the included studies are sufficiently similar if the analyses have been conducted from widely different viewpoints. You need to think through your findings and comment on how choice of perspective can influence the magnitude of the estimated ICERs.

Question 4: How do I make sure that the conclusions of the review are generalizable to all users?

You can't. You can only write your conclusions based on the evidence that is described in your included studies. You need to think about the question that you set out to answer and make sure that you have attempted to do this to the best of your ability, based on the nature and quality of the data that are available to you.

Further Reading and Resources

Drummond, M. and Jefferson, T. (1996) 'Guidelines for authors and peer reviewers of economic submissions to the BMJ', *British Medical Journal*, 313(7052): 275–83.

Heslin, M., Forster, A., Healey, A. and Patel, A. (2016) 'A systematic review of the economic evidence for interventions for family carers of stroke patients', *Clinical Rehabilitation*, 30(2): 119–33.

Husereau, D., Drummond, M., Petrou, S., Carswell, C., Moher, D., Greenberg, D., Augustovski, F., Briggs, A., Mauskopf, J. and Loder, E. (2013) 'Consolidated Health Economic Evaluation Reporting Standards (CHEERS) statement', *Cost Effectiveness and Resource Allocation*, 11(1): 6.

Kobelt, G. (2002) Health Economics: An Introduction to Economic Evaluation (https://www.ohe.org/publications/health-economics-introduction-economic-evaluation-0). (Last accessed March 2017).

Petrou, S. and Gray, A. (2011) 'Economic evaluation alongside randomised controlled trials: Design, conduct, analysis, and reporting', *British Medical Journal*, 342: d1548.

WATCH...	EXPLORE...	READ...
... a video in which the editors answer your FAQ: *"I'm an economics student and have never done a systematic review before. Is it too big an undertaking for me?"*	... the Links Library, which gives you a host of resources to help you tackle the systematic review process.	... online resources such as example reviews, journal articles and further guidance on the review process.

Take your systematic review journey online at:
https://study.sagepub.com/doingasystematicreview2e

Epilogue

We began the epilogue of the first edition with 'Well, you are nearing the end of your systematic review journey. We hope that the experience of completing your review has been both educational and, dare we say, enjoyable.' We then went on to encourage students to disseminate their systematic reviews. However, all of that discussion has now been subsumed into Chapter 10 in this second edition, which left us wondering how best to conclude the second edition of this book. After much deliberation, we decided that, as an epilogue is supposed to be forward-thinking, we want to focus on the future! Specifically, we want to ask for your help to answer two very important questions:

1. What more can we do to help you to successfully complete your systematic review?
2. What can *you* do to help others do the same?

We need you to tell us whether there is any information missing that would help to make your systematic review journey even easier. You can get in touch with us directly via our website (https://study.sagepub.com/doingasystematicreview2e) and ask us specific questions about your review. You and your supervisors can also share with us advice, ideas and tips that have helped you to deal with specific issues that have arisen during the course of your review. We will do our best to respond to individual queries, and we will use your feedback to make our online resources even more comprehensive. If we are lucky enough to be asked to do a third edition of this book, then this feedback will be invaluable in shaping its content.

Selfishly, we would also like to have more personal contact with supervisors who use our book to support students who are conducting systematic reviews as part of their academic accreditations. So, if you are in this category, then please get in touch with us too! The authors of this book often present at national and international conferences, so if we are coming to a place near to you, it would be really useful to spend some time with you and get a sense of how you use the book and how you think it could be improved – and perhaps even talk to some of your students.

So, in conclusion, thank you for continuing to support our endeavours and making this second edition possible. We hope that the changes to this new edition of the book have made it an even more comprehensive resource for both students and supervisors, but we don't want to stop here! We want to expand the resources available to students and supervisors alike, and, where possible, link together like-minded individuals. We hope that you will support our plan and ultimately help us to make it a reality.

Angela, Gemma, Rumona and authors

Glossary

Action research (also known as: participatory action research)   A study that is initiated to generate solutions to practical problems, typically conducted in the field of education. Often called 'participatory' action research because individuals become involved in gathering information about the issue and implementation of solution, thus blurring the distinction between the 'researcher' and the 'researched'.

Allocation bias   A form of bias common to intervention studies, which occurs as a result of methods used to allocate participants to different intervention or treatment comparison groups.

AMSTAR tool   (also known as: A Measurement Tool to Assess Systematic Reviews) An 11-item measurement tool for assessing the quality of systematic reviews.

Analytical data   Qualitative or quantitative study results.

Attrition bias   A form of bias common to intervention studies, which occurs as a result of differences in participant withdrawal rates between intervention or treatment comparison groups.

Backward searching   (also known as: backward snowballing) The process of consulting the bibliography of a key reference to find other relevant research.

Base year   (also known as: base period) A term used in economic studies to refer to the year used as the beginning or reference year for comparison when calculating an economic index.

Bias   Distorted or inaccurate study findings, which occur as a result of systematic flaws in the conduct, reporting or design of the study.

Bibliographic database (also known as: bibliographical database; database of bibliographic records; electronic database; electronic bibliographical database)   A digital collection of references of published and grey literature, including journal articles, theses and dissertations, books, government and legal reports, newspaper articles, conference abstracts and patents.

Bibliographic software (also known as: bibliography generation software; citation management software; reference management software; reference management tool; referencing software)   Commercial reference management software, which allows users to record, organize, manage and report bibliographic citations (references).

Bibliography   A full list of all of the sources that were consulted or used when preparing a document.

Binary data (also known as: dichotomous data)   Data outcomes that can only be expressed as one of two possible responses, for example, dead or alive, success or failure.

Blind assessment (also known as: blinding of outcome assessment; blinded outcome assessment)   An approach commonly used in clinical trials and empirical research to reduce detection bias. Assessors are 'blinded' to (unaware of) the treatment allocated to/received by a particular patient group.

Blog   A type of website which comprises discrete text entries ('posts'), which are usually presented chronologically in reverse date order.

Boolean operators   Words (AND, OR, NOT or AND NOT), which are used to combine or exclude keywords in a search, leading to increased focus and precision.

Burden-of-illness/cost-of-illness study   A study in which the economic burden of a disease is measured and the maximum amount of money that could potentially be saved, or gained, if a disease or condition no longer existed, is estimated.

Campbell Collaboration   A non-profit international research organization that produces and disseminates systematic reviews of the effectiveness of interventions in the social and behavioural sciences.

Case-control study   A comparative study in which a group of participants with a particular condition are 'matched' (i.e. paired on the basis of specific characteristics) with a control group of participants who do not have the condition.

Case series   A study in which a person, or series of people, who have been given a similar treatment are followed for a specific time period.

Critical Appraisal Skills Programme (also known as: CASP) An organization that develops and delivers critical appraisal training via tools and workshops (online and face-to-face).

Centre for Reviews and Dissemination (also known as: CRD) A health services research centre based at the University of York, UK, which carries out systematic reviews and meta-analyses of healthcare interventions and disseminates these findings to decision makers in the National Health Service (NHS).

CERQual (also known as: Confidence in the Evidence from Reviews of Qualitative Research) A system, analogous to the GRADE system for quantitative evidence, for assessing the extent of uncertainty surrounding qualitative review findings.

Citation A reference to a scholarly book, paper or author.

Citation chaining (also known as: snowballing; forward searching; forward snowballing; backward searching; backward snowballing) The practice of looking at the bibliography of one study to find other, related studies.

Clinical effectiveness The extent to which an intervention or programme can be regarded as providing clinical or healthcare advantages.

Clinical heterogeneity Differences in the participants, outcome measures and/or intervention characteristics of individual intervention studies.

Cochrane Collaboration An independent, non-profit, non-governmental organization that produces systematic reviews of primary research in human healthcare and health policy. Reviews are internationally regarded as the highest (gold standard) in evidence-based healthcare resources.

Cochrane Handbook for Systematic Reviews of Interventions (also known as: Cochrane Handbook) A publication that provides guidance to authors preparing Cochrane systematic reviews of healthcare interventions.

Cohort study A study in which a group of participants is identified and followed over time to assess specific outcomes. The study may, or may not, also have a concurrent control group.

Conference proceedings The collection of academic works (i.e. oral or written contributions) presented by delegates attending a conference. Conference proceedings are normally made available either electronically or in print format immediately prior to, or after, a conference.

Confidence interval   A statistic, usually reported alongside the point estimate, used to describe the uncertainty around the estimate by giving the range of values within which the true effect is strongly believed to lie. Confidence intervals can be reported for a number of significance levels; the most common is the 95 per cent confidence interval, which can be interpreted as meaning that we are 95 per cent certain that the true effect lies within the range of the confidence interval.

Constant comparison   A method used in qualitative data analysis whereby themes and concepts in one paper are compared to those in other papers.

Continuous data   Data outcomes measured on a continuous scale, for example, age or height.

Cost analysis   A type of economic study in which there is no mention of outcomes; focus is solely on costs.

Cost–benefit analysis   A type of economic evaluation study in which both benefits and costs are measured in currency (e.g. £ or $).

Cost–consequence analysis   A type of economic study in which the different costs and benefits of the interventions being compared are not aggregated. Benefits are measured in a range of natural units (e.g. number of people cured) and costs are measured in currency (e.g. £ or $).

Cost-effectiveness   The extent to which costs and health effects of an intervention or programme can be regarded as providing value for money.

Cost-effectiveness analysis   A type of economic evaluation study in which benefits are unidimensional and measured in natural units (e.g. cost per life year gained). Costs are measured in currency (e.g. £ or $).

Cost-minimization analysis   A type of economic evaluation study in which benefits are proven to be equivalent and the focus is on costs. Costs are measured in currency (e.g. £ or $).

Cost–utility analysis   A type of economic evaluation study in which benefits are multi-dimensional (e.g. quality and quantity of life) and typically measured in quality-adjusted life years. Costs are measured in currency (e.g. £ or $).

Count data   Data that are expressed as the total number of events experienced by each participant; for example, the number of infections patients experience during a clinical trial.

Critical appraisal The process by which evidence is carefully and systematically assessed in order to determine its relevance, validity, credibility and value.

Critical interpretative synthesis (also known as: CIS) A technique, adapted from meta-ethnography, which incorporates principles of grounded theory and aims to generate theory. Critical interpretative synthesis (CIS) differs from meta-ethnography in that it includes studies that use multiple methods (not just qualitative research) and offers more in-depth critique of material included in the review.

Cross-checking The process by which the accuracy of something (such as extracted data or selected studies) is verified by another person in an attempt to reduce bias and error.

Cross-sectional study (also known as: transverse study) A type of observational study in which data are collected at one point in time.

Data extraction (also known as: abstraction; coding; data abstraction; data coding) The process whereby relevant data are taken from included papers and stored in one single format – usually a data extraction form or data extraction table.

Data extraction form A standardized form, usually developed or modified to fit each individual systematic review, in which relevant data for a particular study can be recorded.

Data extraction table A means of tabulating extracted data from individual studies.

Data synthesis (also known as: data analysis) The process by which relevant data from individual studies are aggregated and synthesized with the goal of answering a review question.

Data tables Tables that describe and summarize extracted data.

De-duplicate The process of removing duplicate copies of identified references.

Descriptive data Data that help to describe or summarize a population's or sample's characteristics in a meaningful way.

Detection bias (also known as: response bias; ascertainment bias; measurement bias) A type of bias that occurs when a phenomenon is more likely to be observed in one group than another (e.g. awareness of treatment allocation may distort the assessment of outcome measures).

Discounting   A technique used to enable comparison of costs and/or benefits occurring in different years.

Discourse analysis (also known as: critical discourse analysis; empirical discourse analysis)   A generic term that encompasses a number of approaches to studying and analysing the use of language. Discourse analysis can be performed on a wide range of data sources including written, spoken and visual or sign language.

Dissemination   The process of tailoring and distributing information to an intended audience.

Dissemination strategy   A written document that: a) identifies the target audience(s) for dissemination; b) clearly defines and prioritizes dissemination methods; and c) defines timelines for the planned dissemination strategies.

ECLIPS(E)   A mnemonic used to guide the development of inclusion and exclusion criteria for qualitative evidence syntheses.

Economic evaluation   An umbrella term that refers to a range of study designs that are used to compare the costs and benefits of different treatments or interventions.

Effect size   A quantitative measure of the difference between two groups. Examples of effect sizes are the mean difference, or the relative risk.

ENTREQ (also known as: Enhancing Transparency in Reporting the Synthesis of Qualitative Research)   A set of guidelines designed to aid clear reporting of qualitative evidence syntheses.

Epidemiological survey   A method used to collect data from specific population samples in order to identify causal disease factors. Findings are then used to inform the development of potential preventative interventions.

EPPI approach (also known as: Evidence for Policy and Practice Information Coding Centre approach)   A form of mixed-methods synthesis in which qualitative and quantitative evidence is synthesized using an approach derived by the Evidence for Policy and Practice Information Coordinating Centre (Institute of Education, University College London).

EPPI-Reviewer   Special software developed by the Evidence for Policy and Practice Information Coordinating Centre (Institute of Education, University College London) for conducting systematic reviews.

Ethnographic studies (also known as: ethnography)   A qualitative study that uses ethnographic research methods to collect and analyse data about different groups or cultures. Researchers completely immerse themselves in the lives, culture or population that they are studying in order to observe society from the point of view of those being studied. Ethnographers typically study social interactions and behaviours among groups or communities through observation and informal interview methods.

Evidence-based   Informed by or derived from objective, current and best available evidence.

Evidence map (also known as: mapping study; mapping exercise; systematic map; evidence-mapping; mapping review)   A method of evidence synthesis in which the current state of an evidence-base is 'mapped out', presented in a user-friendly format, and used to inform future practice by identifying gaps in knowledge or research.

Exclusion criteria   A list of characteristics that disqualify a piece of evidence from inclusion in a systematic review.

Filter   Features of many electronic bibliographic databases that allow searches to be narrowed, or 'filtered', according to, for example, study design.

Fixed effects analysis   A method of conducting meta-analysis in which it is assumed that there is one true effect observed across all studies and that any variability between the studies is due simply to chance.

Focus group   A qualitative research methodology in which the views, opinions or perceptions of a small group of people towards a product, experience or service are collectively solicited.

Forest plot   A graphical display of the results of a meta-analysis, which may be accompanied by a pooled estimate of the effect.

Forward searching (also known as: forward snowballing; citation chaining)   The process of identifying articles that cite a key reference.

Framework synthesis (also known as: framework-based synthesis; best-fit framework synthesis)   An approach to qualitative evidence synthesis that applies 'framework analysis' – a structured and transparent method of analysing primary qualitative data. Framework synthesis starts with an a priori framework of concepts and themes against which data are extracted and synthesized. Although more deductive than other approaches, new themes and topics can be added to the framework during synthesis.

Free-text words   Single or multiple terms and phrases, such as 'cancer' or 'educational intervention', used when searching bibliographic databases.

Full economic evaluation   A method of evaluation that identifies, measures and values both costs and benefits.

Generalizability   To extrapolate research findings from individual study samples to the entire target population of interest.

Gold standard   The highest quality of its type.

Grey literature (unpublished)   A term used to refer to the vast array of evidence not controlled by commercial publishers.

Grounded theory   A qualitative research method that is characterized by simultaneous collection, coding and analysis of data that is repeated until it is possible to discern a theory that explains the phenomenon being studied. Constant comparison is used to compare new categories with existing ones and relate them to the emerging theory. When new data do not change the developing theory, this is known as data 'saturation' and data collection is usually stopped.

Grounded theory synthesis (also known as: grounded formal theory)   A method of qualitative data synthesis derived from grounded theory. The key principles of grounded theory are applied to the synthesis of a body of grounded research to a higher order and more abstract level.

Hand searching   Manual searching of potentially relevant information sources (such as conference proceedings) in an attempt to identify eligible studies for inclusion in a systematic review.

Harvard referencing style (also known as: the Harvard system)   A style of referencing citations or sources in the text and reference list of academic work.

Hazard ratio   A measure of how often an event happens in one group compared to another group over time.

Health economics   A branch of economics concerned with costs, benefits, efficiency, effectiveness, value and behaviour of healthcare systems.

Heterogeneity   Variability in the intervention effects being evaluated in different studies. There are three types of heterogeneity: clinical, methodological and statistical.

Homogeneity   Similarity in the intervention effects being evaluated in different studies.

I^2 statistic   A statistic that describes the percentage of the total variation across studies in a meta-analysis that is due to heterogeneity rather than chance. Possible values range from 0 to 100 per cent.

Impact factor   A term used to refer to the average number of times an article in an academic peer-reviewed journal has been cited (i.e. referenced) over the past year.

Inclusion criteria (also known as: eligibility criteria)   A list of characteristics that a piece of evidence must have to be included in a systematic review.

Incremental cost-effectiveness ratio (also known as: ICER)   Summary of all changes in costs and benefits between the different interventions or programmes being compared.

Incremental cost per life year gained   A type of incremental cost-effectiveness ratio that represents the change in the cost of an intervention divided by the change in life years associated with the intervention.

Incremental cost per quality-adjusted life year (also known as: cost per quality-adjusted life year)   A type of incremental cost-effectiveness ratio that represents the change in the cost of an intervention divided by the change in the quality-adjusted life years associated with the intervention.

Index terms (also known as: subject headings; medical subject headings; MeSH terms)   Words or phrases used to index the content of electronic bibliographic databases.

Inductive approach (also known as: inductive reasoning)   A form of reasoning often used in qualitative research, which allows for themes, patterns and categories to be identified from the data, rather than imposing pre-existing categories or concepts (see deductive reasoning). The researcher typically moves from observation to hypothesis- or theory-generation.

Information specialist   An individual with expert knowledge in bibliographic databases and information retrieval.

Integrative approach (also known as: aggregative approach)   An approach to qualitative evidence synthesis in which emphasis is placed on previous analytical categories obtained from: a theory, a conceptual framework, the researcher's own professional knowledge or even a topic guide.

Integrative review (also known as: mixed-methods review)   A literature review that includes both quantitative and qualitative evidence.

Interface (also known as: platform)   The structure in which bibliographic databases are accessed.

Interpretative approach   An approach to qualitative evidence synthesis, which is concerned with generating concepts and developing theories that link together concepts and which are grounded in the findings of the included qualitative studies.

Interpretative phenomenological analysis (also known as: IPA)   An experiential approach to qualitative research, developed within the discipline of psychology, which attempts to provide a detailed account of the personal lived experience of participants by interpreting how participants make sense of a given phenomenon.

Intervention study   A study in which the impact of an intervention on a population or group is studied.

Inverse variance (also known as: inverse-variance weighting)   A method of combining results from two or more intervention studies, which is commonly used in meta-analysis to combine the results from individual studies.

Joanna Briggs Institute   An international not-for-profit, research and development organization based at the University of Adelaide, South Australia, which promotes and supports the synthesis, transfer and utilization of evidence.

Keywords   A way of classifying and organizing digital content within bibliographic databases according to factors such as the topic being studied and the methodology adopted.

Language bias   Bias resulting from exclusion of evidence written in certain languages from a systematic review (e.g. only considering English-language studies).

Literature review   A common catch-all term for any study that assimilates and synthesizes, or describes, the findings of more than one study and/or review.

Main search (also known as: search; searches)   A term used to refer to a global approach to searching (sometimes called the 'search plan'), which covers all of the activities involved in the main searches (e.g. specific bibliographic databases or other resources to be searched, key search terms and any date limits).

Mean difference (also known as: difference in means)   The absolute difference between the mean values of the outcome in the two treatment groups.

Medical Subject Headings (MeSH) terms   A list of subject headings used for indexing articles for the bibliographic databases MEDLINE and PubMed.

Meta-analysis A statistical technique that allows results from individual studies to be combined to give an overall measure of the effect of one intervention compared with another.

Meta-Analysis of Observational Studies in Epidemiology guidelines (also known as: MOOSE guidelines) A checklist designed to aid clear reporting of meta-analyses and systematic reviews of observational data.

Meta-ethnography A method of qualitative data synthesis, developed as an alternative to meta-analysis, which brings together concepts, themes and metaphors from individual studies (ethnographies) into a 'whole' result, which is greater than the sum of the parts. A meta-ethnography produces a 'higher-order' interpretation and often produces explanatory theory.

Meta-regression A statistical method, often regarded as an extension to meta-analysis, which allows for further investigation of heterogeneity.

Meta-study An interpretative approach to qualitative evidence synthesis, which comprises three components – meta-data analysis, meta-method and meta-theory. The components can be conducted concurrently and aim to reveal similarities and differences in the data, scrutinize the methods and explore theoretical assumptions across the included studies. The synthesis brings together the three elements and provides a new interpretation and/or new or overarching theory of the phenomenon.

Methodological heterogeneity Variability in the design and quality of intervention studies.

Methodological quality (also known as: study quality) The extent to which a study takes steps to minimize bias and error in its conduct, analysis and reporting.

Microblogging (also known as: tumblelogs) A type of blogging that allows users to exchange short messages (e.g. sentences, individual images or video links). Examples include Twitter, Tumblr, FriendFeed and Plurk.

Mind map (also known as: spider diagram) A hierarchical diagram that can be used to organize information and show relationships between ideas or constructs.

Narrative review (also known as: literature review) A study that assimilates and synthesizes, or describes, the findings of more than one study and/or review, using words.

Narrative synthesis (also known as: qualitative synthesis) A term used to refer to any write up of results using words only (with reference to data in tables).

National Institute for Health and Care Excellence (NICE)   An independent UK organization that determines which drugs and treatments are available on the National Health Service (NHS) in England and Wales.

Non-randomized study   A study in which participants are assigned to two or more treatment groups but randomization methods are not used in the allocation process.

NVivo (also known as: CAQDAS)   A type of computer-assisted qualitative data analysis software (CAQDAS) which helps researchers to manage and organize qualitative data by using functions such as coding, searching, retrieving and grouping data. It is an 'aid' to qualitative data analysis, helping the researcher to interrogate the data in order to discover connections and find insights.

Observational study   A type of non-intervention study in which phenomena are observed rather than manipulated. The most common examples are cohort studies, case–control studies and cross-sectional studies.

Odds ratio   The odds of an event occurring in one group divided by the odds of an event occurring in another group, where odds are defined as the ratio of the probability of the event occurring relative to the probability of the event not occurring.

Ordinal data   Data that fall into ordered categories, for example, mild, moderate and severe.

Partial economic evaluation   A method of economic evaluation that addresses either costs or benefits (e.g. a cost analysis).

Patient and public involvement (also known as: PPI)   The process of considering key stakeholders' views in the research process.

Peer-reviewed academic journal   A publication containing journal articles that have been subjected to scholarly peer review (also known as refereeing).

Perspective   The viewpoint adopted in economic evaluations. Examples include patient, health service and society.

Phenomenological study (also known as: phenomenology)   A qualitative study that makes use of phenomenological theory. Such studies explore how individuals make sense of the world and aim to produce accounts of the lived experience of participants. Studies tend to use in-depth interviews and diaries to track individual stories and the way that participants make sense of their experiences. Phenomenological studies focus on providing accounts of individuals' experiences within a specific setting rather than being more widely generalizable.

PICo   A mnemonic used to guide the development of inclusion and exclusion criteria for qualitative evidence syntheses.

PICO   A mnemonic used to guide the development of inclusion and exclusion criteria for quantitative evidence syntheses.

PICOSS   A mnemonic used to guide the development of inclusion and exclusion criteria for quantitative evidence syntheses.

Pooled measure of effect (also known as: pooled effect size)   Overall measure of the effect of one group compared with another, which is calculated by combining studies in a meta-analysis.

Pooled standard deviation   The weighted average of standard deviations for two or more groups.

Practitioner   Any person actively engaged in a discipline. Practitioners include healthcare professionals, teachers/educationalists, policymakers, criminologists and information technology consultants.

Primary research   Original research that results in first-hand data acquisition or theory development.

PRISMA statement (also known as: Preferred Reporting Items for Systematic Reviews and Meta-Analyses)   A 27-item checklist and a four-phase flow diagram that outlines all aspects of the conduct of a systematic review.

Prospective study   A longitudinal study that prospectively follows a group (or groups) of people over time.

PROSPERO   An international database of prospectively registered systematic review protocols relevant to a number of subject areas.

Protocol (also known as: study protocol; review protocol)   A written document that clearly states the methods to be used in the systematic review.

Publication bias   A form of bias that occurs when published evidence is not representative of the entire body of evidence in an area. This arises because negative or null findings are less likely to be published by commercial publishers than positive findings.

Published evidence   A term used to refer to evidence from commercial publishers.

Purposive sampling   A sampling technique in which researchers select particular 'information-rich' studies for inclusion in a qualitative evidence synthesis.

Qualitative Assessment and Review Instrument (also known as: QARI)   Specific software developed by the Joanna Briggs Institute to support meta-aggregation of the findings of qualitative research.

Qualitative data   Data that approximate or characterize. These data are usually, but not always, non-numeric. Qualitative research generates large amounts of textual data, which may include: verbatim transcripts of interviews or focus groups, notes or field observations, participant diaries, as well as the researcher's own notes reflecting on the research process. Transcripts and notes represent the raw data of qualitative research, which the researcher makes sense of using a specific analytical process of organizing, sifting and interpreting.

Qualitative evidence synthesis (also known as: QES; qualitative systematic review; qualitative meta-aggregation; qualitative meta-narrative; qualitative meta-ethnography; qualitative meta-summary; qualitative meta-synthesis; qualitative synthesis)   A means of identifying, appraising and synthesizing qualitative data pertaining to a specific review question from a range of sources. Ultimately, the value of qualitative evidence synthesis lies in being able to produce new understandings of a topic or area from primary qualitative research.

Qualitative meta-aggregation   A pragmatic and process-driven approach to qualitative evidence synthesis that avoids re-interpretation and instead presents the findings of included studies accurately and as intended by the original authors. Meta-aggregation assembles the conclusions of primary studies (however reported) and pools them on the basis of similarity in meaning; it is analogous and predicated on meta-analysis. The output tends to be generalizable recommendations for policy and practice.

Qualitative meta-narrative   An approach to qualitative evidence synthesis that involves interpretative synthesis, in which primary sources are read and narratives are used to summarize their key methods and findings. A meta-narrative review seeks to explore a topic area by highlighting the contrasting and complementary ways in which researchers have studied the same or a similar topic. As such, it's often considered to be a means of identifying 'storylines' across different qualitative research. This approach to the synthesis of qualitative data is traditionally used to inform policymaking.

Qualitative meta-summary   An aggregative method of qualitative data synthesis in which findings from individual studies are accumulated and summarized rather than transformed into a higher-order theory or interpretation. The approach produces a map of the content of included qualitative studies and attempts to 'quantify' the frequency of each finding, even going as far as calculating 'effect sizes'.

Quality-adjusted life year (also known as: QALY)   Outcome measure that captures both length of life and quality of life.

Quality assessment (also known as: quality appraisal; risk of bias assessment)   The process of determining the quality of the evidence included in a systematic review.

Quality assessment tool (also known as: quality appraisal tool; risk of bias assessment tool)   A (normally) standardized measure of assessing the quality of the evidence included in a systematic review.

Quantitative data   Data that can be quantified, verified and manipulated using statistical techniques (e.g. height, distance, duration of survival).

Quantitative evidence synthesis (also known as: quantitative systematic review)   A means of identifying, appraising and synthesizing quantitative data pertaining to a specific review question from a range of sources.

Random effects analysis   A method of conducting meta-analysis in which it is assumed that the true effect varies from study to study, but is centred on some overall average effect.

Randomized controlled trial (also known as: RCT)   A study in which participants are randomized to two or more treatment groups using robust methods of randomization.

Rapid review   A type of systematic review in which researchers utilize time-saving shortcuts so as to deliver findings rapidly.

Realist review (also known as: realist synthesis; realist evidence synthesis)   An evidence synthesis approach that focuses on identifying what works, for whom, in what circumstances, in what respects and how.

Reference list   A full list of all of the sources referenced within a document.

Relative risk   The risk of an event occurring in one group divided by the risk in the other group, where the risk is defined as the probability of the event occurring.

Reporting bias (also known as: outcome reporting bias)   A form of bias that occurs as a result of selective reporting of data (either by participants themselves or by study authors).

Research question (also known as: review question)   A formal statement of the intent of a piece of research.

Retrospective study   A study which looks backwards at a group (or groups) of people to examine whether a suspected risk or protection factor has had an influence on an outcome specified at the start of the study.

Review question (also known as: research question)   A formal statement of the intent of a review.

Risk difference   The risk of an event in one group minus the risk in another group, where risk is defined as the probability of the event occurring.

Scoping review (also known as: scoping study; scoping project; scoping exercise, scoping report; scoping method; scoping exercise method)   A form of literature review which follows a similar process to a systematic review but which is performed to rapidly outline the breadth, depth and type of literature available pertaining to a certain topic, and/or the key constructs underpinning it.

Scoping searches   Relatively brief searches that are performed to help determine whether a topic area is suitable for a review by providing a snapshot of the volume and type of evidence available for synthesis.

Screening (also known as: first and second stage screening; first and second level screening; Stage 1 and Stage 2 screening; title and abstract screening)   The process by which potentially eligible studies are screened against inclusion and exclusion criteria to determine their eligibility for inclusion in a systematic review.

Screening and selection tool (also known as: study screening tool; study screening form; selection tool; selection form)   An electronic or paper 'tool' that enables studies to be easily screened against inclusion and exclusion criteria.

Search strategy (also known as: search syntax; search terms; search criteria)   The specific syntax used when searching a single database (e.g. key search terms or specific years to be searched).

Search terms (also known as: keyword; key word; search query)   Terms, words or phrases that can be used to electronically identify relevant data from bibliographic databases, Internet web pages or other information sources.

Searching (also known as: search process; literature searching; systematic review searching)   An umbrella term to refer to the process by which relevant data or evidence sources are identified for inclusion in a systematic review.

Secondary research Summation, collation and/or synthesis of primary research findings.

Selection bias (also known as: selection effect) Bias arising as a result of unrepresentative sampling or selection of participants, groups or data.

Sensitivity analysis Additional analysis used to test the robustness of results to uncertainty in parameters or methodologies.

Skewed data Data that are not evenly distributed around a central point but rather are clustered to either the left or right of a distribution curve.

SPICE A mnemonic used to guide the development of inclusion and exclusion criteria for qualitative evidence syntheses.

SPIDER A mnemonic used to guide the development of inclusion and exclusion criteria for qualitative evidence syntheses.

Standardized mean difference A measure of the treatment effect that takes into account the variability observed across the participants (i.e. when studies assess the same outcome but measure it using different scales).

Standardized systematic review checklist A set of standards or quality criteria for the conduct and reporting of systematic reviews (and sometimes meta-analyses).

Statistical heterogeneity Variability between intervention study results that is more than would be expected due to chance alone.

Subgroup analysis Analysis used to determine whether different effects are observed in different subgroups of participants.

Subject headings (also known as: index terms; medical education subject headings; MeSH terms) Words or phrases used to index the content of electronic bibliographic databases.

Summary statistic A point estimate that is the 'best guess' of the direction and size of the treatment effect.

Survival analysis A method for analysing time-to-event data.

Systematic review A literature review that is designed to locate, appraise and synthesize the best available evidence relating to a specific research question to provide informative and evidence-based answers.

Textual narrative synthesis   An approach to synthesis that can be used to combine different types of evidence. Rather than identifying themes or concepts, narrative synthesis prepares narrative summaries of included studies. Typically, the study characteristics, design, methods and findings are reported in a standardized way in tables so that commonalities and differences can be identified.

Thematic analysis   One of the most common forms of primary qualitative data analysis. Themes or patterns of relevance to a particular review question are identified, examined and scrutinized across data sets.

Thematic synthesis   An approach to qualitative evidence synthesis that borrows from methods used to analyse primary research and has been applied to reviews of acceptability and appropriateness of health interventions. In thematic synthesis, codes are identified inductively, and constantly compared and regrouped into themes. Descriptive themes are further developed into analytical themes, similar to higher-order interpretation in meta-ethnography.

Theoretical sampling   A sampling technique used to generate theory.

Thesis archiving/indexing (also known as: thesis indexing; thesis archiving)   The process of electronically preserving and promoting a thesis in an online repository.

Time-to-event data (also known as: survival data)   Data outcomes that measure the time taken for each participant to experience an event from a specified starting point (e.g. months of survival).

Utility   A measure of well-being or benefit gained from a healthcare intervention or programme.

Vancouver referencing style   A style of referencing citations or sources in the text and reference list of academic work.

Weighted average   A method of computing an arithmetic mean whereby certain values in a dataset are given more influence than others, according to some attribute of the data.

References

Altman, D. G. (1991) *Practical Statistics for Medical Research*. London: Chapman and Hall.

American Educational Research Association (AERA) (2013) Standards for Reporting on Empirical Social Science Research in AERA Publications (www.aera.net/Research PolicyAdvocacy/AERAShapingResearchPolicy/tabid/10297/Default.aspx). (Last accessed January 2017).

Anderson, R. (2010) 'Systematic reviews of economic evaluations: Utility or futility?', *Health Economics,* 19(3): 350–64.

Arksey, S. and O'Malley, L. (2005) 'Scoping studies: Towards a methodological framework', *International Journal of Social Research Methodology*, 8: 19–32.

Barnett-Page, E. and Thomas, J. (2009) 'Methods for the synthesis of qualitative research: A critical review', *BMC Medical Research Methodology*, 9: 59.

Bax, L., Yu, L., Ikeda, N. and Moons, K. (2007) 'A systematic comparison of software dedicated to meta-analysis of causal studies', *BMC Medical Research Methodology,* 7(40).

British Library Archives (2013) The British Newspaper Archives (www.bl.uk/). (Last accessed February 2017).

Britten, N., Campbell, R., Pope, C., Donovan, J., Morgan, M. and Pill, R. (2002) 'Using meta-ethnography to synthesise qualitative research: A worked example', *Journal of Health Service Research*, 7: 209–15.

Brown, T., Pilkington, G., Bagust, A., Boland, A., Oyee, J., Tudur-Smith, C., Blundell, M., Lai, M., Martin Saborido, C., Greenhalgh, J., Dundar, Y. and Dickson R. (2013) 'Clinical effectiveness and cost-effectiveness of first-line chemotherapy for adult patients with locally advanced or metastatic non-small cell lung cancer: A systematic review and economic evaluation', *Health Technology Assessment,* 17(31): 1–278.

Campbell Collaboration (2012) The Campbell Collaboration (www.campbellcollaboration.org). (Last accessed October 2016).

Carrigan, M. (2016) *Social Media for Academics*. London: SAGE.

CASP (2002). *Ten Questions to Help You Make Sense of Qualitative Research*. Oxford: CASP International Organisation (https://hhs.hud.ac.uk/lqsu/Useful/critap/Qualitative%20 Research%20Checklist/CASP-Qualitative-Research-Checklist-31.05.13.pdf). (Last accessed January 2017).

CASP (2013) *Critical Appraisal Skills Program: Making Sense of Evidence*. Oxford: CASP UK (www.casp-uk.net/). (Last accessed January 2017).

Centre for Reviews and Dissemination (CRD) (2009) Systematic Reviews: CRD's Guidance for Undertaking Reviews in Health Care (https://www.york.ac.uk/media/crd/Systematic_Reviews.pdf). (Last accessed February 2017).

Chalmers, I., Enkin, M. and Keirse, M. (eds) (1989) *Effective Care in Pregnancy and Childbirth*. Oxford: Oxford University Press.

Chalmers, I., Hedges, L.V. and Cooper, H. (2002) 'A brief history of research synthesis', *Evaluation and the Health Professions*, 25(1): 12–37.

Chalmers, I., Hetherington, J., Newdick, M., Mutch, L., Grant, A., Enkin, M., Enkin, E. and Dickersin, K. (1986) 'The Oxford Database of Perinatal Trials: Developing a register of published reports of controlled trials', *Journal of Controlled Clinical Trials*, 7(4): 306–24.

Cherry, M.G. (2013) 'Exploring the relationships between attachment style, emotional intelligence and patient–provider communication', PhD thesis, University of Liverpool, Liverpool.

Cherry, M.G., Fletcher, I., O'Sullivan, H. and Shaw, N. (2012) 'What impact do structured educational interventions to increase emotional intelligence have on medical students? BEME Guide No. 17', *Medical Teacher*, 34: 11–19.

Cherry, M.G., Taylor, P.J., Brown, S.L., Rigby, J.W. and Sellwood, W. (2017) 'Guilt, shame and expressed emotion in carers of people with long-term mental health difficulties: A systematic review', *Psychiatry Research*, 249: 137–51.

Cochrane, A.L. (1972) *Effectiveness and Efficiency: Random Reflections on Health Services*. London: Nuffield Provincial Hospitals Trust.

Cochrane, A.L. (1979) *1931–1971: A Critical Review. Medicines for the Year 2000*. London: Office of Health Economics.

Cochrane Collaboration (2017) The Cochrane Collaboration (www.cochrane.org/). (Last accessed January 2017).

Cohen, J. (1988) *Statistical Power Analysis in the Behavioral Sciences*. 2nd edn. Hillsdale, NJ: Lawrence Erlbaum Associates, Inc.

Colvin, C.J., Smith, H.J., Swartz, A., Ahs, J.W., de Heer, J., Opiyo, N., Kim J.C., Marraccini, T. and George, A. (2013) 'Understanding careseeking for child illness in sub-Saharan Africa: a systematic review and conceptual framework based on qualitative research of household recognition and response to child diarrhoea, pneumonia and malaria', *Social Science and Medicine*, 86: 66–78.

Cooke, A., Smith, D. and Booth, A. (2012) 'Beyond PICO: The SPIDER tool for qualitative evidence synthesis', *Qualitative Health Research*, 22(10): 1435–43.

Cooper, H. (2010) *Research Synthesis and Meta-Analysis: A Step-by-Step Approach*. London: SAGE.

Cowley, D.E. (1995) 'Prostheses for primary total hip replacement: A critical appraisal of the literature', *International Journal of Technology Assessment in Health Care*, 11: 770–8.

Deeks, J., Dinnes, J., D'Amico, R., Sowden, A., Sakarovitch, C., Song, F., Petticrew, M., Altman, D.G., International Stroke Trial Intervention Group and European Carotid

Surgery Trial Collaborative Group (2003) 'Evaluating non-randomised intervention studies', *Health Technology Assessment*, 7(27): 1–173.

Department for International Development (DfID) (2012) Systematic Reviews in International Development: An Initiative to Strengthen Evidence-informed Policy Making (www.dfid.gov.uk/what-we-do/research-and-evidence/case-studies/research-case-studies/2011/systematic-reviews-background/). (Last accessed October 2016).

Dixon-Woods, M., Agarwal, S., Jones, D., Young, B. and Sutton, A. (2005) 'Synthesising qualitative and quantitative evidence: A review of possible methods', *Journal of Health Services Research and Policy*, 10(1): 45–53.

Dixon-Woods, M., Cavers, D., Agarwal, S., Annandale, E., Arthur, A., Harvey, J., Hsu, R., Katbamna, S., Olsen, R., Smith, L., Riley, R. and Sutton A.J. (2006) 'Conducting a critical interpretive synthesis of the literature on access to healthcare by vulnerable groups', *BMC Medical Research Methodology*, 6: 35.

Downs, S.H. and Black, N. (1998) 'The feasibility of creating a checklist for the assessment of the methodological quality of both randomised and non-randomised studies of health care interventions', *Journal of Epidemiology and Community Health*, 52: 337–84.

Drummond, M. and Jefferson, T. (1996) 'Guidelines for authors and peer reviewers of economic submissions to the BMJ: The BMJ Economic Evaluation Working Party', *British Medical Journal*, 313(7052): 275–83.

Drummond, M., O'Brien, B., Stoddart, G. and Torrance, G. (1997) *Methods for the Economic Evaluation of Health Care Programs*. Oxford: Oxford University Press.

Eaves, Y. (2001) 'A synthesis technique for grounded theory data analysis', *Journal of Advanced Nursing*, 35: 654–63.

Egger, M., Smith, G. and Altman, D. (2001) *Systematic Reviews in Health Care: Meta-Analysis in Context*. 2nd edn. London: British Medical Journal Books.

Ellis, P.D. (2010) *The Essential Guide to Effect Sizes: Statistical Power, Meta-analysis, and the Interpretation of Research Results*. Cambridge: Cambridge University Press.

EQUATOR (2017) EQUATOR Network website (www.equator-network.org/home/). (Last accessed January 2017).

Estabrooks, C., Field, P. and Morse, J. (1994) 'Aggregating qualitative findings: An approach to theory development', *Qualitative Health Research*, 4: 503–11.

Finfgeld-Connett, D. (2008) 'Meta-synthesis of caring in nursing', *Journal of Clinical Nursing*, 17: 196–204.

Flemming, K. and Briggs, M. (2007) 'Electronic searching to locate qualitative research: Evaluation of three strategies', *Journal of Advanced Nursing*, 57: 95–100.

Glaser, B. and Strauss, A. (1967) *The Discovery of Grounded Theory*. Hawthorne, NY: Aldine Publishing Company.

Glass, G.V. (1976) 'Primary, secondary, and meta-analysis of research', *Educational Researcher*, 5(10): 3–8.

Greenhalgh, T., Robert, G., Macfarlane, F., Bate, P., Kyriakidou, O., Peacock, R. (2005) 'Storylines of research in diffusion of innovation: a meta-narrative approach to systematic review', *Social Science & Medicine*, 61(2): 417–30.

Greenhalgh, J., Bagust, A., Boland, A., Martin Saborido, C., Oyee, J., Blundell, M., Dundar, Y., Dickson, R., Proudlove, C. and Fisher, M. (2011) 'Clopidogrel and modified-release dipyridamole for the prevention of occlusive vascular events (review of Technology Appraisal No. 90): A systematic review and economic analysis', *Health Technology Assessment*, 15(31): 1–178.

Greenhalgh, J., Dickson, R. and Dundar, Y. (2009) 'The effects of biofeedback for the treatment of essential hypertension: A systematic review', *Health Technology Assessment*, 13(46): 1–104.

Hannes, K. and Macaitis, K. (2012) 'A move to more systematic and transparent approaches in qualitative evidence synthesis: Update on a review of published papers', *Qualitative Research*, 12: 402.

Higgins, J.P.T. and Green, S. (2011) Cochrane Handbook for Systematic Reviews of Interventions (www.handbook.cochrane.org). (Last accessed February 2017).

Hill, J., Hoyt, J., van Eijk, A.M., D'Mello-Guyett, L., ter Kuile, F.O., Steketee, R., Smith, H. and Webster, J. (2013) 'Factors affecting the delivery, access and use of interventions to prevent malaria in pregnancy in sub-Saharan Africa: A systematic review and meta-analysis', *PLoS Medicine*, 10(7): e1001488.

Holmes, F.L. (1993) *Hans Krebs: Architect of Intermediary Metabolism 1933–1937, Volume II*. New York and Oxford: Oxford University Press.

Joanna Briggs Institute (2014) Reviewers' Manual (www.joannabriggs.org). (Last accessed February 2017).

Kearney, M. (1988) 'Ready-to-wear: Discovering grounded formal theory', *Research on Nursing and Health*, 21: 179–86.

Khan, K., Kunz, R., Kleijnen, J. and Antes, G. (2003) *Systematic Reviews to Support Evidence-Based Medicine: How to Review and Apply Findings of Healthcare Research*. London: Royal Society of Medicine Press.

Lavis, J. (2009) 'How can we support the use of systematic reviews in policymaking?', *PLoS Med*, 6(11): e1000141.

Levac, D., Colquhoun, H. and O'Brien, K. (2010) 'Scoping studies: Advancing the methodology', *Implementation Science*, 5: 69.

Lewin, K. (1946). 'Action research and minority problems', *Journal of Social Issues*, 2(4): 34–46.

Liberati, A., Altman, D.G., Tetzlaff, J., Mulrow, C., Gøtzsche, P.C., Ioannidis, J.P.A., Clarke, M., Devereaux, P.J., Kleijnen, J. and Moher, D. (2009) 'The PRISMA statement for reporting systematic reviews and meta-analyses of studies that evaluate healthcare interventions: Explanation and elaboration', *British Medical Journal*, 339: b2700.

Library of Congress (2013) Chronicling America – Historic American Newspapers (http://chroniclingamerica.loc.gov/). (Last accessed February 2017).

Lockwood, C., Munn, Z. and Porritt, K. (2015) 'Qualitative research synthesis: Methodological guidance for systematic reviews utilizing meta-aggregation', *International Journal of Evidence Based Healthcare*, 13: 179–87.

Lucas, P., Baird, J., Arai, L., Law, C. and Roberts, H. (2007) 'Worked examples of alternative methods for the synthesis of qualitative and quantitative research in systematic reviews', *BMC Medical Research Methodology*, 7(4).

Meremikwu, M. and Oyo-Ita, A. (2003) 'Physical methods for treating fever in children', *Cochrane Database of Systematic Reviews*, 2003(2): CD004264.

Miake-Lye, I., Hempel, S., Shanman, R. and Shekelle, P. (2016) 'What is an evidence map? A systematic review of published evidence maps and their definitions, methods, and products', *Systematic Reviews*, 5(28).

Moher, D., Liberati, A., Tetzlaff, J. and Altman, D.G. (2009) 'Preferred reporting items for systematic reviews and meta-analyses: The PRISMA statement', *British Medical Journal*, 339: b2535.

Mullins, G. and Kiley, M. (2002) '"It's a PhD, not a Nobel Prize": How experienced examiners assess research theses', *Studies in Higher Education*, 27(4): 369–86.

National Institute for Health and Care Excellence (NICE) (2014) Developing NICE Guidelines: The Manual (http://nice.org.uk/process/pmg20). (Last accessed February 2017).

Noblit, G. and Hare, R. (1988) *Meta-Ethnography: Synthesizing Qualitative Studies*. London: SAGE.

Noyes, J. and Lewin, S. (2011) 'Supplemental guidance on selecting a method of qualitative evidence synthesis and integrating qualitative evidence with Cochrane Intervention Reviews', in J. Noyes, A. Booth, K. Hannes, A. Harden, J. Harris, S. Lewin and C. Lockwood (eds), *Supplementary Guidance for Inclusion of Qualitative Research in Cochrane Systematic Reviews of Interventions. Version 1* (updated August 2011). Cochrane Collaboration Qualitative Methods Group (http://cqrmg.cochrane.org/supplemental-handbook-guidance). (Last accessed February 2017).

Noyes, J., Hannes, K., Booth, A., Harris, J., Harden, A., Popay, J., Pearson, A., Cargo, M. and Pantoja, T. on behalf of the Cochrane Qualitative and Implementation Methods Group (2015) 'Chapter 20: Qualitative research and Cochrane reviews', in J.P.T. Higgins and S. Green (eds), *Cochrane Handbook for Systematic Reviews of Interventions* Version 5.3.0 (updated October 2011). The Cochrane Collaboration (http://qim.cochrane.org/supplemental-handbook-guidance). (Last accessed February 2017).

Oliver, S., Rees, R., Clarke-Jones, L., Milne, R., Oakley, A., Gabbay, J., Stein, K., Buchanan, P. and Gyte, G. (2008) 'A multidimensional conceptual framework for analysing public involvement in health services research', *Health Expectations*, 11: 72–84.

Paltridge, B. (2013) 'Referees' comments on submissions to peer-reviewed journals: When is a suggestion not a suggestion?', *Studies in Higher Education*, 40(1): 106–22.

Paterson, B., Thorne, S., Canam, C. and Jillings, C. (2001). *Meta-study of Qualitative Health Research: A Practical Guide to Meta-analysis and Meta-synthesis*. Thousand Oaks, CA: SAGE.

Pawson, R., Greenhalgh, T., Harvey, G. and Walshe, K. (2005) 'Realist review – A new method of systematic review designed for complex policy interventions', *Journal of Health Services Research and Policy*, 10(1): 21–34.

Philips, Z., Ginnelly, L., Sculpher, M., Claxton, K., Golder, S., Riemsma, R., Woolacott, N. and Glanville, J. (2004) 'Review of guidelines for good practice in decision-analytic modelling in health technology assessment', *Health Technology Assessment*, 8(36): 1–158.

Pope, D.P., Mishra, V., Thompson, L., Siddiqui, A.R., Rehfuess, E.A., Weber, M. and Bruce, N.G. (2010) 'Risk of low birth weight and stillbirth associated with indoor air pollution from solid fuel use in developing countries', *Epidemiologic Reviews*, 32(1): 70–81.

Reisch, J., Tyson, J.E. and Mize, S.G. (1989) 'Aid to the evaluation of therapeutic studies', *Pediatrics*, 84: 815–27.

Review Manager (RevMan) Version 5.3 (2014) [Computer program]. Copenhagen: The Nordic Cochrane Centre, The Cochrane Collaboration.

Ring, N., Ritchie, K., Mandava, L. and Jepson, R. (2011) A Guide to Synthesising Qualitative Research for Researchers Undertaking Health Technology Assessments and Systematic Reviews (www.healthcareimprovementscotland.org/programmes/clinical__cost_effectiveness/programme_resources/synth_qualitative_research.aspx). (Last accessed September 2016).

Saborido, C.M., Hockenhull, J., Bagust, A., Boland, A. and Dickson, R. (2010) 'Systematic review and cost-effectiveness evaluation of "pill-in-the-pocket" strategy for paroxysmal atrial fibrillation compared to episodic in-hospital treatment or continuous antiarrhythmic drug therapy', *Health Technology Assessment*, 14(31): 1–75.

Sandelowski, M. and Barroso, J. (2007) *Handbook for Synthesizing Qualitative Research*. New York: Springer Publishing Company.

Sandelowski, M., Barroso, J. and Voils, C. (2007) 'Using qualitative metasummary to synthesize qualitative and quantitative descriptive findings', *Research in Nursing and Health*, 3(1): 99–111.

Shea, B., Grimshaw, J., Wells, G., Boers, M., Andersson, N., Hamel, C., Porter, A., Tugwell, P., Moher, D. and Bouter, L. (2007) 'Development of AMSTAR: A measurement tool to assess the methodological quality of systematic reviews', *BMC Medical Research Methodology*, 7(10).

Smith, H., Colvin, C., Richards, E., Roberson, J., Sharma, G., Thapa, K. and Gülmezoglu, A. (2016) 'Programmes for advance distribution of misoprostol to prevent post-partum haemorrhage: A rapid literature review of factors affecting implementation', *Health Policy and Planning*, 31(1): 102–13.

Social Care Institute for Excellence (2010) SCIE Systematic Research Reviews: Guidelines (www.scie.org.uk/publications/researchresources/rr01.pdf). (Last accessed February 2017).

Sterne, J.A.C., Hernan, M.A., Reeves, B.C., Savovic, J., Beckman, N.D., Viswananthan, M., et al. (2016) 'ROBINS-1: A tool for assessing risk of bias in non-randomized studies of interventions', *British Medical Journal*, 355: i4919.

Stroup, D., Berlin, J., Morton, S., Olkin, I., Williamson, G., Rennie, D., Moher, D., Becker, B., Sipe, T. and Thacker, S. (2000) 'Meta-analysis of observational studies in epidemiology: A proposal for reporting', *Journal of the American Medical Association*, 283(15): 2008–12.

Thomas, H. (no date) *Quality Assessment Tool for Quantitative Studies. Effective Public Health Practice Project.* Toronto: McMaster University.

Thomas, J. and Harden, A. (2008) Methods for the thematic synthesis of qualitative research in systematic reviews. *BMC Medical Research Methodology*, 8(45) (http://bmcmedresmethodol.biomedcentral.com/articles/10.1186/1471-2288-8-45). (Last accessed May 2017).

Tong, A., Flemming, K., McInnes, E., Oliver, S. and Craig, J. (2012) 'Enhancing transparency in reporting the synthesis of qualitative research: ENTREQ', *BMC Medical Research Methodology*, 12: 181.

Vergnes, J., Sixou, C., Nabet, C., Maret, D. and Hamel, O. (2010). 'Ethics in systematic reviews', *Journal of Medical Ethics*, 36: 771–4.

Wells, G., Shea, B., O'Connell, D., Peterson, J., Welch, V., Losos, M. and Tugwell, P. (2012) The Newcastle–Ottawa Scale (NOS) for Assessing the Quality of Nonrandomised Studies in Meta-analyses (www.ohri.ca/programs/clinical_epidemiology/oxford.asp). (Last accessed January 2017).

Wildrige, V. and Bell, L. (2002) 'How CLIP became ECLIPSE: A mnemonic to assist in searching for health policy/management information', *Health Information and Libraries Journal*, 19(2): 113–15.

Zaza, S., Wright-de Aguero, L.K., Briss, P.A., Truman, B.I., Hopkins, D.P., Hennessy, M.H, Sosin, D.M., Anderson, L., Carande-Kulis, V.G., Teutsch, S.M. and Pappaioanou, M. (2000) 'Data collection instrument and procedure for systematic reviews in the Guide to Community Preventive Services', *American Journal of Preventative Medicine,* 18(1): 44–74.

Index